IF I FORGET YOU, O JERUSALEM

THE LOVE STORY OF A MODERN CHRISTIAN ZIONIST

HELLEN BATTLE KOSAK

If I Forget You, O Jerusalem
The Love Story of a Modern Christian Zionist
by Hellen Battle Kosak

Printed in the United States of America

ISBN 978-1-60647-033-6

www.xulonpress.com

Dear Marion + Andrew.
This is to say thankyou both
for years of good memories
and much Christian love.
Gavin (BRONISON)
14th Oct. 2008

ACKNOWLEDGEMENTS

No words are adequate to express the depth of love and gratitude that I have for Naomi (not her real name). She was the mother that my own mother was unable to be and became the closest spiritual sister I have ever had! She was also a Holocaust survivor, who had hidden in the bottom of a boat for three years in Europe. A Gentile had saved her life. Years later she brought him into a relationship with the God of Israel. Despite the desperation and cruelty she had suffered, she survived to rise above the gall of bitterness and hatred of her tormenters and return to *Eretz Israel.*

Dear Frau Herz, my "German Jewish grandmother," who was able to escape from the German Nazis twice, was my steadfast protector who taught me how to stand tall in the face of the tyranny of evil. I will always admire her courage.

I am very grateful to General Uzi Narkiss and his staff at the Jewish Agency who went above and beyond the call of duty to offer me the opportunity to become a "Ruth" to the nation of Israel.

I will never stop admiring the IDF. I always felt safe during the Yom Kippur War. The unselfish generosity of the soldiers at the Suez Canal Zone, when they shared their own food and gasoline with me out on the battlefield, made a deep impression on me.

One of my greatest thrills is the joy of the memory of marching down the streets of Jerusalem at the time of the Feast of Tabernacles celebration with a huge banner proclaiming, "Israel, you are not alone!" "We love you," I shouted! Multitudes of Israelis who lined the streets of Jerusalem shouted back, "*We love you, too*!"

Also, I owe much gratitude for the encouragement of my dear Israeli "brother and friend," Michael, who read my manuscript for me. When he told me he "loved it" and felt it had to become a "movie," I had confidence to move forward and publish it!

Last, but not least, I am eternally grateful for my husband, Gary, whom I met some years after the time of this story. I am thankful that he shares my love for Israel and her people. Without his patience and acceptance of my sharing this story, and his help with computer assistance, I could not have managed to accomplish this task.

This book is dedicated
With love
To All Israel
For THE BLESSINGS
You Have Brought
To the Christians
Through Your GOD

FOR ZION'S SAKE I WILL NOT KEEP SILENT,
FOR JERUSALEM'S SAKE I WILL NOT REMAIN QUIET,
TILL HER RIGHTEOUSNESS SHINES OUT
LIKE THE DAWN,
HER SALVATION LIKE A BLAZING TORCH.
THE NATIONS WILL SEE YOUR RIGHTEOUSNESS,
AND ALL KINGS YOUR GLORY;
YOU WILL BE CALLED BY A NEW NAME
THAT THE MOUTH OF THE LORD WILL BESTOW.
YOU WILL BE A CROWN OF SPLENDOR
IN THE LORD'S RIGHT HAND,
A ROYAL DIADEM IN THE HAND OF YOUR GOD.
NO LONGER WILL THEY CALL YOU DESERTED,
OR YOUR NAME DESOLATE.
BUT YOU WILL BE CALLED HEPHZIBAH,
AND YOUR LAND BEULAH;
FOR THE LORD WILL TAKE DELIGHT IN YOU,
AND YOUR LAND WILL BE MARRIED.
AS A YOUNG MAN MARRIES A MAIDEN,
SO WILL YOUR SONS MARRY YOU;
AS A BRIDEGROOM REJOICES OVER HIS BRIDE,
SO WILL YOUR GOD REJOICE OVER YOU.

(THE PROPHET ISAIAH 62:1-5)

CONTENTS

BOOK III

"Christians Are The Antidote to Anti-Semitism"

I was present at a goodbye party in Washington, D.C. for the Ambassador of Israel, Daniel Ayalon, when the U.S. Representative from California, Tom Lantos, a Holocaust survivor, made an unforgettable statement to the audience gathered: "Christians are the antidote to anti-Semitism"! How well I knew, because in 1973, I had followed what I considered "a divine mandate" to become a *Christian Zionist* and leave my family and friends in America in order to join with the Israeli people. The biblical Moabite woman, Ruth, was my role model when she proclaimed to the Jewish people "*Let your people be my people, and your God, my God.*"

I knew that as a Christian, I already have a "love debt" to the Jewish people. They had greatly suffered in the past in order to bring God's Word and reality to the world. The Bible is the foundation of my own faith and as a Christian, I believe in a Jewish Messiah. I also believe that generations of persecution of Jews from those who called themselves "Christian," had deeply wounded the hearts and lives of many Jewish people. Apostate Christianity and anti-Semitism are the source of this rejection and persecution. Consequently, there is a need for genuine reconciliation between Christians and Jews. Words are not enough. It must occur through *"osmosis*" an Israeli leader advised.

From the Christian side there also needs to be an honest humility, repentance, and real love in action in order to heal the scars of persecution and rejection the Jews have suffered from so-called Christians throughout history. There is a growing multitude of Christian believers who have never been anti-Semitic, but have been awakened to the Jewish roots of their faith with recognition and gratitude of what price the Jews have paid for the faith we share together in the same God. These people are *Christian Zionists*. They desire to bless and serve the nation of Israel and the Jewish people. In 1973 a Christian stranger called me forward in a meeting and spoke the words: "*Like Abraham, I have called you from your father's house to leave all and follow me to the Land I will show you— Israel!* Shortly thereafter, a Christian friend came to me and said "*If you want to be in the center of the heart of God, you will be in Israel*"! I knew that Israel was where I wanted to be!

IF I FORGET YOU, O JERUSALEM is a book about war and peace, pride and passion, love and hate, and most of all reconciliation. After more than two thousand years of fear, mistrust, prejudice and persecution, two estranged members of the same family of God can begin to come together and be healed. This book is also a love story of an Israeli man and a Christian woman, both deeply committed to their God, but torn by the fears and prejudices of the people who surrounded them. The distrust of the Jews was the suspicion that she was a "*missionary*" who had come to steal the identity of his people with another religion. The Christians who surrounded her suspected him of being the *charming philanderer* who would take advantage of her innocence and good will. However, both were magnetically drawn to each other, but continually repelled through fear. *Even those who knew them best failed to recognize or understand that underneath their love, sustaining their relationship was a greater love story of the Spirit of God, wooing the spirit of Israel, and Israel's God, drawing the Gentile Church into her loving heritage from the Jews!* The Prophet Isaiah declared: *"Let no foreigner who has bound himself to the LORD say, 'The LORD will surely exclude me from His people"*. (Isa. 56:3)

My fourteen months as a political prisoner of the East German Communists from November 1965, to February 1967 was part of my preparation to enter and identify with the world of Israel. (I have written this story in a previous book, Every Wall Shall Fall). Israel is a nation of Holocaust survivors and immigrants from the entire world who have endured much rejection and persecution in fulfilling the biblical promises of God's mercy, justice, and blessing for all mankind. The Jewish people were and still are chosen by God to bring His redemption to the entire world. Hence when God's Spirit spoke deeply to my heart, "would you be willing to sacrifice yourself for my people Israel and become a bridge of reconciliation?" My immediate answer was "yes"! I was instantly filled with the most wonderful love for a nation that I had never even visited. *Little did I know how much it would cost me!*

Miraculous events began to occur. This is where my story begins—in the nation of Israel from 1973 to 1976.

INTRODUCTION

In these uncertain times we are living, hardly a day passes without hearing of some tragedy or random violence erupting in the State of Israel. Her citizens have faced death almost daily since the inception of her political rebirth as a sovereign State in 1948. For most people the issues that are spewed from this erupting volcano of hatred and terror from her enemies are an enigma, but their irrational rage is a personal and national threat to Israel's very existence and the peace of the whole world. All the nations seek to solve Israel's problems from their own perspective. Yet, very few either know or comprehend the transcendent power of her spiritual heritage. In fact, multitudes of her people, the Jews, are often in disagreement or even oblivious to these matters. From whatever lens one views her existence and destiny, it is evident that the reality of Israel has an impact on the whole world. Geographically, she is the navel of the world. Spiritually and politically this tiny nation has a far greater influence on everyone than can be attributed to her size, both in land and population!

Israel is the only nation that has suffered both exile and dispersion from her land for generations and yet has remained a nation which has been reborn into a contemporary state. Since her rebirth, she has suffered the ravage of wars, violence and hatred from her enemies which surround her, and unrelenting anti-Semitism from the whole world. The saga of her history and spiritual struggle is recorded in the Bible, which is the foundation of faith for both Christians and Jews. Therein, it is written that Israel is the only nation of which

God Himself says that Israel is His Land, and He will judge those who divide it. (Joel 3:2).

The Jewish people have engaged in hundreds of years of struggle and enmity with their enemies, including the world of Christendom, culminating in one of the most catastrophic events in Jewish history, the Holocaust. Most educated people in the Western world are familiar with the brutal and senseless massacre of six million Jews under the hatred of Adolph Hitler and Nazi Germany. The Jews' only crime against that evil regime was that *they were born Jewish!* Modern Israel was reborn as a nation in her ancient homeland out of the ashes and blood of this horrendous tragedy which attempted to annihilate all the Jewish people. Modern Israel is a nation of refugees and survivors! They have tasted poverty, rejection, homelessness, abuse, imprisonment, and even death for simply being Jewish!

These refugees did not even have time to dry their tears or heal their broken bodies. When they entered their God-given resurrected State of Israel in 1948, they were met with another chapter of hatred, terror and war that continues until this day. The surrounding Moslem nations sought to annihilate them. Even though Israel was enormously outnumbered by her enemies when they attacked, she prevailed against them with barely any weapons or even a well established military. To this day, these same enemies of Israel are determined to destroy her and her right to exist in her own God-given homeland.

I was personally thrust into the cauldron of the Middle East and entwined with Israel's destiny in 1973, when I sought to immigrate to Israel as an American social worker. Israel was in great need of social assistance at a time when droves of Russian Jews were beginning to immigrate to Israel. There was only one problem. I am a Christian and have no Jewish roots in my family tree. However, in 1967, at the time of the miraculous Six Day War in Israel, while I was in South Florida, I experienced a beautiful and life transforming encounter with the God of Israel and the one whom I believe to be His Messiah, Jesus. When this glorious epiphany occurred, I was in Miami, staying with friends and writing my first book, Every Wall Shall Fall. I had just come out of fourteen months in a communist prison in East Germany, a political prisoner of the Cold War because of my strong belief in personal freedom and desiring to help a captive East German. While in prison, my time in solitary confinement brought me into one of the darkest nights of my soul. There were even times I desired to die. However, even this atrocity in my life held a link of preparation for me to begin to enter into the broken heart of Israel.

In the midst of desperation while in three months of solitary confinement, the Spirit of God poured the liquid presence of His love into me when I felt I could not go on. I instantly knew that never again could I doubt the reality of God's existence or His personal love for me, as well as for all mankind! I was empowered *to love and forgive* my enemy! I knew that this love is the nature of God, who wants to bless and heal His creation and engage in a personal spiritual relationship with all those who want Him in their lives. I also discovered that this love is perfect and forgiving and infinitely greater than hatred. It is more powerful than all the weapons of destruction. It is a love that not only reconciles a person to God, but also to other human beings, including one's enemies who are willing to receive it.

At that time I had a revelation of the Hebrew word, *Messiah*, which means, *Anointed One*. This *anointing* is the pouring of God's Spirit upon or into an individual's life for God's purpose, His character, or His indwelling presence. For me it provided not only a spiritual rebirth, but a revelation of the presence of Messiah Himself.

For generations Jews have longed for a time when the world could live in love, peace and brotherhood with one another. Just one infusion of God's Spirit, living in and through people, gave me hope that a Messianic Age could and would one day become a reality. The nation of Israel was born into my heart at this time and I became a *Christian Zionist,* a person who believes in the Biblical promises of God to the nation of Israel and Jerusalem, and is engaged to walk alongside the Jewish people in their love and struggle for the restoration of their God given homeland.

When the stranger spoke to me: "*Like Abraham, I have called you to leave your father's house and go to the Land of Israel!*" I began to search the Scripture about Israel and pray about God's direction for my life. After much praying, reading the Bible and seeking counsel with other believers. I finally decided to go to the *aliyah* office in Miami, which is the agency that helps Jews immigrate to Israel. I inquired about how I might immigrate to Israel. I left there very disappointed when I was told that they "certainly needed social workers in Israel, but they could not help me because I am *not Jewish.*" A few days later, I received an invitation to a Jewish event where General Uzi Narkiss would be speaking. He was one of the generals who recaptured Jerusalem in the Six Day War of 1967. The meeting was to be held in a large Jewish synagogue in Miami Beach.

My Jewish friend, Ellen, and I entered the synagogue together. We were both amazed at how many people were there. We took a seat and quietly began to ask God "to reveal to us what we need to know." Instantly, a wonderful invisible cloud of the sweetest presence I had ever experienced filled the sanctuary. We were both struck with awe. I was afraid to speak, or even say the wrong thing. I finally asked God to show me that night, whether He wanted me to go to Israel.

As General Narkiss told us about numerous Russian Jews who were immigrating to Israel at that time, he suddenly stopped speaking, as if he were listening to an unseen voice. He instantly said, "We especially need *Americans in the field of social work in Israel!"*

I gasped. My friend, Ellen, spoke, *"That's your cue!"*

"But what about only wanting Jewish people in Israel?" I queried out loud. *"God if you really want me to go to Israel, show me about this issue of not being Jewish, and open the door tonight!"*

When General Narkiss finished his talk, he opened the meeting to questions from the audience. The first question came from a man who appeared to be an ultra Orthodox Rabbi from the way he was dressed. He was extremely angry and upset about the General's answer to his question about assisting non Jews to go and live in Israel. I sat on the edge of my seat waiting for the General's response to the rabbi.

"I believe that there is a place for *everyone* in Israel," General Narkiss firmly announced. The rabbi was enraged and wanted to argue right there on the spot. This infuriated the other Jews in the audience, who finally admonished the rabbi to "shut up or leave the meeting."

The rabbi immediately stormed out and the meeting was formally closed later. I rose and walked up to General Narkiss, "I'm an American social worker and I would like to immigrate to Israel, but your Miami office said they could not help me because I am not Jewish."

"That's no problem," he stated, immediately barking an order to the Miami representative, "Get this lady to Israel!"

In the following weeks I filled out papers, including giving references of anyone I knew in Israel. I only knew of two American Jews who had immigrated there. The fact that they were Messianic Jews —those who believe in Yeshua, which is Jesus name in Hebrew, did not appear to be important to me, since I knew that Israel always boasted of being a democracy. I was somewhat aware that there were ultra religious and extremist Jews who rejected these Jewish believers, but I assumed that the government protected religious freedom as its constitution proclaims. I was greatly astonished when a response came back from Jerusalem to the Miami office declaring that the Government did not like my references. They said, "It seems that these references are *members of a group that believe in Yeshu, and the Government does not want any trouble in Israel."* The Miami director of the Agency then warned me; "*If you want to go to Israel, you must assure us that you are not going as a missionary!*" He appeared to be very fearful and disturbed that he had to deal with me.

I was shocked! "Sir, I am going as a *social worker."* I replied. Then I was the one who became disturbed and fearful. Were they going to *discriminate against me for being a Christian?* In two weeks, the Interior Ministry of Israel sent a letter to the a*liyah* office in Miami, telling the director that they "*did not want me in* Israel!" I was crushed when I heard the words of rejection. Then, something happened that gave me a surprising clue about the Israelis. Little did I realize that I was in the middle of a "cultural war" which was taking place in Israel. After the Miami director announced the "bad news", he quickly stated "Don't worry! We'll get you there some other way! Uzi Narkiss will be coming to America again soon, and we will discuss your case!"

I was both surprised and amused to see that the same person who had initially turned me away from his office because I was not Jewish was now telling me that he was going to do his best to "get me to Israel." After a couple of weeks I was informed that they were sending me to Israel through the kibbutz *aliyah* desk, which was not sympathetic to the militant extreme of the religious Jews! That was my rocky beginning with the tiny nation of Israel. Generations of anti-Semitism and persecution from so-called Christians had wounded and scarred the Jewish hearts of that nation of survivors, so that it was almost impossible to trust an outsider, especially one that was a genuine Christian!

Little did I know that I was walking into the midst of a vicious family feud among the Jews themselves, concerning *"Who is a Jew?"* and also into the arms of the romantic conflict of two people whose love was forbidden. The Yom Kippur War and the fierce civil war over "Who is a Jew?"were the backdrops of my drama within Israel.

King Solomon said, *"There is a time to keep silence and a time to speak.*" For over thirty years I have kept silent about the true story I am now going to relate in this book. In recording the events of this story, I have a deep and overwhelming awareness that I am dealing with a subject that transcends my capacity to interpret adequately. For two thousand years there has been a wall of partition between Jews and Christians. Enmity, hostility, hatred, and bitterness are only a few of the negative attributes which have accumulated on this wall. Perhaps, more than any characteristic, *fear* underlies the mistrust and misunderstanding that have caused so much pain and alienation in Christian-Jewish relations. We have made tremendous inroads in healing and reconciliation but we still have some distance to go. In spite of the enormous gulf that has separated these cultures; I want to dare to build a bridge between them. I am of the genuine conviction that there is more that should unite us than should divide us! I have lived this story myself, through the eyes of both worlds. In fact, at the time of a major turning point in my own spiritual journey as a deeply committed Christian, which was at the time of Israel's

Six Day War, I felt a sacred mandate to make a wholehearted and honest attempt to enter fully into the world of the Jew. The roots of Christianity are unquestionably Jewish. True biblical Christianity, unfortunately tainted by two thousand years of syncretism with paganism, is clearly Jewish in its nature. All of the writers of the New Testament, with one possible exception are Jews. In the case of Luke, the Gentile physician, some scholars feel he might have been a second generation Christian of Jewish origin.

It is unfortunate that I have to confide the adverse behaviors of some prominent personalities in an identifiable way. When I can avoid this or disguise identities, as well as names and locations and remain true to my narrative, I do so. Therefore, I have changed names and locations and left some people nameless. Finally, I offer my own conclusions. I invite readers to formulate their own. Above all, whatever one's background or conviction, I encourage all Jews, Christians, and others who want to expand their vision of those who differ and enlarge their hearts toward them, to share this story with me—*to become both reconcilers and peacemakers in a world torn by fear, hatred, strife and enmity.*

FOREIGNERS SHALL REBUILD YOUR WALLS

**"Foreigners will rebuild your walls,
and their kings will serve you."
(Isaiah 60:10)**

The year was 1973. My inauguration into the pioneer life of the early Zionists in Israel came through Yossi. The moment I met him I knew he was a "super" Jew. No, he was not the kind with all the black religious clothes and the long, curly side locks. He was a gangly young man with a visionary spirit and a big heart. The kibbutz housemother for the foreigners' group must have secretly had matchmaking on her mind when she immediately decided to station Yossi and myself as neighbors in the kibbutz housing. Yossi was a Jew from Argentina. There was nothing religious about him, except his generous compassionate heart. He had spent many years in the States. "Jose" was his birth name, but like many immigrants, he took a Hebrew name when he came to Israel. He was doing his second "tour of duty" like a true Zionist in an Israeli kibbutz, which was one of the agricultural development communities south of Ashkelon in Israel.

Yossi was the very first person with whom I spent more than five minutes in conversation in a strange new culture. That made it natural for me to cling to him for support. Yossi appeared to like it when I did. He secretly admired me for being the bold and daring Christian Zionist who had burned all my bridges behind me in order to rebuild the brave new world of Zion. As a Gentile Christian, I barely had my big toe inside of the world of the Jew. I was both excited and scared. According to my Southern lingo, I looked just like the "sweet petunia in the middle of the pea patch", and I felt like "little girl lost." My upswept blond hair with a French twist, and with a touch of light makeup, made me a stark contrast to the raggedy Ann rumpled look of the average female kibbutznik. Since Yossi had arrived the same day I did, he had probably been ordained as the most likely candidate to latch on to for security. Yossi had already conquered a good chunk of his basic Hebrew vocabulary, and he knew how to find his way to the central dining hall, so I invited myself as his tagalong.

The Miami Jewish Agency Director had warned me of the severity of the struggle for survival on the Israeli pioneer frontier, but I was truly caught off guard by the austerity of communal life on the kibbutz. Part of the atmosphere was rooted in ideology as well as the challenge of causing the Middle Eastern desert to bloom.

In some strange way, I felt that the year I had spent in a Communist prison as a political hostage had been a vital preparation for the survival skills I needed. My first lonely night on a cot in a drab square room reminded me of my prison cell. I stumbled in the dark, traipsing out into the cold black night with my flashlight to find the community latrine. I had never heard a hoot owl screeching in the night, either, so the eerie sounds sent shudders down my spine. Before the dawn cracked through the gloom, entire antiphonal choruses of birds were busy saluting the new day. It sounded as if hundreds of them had gathered for their hallelujah chorus just outside my window. I hopped straight up from the bed with my knit jacket wrapped around me and fired up the kerosene stove. "Brrrrr." I had already decided I would rather choke to death on the fumes than sleep in a cold room all night.

"Some pioneer you'll make," I thought to myself as I picked up the big kerosene container to fill it with fuel. I was consoled by the reminder that the founding fathers had suffered much greater hardships, and if they had survived, I was determined nothing would stop me, either.

The arrival on the kibbutz in the wilderness had provided a crass contrast to the fast moving, mod, disco, materialistic world of glitz and glamour I had been exposed to on the Israeli ship which brought me across the Mediterranean. It was a battle all the way, surviving a bronchial infection, conjunctivitis, and two days of vomiting. These trials were nothing compared to the aggressive and amorous advances of the fevered seamen. The monastic simplicity of the kibbutz was a welcomed relief. I felt I was home.

It took little time to discover that kibbutz life was the backbone of the early Zionist spirit which rebuilt the ruins of Israel and upheld her agricultural economy from the end of the 19th Century. Waves of brave settlers had come from Eastern Europe and later from North Africa, South America and the States. Their communal life was built upon survival from outside enemies, the common cultivation of their food, and the simplicity of the ideology they had brought with them from abroad. No one owned private property, except maybe the shirts on their backs, and in later years, their television sets. Cars were not allowed as personal possessions, except for rare exceptions.

Quickly I caught on that the "god of work" was exalted. In fact, I learned that one word for work in Hebrew was also one of the words for "worship". Though I initially found great joy in the dedication and sweat I spilled to rebuild the walls of Zion, I quickly discovered that life was lopsided. Feelings were luxuries that no one could afford, and for a great romantic like me, it was sheer torture to have to live without them. Even the kibbutz dogs were stoic and undemonstrative, like most of the people appeared to be on the outside. Later, though, I learned that with a voluminous turnover of outsiders coming through the small closed community regularly, people had stopped risking themselves to discover one another.

The Jewish Agency in America had suggested that I begin my pilgrimage in Israel just like the pioneers on this particular kibbutz. I was a part of a group from ages 18 to 35 who came every six months to learn Hebrew half a day and work the other half. In turn, the group received a token of pocket money each month, room and board, work clothes, and medical coverage. All the basics of survival were there, but I felt an incredible emotional pain from being locked up in a spiritual vacuum. Perhaps the emptiness I perceived was really filled with the adoration of mother earth—the love of the soil, the land, Eretz *Israel.* Her biblical prophets had proclaimed that when her God brought her back to the Land, "her sons would be married to her land." So they were. There was a mystery how her people were inextricably bound to her matrix with a deep cord. Sometimes, it seemed, especially with the old timers, that Israel was the god her sons worshipped on the kibbutz, and not the God of Israel! Yet, I, too, began to feel the compelling attraction of a love affair with her land.

Out in the raw open fields of the kibbutz more than anywhere else, I sensed and felt that Israel was being rebuilt by those who had been grasped by some powerful vision of what she was yet to become. In spite of odds, obstacles, and opposition, these rugged visionaries had persevered with the impossible dream that her prophets had foretold. Their blood, sweat, tears, and sacrifices were wrapped up in the wilderness that was now in full bloom! It thrilled me to experience it with them. I was somehow fascinated, too, by all the blending of the human fabric which consisted of our group of foreign volunteers. We were mostly divided into Russians and Americans—mainly for language purposes. The colorful Russian Jewish soul with its vision, intensity, passion and intolerance immediately clashed with the American casual, happy-go-lucky, nigh anarchistic love of personal freedom. The Russians were unaccustomed to "doing their own thing", and the Americans were bound and determined that nobody was going to stop them from smoking their pot or shacking up with someone! The Russians were appalled, and my little Russian *yenta* roommate always spit in spontaneous disapproval when she described some of the American malcontents who had landed on our kibbutz.

In fact, observing the behavior of some of the Americans in our Hebrew class, I concluded that the kibbutz must offer a treatment center for wayward American kids from dysfunctional families. We were indeed an odd hodgepodge of social radicals who were living the communal lifestyle; the idealists like Yossi who saw the dream of Zionism; devoted youth fulfilling their duty of Jewish *mitzvoth* by helping Israel; confused Gentile seekers in search of their identity; troublemakers who had been shipped out of the States by frustrated parents; restless adventurers; and simply those who did not know why they were there. In any case, it appeared that everyone was searching for something by being in Israel.

The Russians, on the other hand, had paid a great price for their liberation and took to heart that they had come to *Eretz Israel* to rebuild their lives in freedom. The initial adjustment was more difficult for them, especially when they saw the unbridled self expression of the libertine Americans, and when they struggled with the language. For a city gal who had lived in many major world cities—Berlin, Madrid, New York, Los Angeles, Miami—the rugged life of the pioneer frontier offered a new challenge for me. I felt trapped when the work leader assigned me to the dining hall to clean tables, scrub floors, and serve the kibbutzniks. I had yearned to breathe the fresh free air of the open meadows, but I also sought connection to the people. The need to communicate and articulate with others was as strong in me as breathing. I found it excruciating when my lack of Hebrew hindered me.

I dove into my work with all the "worship" I knew how. I was gravely disappointed when I got nothing in return but North African women screaming at my ineptness. No one gave me or any other person, an orientation. They told us to "just jump in" and we would learn after a while. A middle aged Belgian volunteer saw my dismay one day and decided to teach me my initial Hebrew lesson before the real classes began. He gave me the first new word in my vocabulary, "*savlanoot*", which means "patience" in English. All the cartoonists in Israel depict every new immigrant learning this word first. The Israelis were famous for preaching *savlanoot* to the immigrants, but it was the standing joke in Israel that *no one* practiced patience!

On the kibbutz work was so sacred that it had to be maintained even on the Sabbath. I found myself resenting those sweet days of rest which were robbed from me from time to time. Most of the kibbutz members were socialist settlers who were basically anti-religious in their outlook. I had heard tales of how in the early days on the kibbutz, they refused legal wedding ceremonies. All official marriages had to pass through the religious authority in Israel, so the hardnosed founders of kibbutz life chose common law marriage instead.

The funniest story I had heard was whispered behind closed doors and was about how the kibbutz in its first years of survival had secretly raised pigs, which was contrary to Jewish religious law and an abomination to the religionists. Pork was still tasty to the non religious Jews, although they were forced to call it "white steak" in Israel, so as not to offend the sensibilities of their opponents! The local rabbi was required to pay regular calls to inspect the poultry and dairy products on the kibbutz in order to grant them kosher status. Each time the rabbi was scheduled for a visit, the kibbutzniks hid their pigs behind a mound outside their complex, so that their other products would not be rejected by the rabbinical inspectors. Either the "wind" or the word got out to the authorities, and the rabbis began to boycott the other kibbutz products.

The clever kibbutzniks merely got around the issue, which stated that it was illegal "to raise pigs on Jewish soil". They built a platform up above the ground. They then informed the religious authorities that the pigs were no longer on Jewish soil and continued their commerce with pork. The authorities did not find this amusing and threatened to block the sale of all their products if the pigs were not permanently removed. The rabbis naturally won. I was beginning to learn that Israel is a nation of colorful contrasts.

HEPHZIBAH AND BEULAH

**"You will be called Hephzibah, ("My delight is in her"),
and your land Beulah ("Married"),
for the Lord will take delight in you and your land
will be married. As a young man marries a maiden,
so will your sons marry you."
(Isaiah 62:4-5)**

My first encounter with the Hebrew language was a fiasco! I distinctly felt a wall of conspiracy around the language and the culture. An impenetrable barrier seemed to shut out the rest of the world! It could not be broken by sheer effort. The vocabulary I learned immediately bounced off my brain the moment I received it. I was baffled because I usually had facility with languages, speaking Spanish, German, and some French. The more I tried, the harder it became. For the first time in my life I knew what the frustration of a learning disabled person could be!

Completely isolated from other Christians, I sometimes felt I was a member of the "out-group", experiencing some of the loneliest moments ever. When I did not desperately cling to the Lord in my prayer corner, I was holding tightly to Yossi, whom I trusted. Great tenderness and affection flowed between us, and for the first time in my life I began to feel completely loved by a man who was not demanding anything at all from me. Yossi, who was a couple of years my junior, cared for me "pure and chaste from afar". His rugged youthful look with a well defined "Jewish nose," long full hair, and a generous beard gave him the appearance of a Hebrew prophet.

When Yossi strummed the strings of his expressive guitar in the group circle each evening, he plucked a deep chord in my own heart which vibrated with life. I loved to hear him sing and run through his repertoire of all my favorite songs, especially those of Spanish flavor! Without even realizing it, I had become emotionally attached to him.

One Sabbath afternoon, Yossi and I decided to take a hike over the wooded hill behind the kibbutz. The mound was sprinkled with olive trees, clinging to the dry tan sandy soil. Suddenly we discovered a tent of Bedouins camped on the hillside. One of my secret desires was to visit these tribal nomads. As Yossi and I ambled closer, an old patriarchal looking man was arriving home on his donkey. We mutually exchanged customary nods of greeting. The man motioned to us to enter his tent. Of course, we complied. His wife, robed and veiled, and loaded with gold colored bangles, pulled out cushions on the dirt floor and disappeared into another partition of the tent. A dirty, bare bottomed toddler tumbled into the area, and the mother quickly snatched him away. I concluded that the women must not be included on such visits.

The old Bedouin with weather parched skin appeared as I had imagined some of the ancient biblical characters. He proceeded to grind coffee before our eyes, and then roast it over a fire. We traded broken comments in bits and pieces of Hebrew, which was inadequate for us all. Most Bedouins spoke a dialect of Arabic. When we finished this ceremony, his wife brought us some fresh oranges. I delighted watching the couple enjoy providing us with genuine Middle Eastern hospitality. As soon as the old man saw us satisfied with food, he offered his bed to us, indicating he would depart. Yossi explained that we had to return to the kibbutz soon.

When we rose to leave, as if reading my mind, the patriarch offered me a ride on his donkey. I nodded to him that I would relish the opportunity. I sensed I was riding off into the time clock of another world. Unfortunately, I did not realize that the blanket saddle was only loosely secured. Suddenly, the animal began to trot and at once I was slung flat on my back on the hard ground. I lay paralyzed for a few minutes, out of the view of the tent, fearing I might never walk again. After some time I limped back to the tent. I had to lean on Yossi all the way back to the kibbutz. I resolved not to be so adventurous in the future.

Increasingly, the lack of appreciation for my overexertion in the dining hall and the yelling of the North African women began to get under my skin. I requested a transfer in my work assignment, convinced that I was not cut out to be a waitress—at least, not in the Middle East. I was immediately reassigned to the hot house where roses were grown. A week later the word got back to me that I had been one of the best workers the dining room ever had!

Initially, I found hot house duty dangerous. The beauties were deadly in their attacks. Their long claws ripped into my clothes and body. Gradually I learned to maneuver my path through their thorny territory, and I began to enjoy their companionship. As deadly as their defensive barbs were, the roses were less threatening than the spicy and unpredictable human temperament I had encountered in the dining hall. While I was alone with them, I could enjoy the mental leisure to meditate, and sing and worship their wonderful Creator with no one around to bother.

One evening, after I returned to my drab room, Yossi came running to my door. "Come on! Let's go! A calf is being born!" I was as excited as Yossi was to embark on this agriculture adventure. We raced together to the stall.

I cringed as I watched. Two kibbutzniks took a stick, tied it to the legs of the calf, which was still inside its mother, and began jerking. I felt so sorry for the poor mom. After they finally pulled the baby out, they kicked mom in the stomach and hit her with the stick because she refused to stand up and take care of new born calves. Tears ran from my eyes because this seemed cruel to me. I determined that if life on the kibbutz produced this hardness to feeling, it was not the place for me.

Gradually, in the strange blend of mixing cultures on the kibbutz, I decided that Rudyard Kipling, the poet, was wrong when he declared "East is East and West is West and the twain shall never meet." They had met, and even collided, on a tiny strip of land called

Eretz Israel! Nowhere was it more evident than when I visited one of the surrounding villagers' homes outside the kibbutz.

Isaac, a kind older Israeli, offered me a ride home from the Ashkelon garage one day. As soon as I set foot in his car, I had the feeling of being in the presence of the ancient patriarchs of his people. I felt some kind of mystical bond of continuity with his land and heritage. As he shared his vision of Zion with me, I confided my own love for his Land and people, informing him I was an American Christian. He appeared to be thrilled to discover my heart for his country, especially since he felt that this trait was absent in the younger generation of Israelis. He insisted that I go home with him to meet his son.

I felt completely safe going home with this Hebrew stranger. When I met his son, I sensed that the young man had lost something of his own heritage, embracing all of the baser side of the American culture. This youth who appeared around eighteen years old was completely enamored with the psychedelic, disco American musical culture with its noisy confusion. I sensed a disdain in him for his Hebrew heritage with a complete indifference about the future of his Land. I silently hoped that he was not characteristic of his generation, for I felt Israel had a higher calling, not only to its own people, but the world. *I held a deep conviction that what most early pioneers had called "Zionism" was really a move of the Spirit of God, restoring Israel back to her land according to the promise of God through her prophets.*

I mulled this over in my mind when I returned to the kibbutz. I wondered whether once Israel had been physically rebuilt, where she was going to go from there. Even though her material prosperity was essential to rebuild the nation, would she be pulled into a materialistic existence alone, or would she arise to her God given call to the spiritual purpose she had received from the beginning? Zionism alone, without the recognition of the God behind it, was a more subtle form of atheistic materialism which many secular idealists could espouse. Israel needed more than faith in her land and her destiny in order to survive. *She needed reconciliation with her God who had promised her through her prophets that His glory would shine upon her and that nations would come to her light. He had promised that her redeemer would come to Zion and His Spirit would be poured out upon her! I longed to see that day!*

Gradually, I got to know the older members of the kibbutz. One by one they confided in me their own disillusionment of their earlier Zionist dream. There were two routes these old-timers seemed to travel. Those whose hearts had been pruned by suffering offered streams of compassion for others. Those hardliners who refused to buckle and bend with the struggle only became harder and harder. Their attitude was "we did it and endured more severe hardships than the next generation is undergoing, so why complain?"

It seems that the hardliners had forgotten that when they had sacrificed and suffered, it had been because they were reaching toward a vision. The vision had become sullied with time and the weariness of endless warfare. The younger generation refused to see why anyone could ever deliberately choose hardship. For that reason young people were leaving kibbutz life by the hoards and fleeing to the city. Kibbutz life was the agriculture backbone of Israel.

In those moments when I felt some of the spiritual emptiness in the lives around me, I sensed that the loneliest heart in the world must be God's own. The "people whom He had formed for Himself to proclaim His praise" according to the prophet Isaiah, "were neither seeking nor relying on Him, so that God might bless them in every way." I was also concerned that they were looking toward America for their example, and I knew that our nation was capable of failing them! America had her own problems and sins that she needed to deal with. God had never called her to be the "redeemer of Israel," but to stand with Israel and be her friend.

Another aspect of kibbutz life troubled me as well, although this problem has greatly diminished today. On many kibbutzim children were not allowed to live with their parents. Although parents and children visited daily, they slept in different houses. From psychologists we now know that the earliest years of a child's life are crucial in developing trust. The close affection and personal protection of their parents plays a great role in this development. I asked one of the adult kibbutzniks what her feelings were from growing up apart from her family. She was not even aware that she had feelings! So often I felt that the message that had been imparted to them in the presence of struggle and opposition on the pioneer frontier was denial. "Nothing matters." "If it hurts inside, it doesn't matter. Just get the job done!"

I felt very sad for these beautiful pioneers who had sacrificed so much for the rebuilding of their nation. I knew that it *does matter to their God.* He deeply cares for their needs and their pain, and wants each one to know His personal love. Their early idealism was not enough to sustain them. It had run dry. I prayed for their needs in the silence of my room. One day, I was greatly encouraged when I read in a book that Theodore Herzl, the father of modern Zionism, had received a revelation of Messiah when he was twelve years old! (I had no way of verifying its accuracy). However, I did believe that the true spirit of Zionism and the Spirit of God were one! It was all about the restoration of Israel promised in the sacred Scripture.

Yossi and I were growing closer daily, so much so that others saw the beautiful bond of friendship we had and became jealous. One little schoolgirl was madly in love with Yossi and his singing guitar. She began to express hatred toward me because of my relationship with him! I felt that Yossi and I had the beauty of loving and being loved in pure unselfish friendship that the lonely envied. I recognized that it was a spiritual bond of deep friendship that linked our hearts!

Divine love is inclusive and not exclusive —different from romantic love. I wanted very much to build closer relationships with others, as well, but they appeared unreceptive. Their walls had long been erected for survival. However, the newly arrived Russian immigrants appeared to be both eager and receptive for friendship. One of the kibbutzniks appeared amazed that I was inviting my little Russian peasant roommate to travel with me to the Sinai in my VW station wagon. It was impossible for her to believe that anyone could genuinely care about this ugly young woman.

As I was trying to explain this to the baffled kibbutznik, I suddenly realized the foolishness of love! God's love had never been based on reason or logic. The little Russian reject, Sonja, said that no one had ever given her anything in her life without expecting something in return. "How sad," I thought. I told her I wanted to give her something with no strings attached by inviting her to join me on this trip to the Sinai. She immediately confided that she had never traveled outside her Russian village. Big tears rolled down her cheeks when I told her I *really* wanted her to go with me.

Camping out in the Sinai, which was still under Israel's control, was an adventure for us all. Five of us had piled into my little VW station wagon. We were a Russian, a Brazilian immigrant, and three Americans bouncing across the hot desert. We were a scraggly looking lot as we slept on the beaches. The moment we crossed over from the Negev into the desert of Sinai we entered another era of civilization. From the majestic royal palm lined beaches of El Arish to the world's most magnificent coral reefs in Sharm el Sheik, we were all enthralled by the many colors and textures of the desert.

A giant sandstorm whipped up unexpectedly while we camped near the oil fields of Abu Rhodeis. I feared we would be swept up into the Gulf of Suez while the ferocious wind shook the car. It was even scarier for those who were camped outside with lean-to blanket tents, being blasted with sand and grit. Water supplies were nonexistent in our barren wasteland. We continued on our trip pasted with dust. Everyone had an eerie feeling when we drove into one of the many ghost towns along the Gulf. Entire villages and cities had been left deserted overnight when the Israelis took the territory in the Six-Day War of 1967. A strange beauty in all of the patterns and textures of the desert made a memorable impression upon me, and I wanted to visit it again.

Back in the world of the kibbutz, there were days when I had feelings and impressions I had never before experienced. Often when I was outdoors, I felt a sense of timelessness, as if I were carried by the wind. Sometimes, strange new emotions rolled over me like sheets of a midnight fog. I felt one such sensation on the day of the commemoration of the Holocaust.

I lived on a kibbutz where many survivors lived. Some had lost relatives in the atrocities of Hitler. Many were Eastern Europeans who had been persecuted by so-called Christians. What I felt on that day of commemoration could only be described as an intense hatred and rejection toward the non Jews who had persecuted these victims. It was such a cloud of hostility that I felt paranoid, although I knew it was not personally directed at me. From time to time I felt very much like an unwelcome outsider, who would never be embraced into their world. Perhaps it was a parallel or counter response to the anti- Semitism these settlers had suffered.

Early one morning, I awoke to the distant sound of a busy tractor in the pear orchard. I looked at my calendar because I thought it was a holiday. Why it was May 1st, the workers international holiday, and still not sacred! I was also scheduled to work on that holiday. After working three Sabbaths in a row, I began to resent the "religion of work". Initially, I had come to love to dig my fingers into the soil, embrace the armloads of fruit in picking season, or drink in the aroma of budding roses at dawn. I had arrived at the point of looking forward to collapsing into my bed at night. Suddenly, I was beginning to balk at the worship of the god of *avodah,* work! I did not want to become its slave by submitting to the guilt and fear of begging permission to allow myself some rest. This kind of life for me represented the "curse of Cain". Cain had worshipped the production of his own hands. I requested a day off and decided to go up to Jerusalem and think about relocating.

"Going up to Jerusalem" as the Israelis always said, was a mixed emotion for me. The Golden City had a special charm and attraction as the capital of "God's Land". More had been written about Jerusalem in the Bible than any city in the world, including about its future glory. It also possessed an atmosphere of great religious darkness that permeated it. There was multicultural mystery, intrigue, and deception in the air. Moslems, Orthodox Jews, Catholics, Russian and Greek Orthodox were all vying for political power over it.

This trip I felt different about going. It was Israel's Independence Day celebration. There would be rejoicing, dancing in the streets and colorful parades. I had also been wrestling with some soul-searching before I departed the kibbutz. Yossi and I were now getting much too close to each other for comfort. Our inner lives were becoming inseparable. The moment I felt I needed him, he appeared at my doorstep. The warm evenings with the melodic guitar began to "get under my skin". Almost everyone in our kibbutz Hebrew class felt the need to pair off as couples and some were already living together. This did not run counter to the kibbutz ethic. Yossi and I both were feeling the pressure. Neither of us wanted to conform to the pressures of emotional involvement which came from the insecurity that surrounded the lonely life in another world, one that rejected the luxury of feeling. Men and women were being thrown into each others' arms as an outlet of support and consolation.

I sent my most urgent SOS up to the Almighty for discernment. I begged Him to show me whether He had more permanent plans for the relationship between Yossi and me. Twice I uttered this cry, and twice another girl came to visit him on the kibbutz. I decided that it must be time for a change of my course in Israel.

Independence Day in Jerusalem was the exact prescription my ailing heart needed! I literally went "bonkers" running around the City with a tiny plastic squeaky hammer, hitting everyone I saw on the head. This fun little ceremony was the way Israelis celebrated their birthday, as well as dancing in the streets. Like all the Israelis I yelled *"hag sameach"* ("happy holiday") as I conked strangers on the head with my plastic hammer. They did not hesitate to conk me back!

Zion Square in downtown Jerusalem was sectioned off and crowds were milling around, munching all the goodies the street vendors were peddling. Here and there groups of folk dancers enlivened street corners. When an exotic looking Sephardic Jew bumped into me, I knew it was not accidental. I had seen him observing me for some time. When he learned I was an American, he invited himself to escort me on a personal introduction of the City of Gold. He seemed to be very nice. Why not?

Alon, like most all of the Israeli *sabra* men I had met, appeared to be a delicate blend of masculine warrior and tender lover. This contrasting combination was fascinating to me, since so many men I knew from my own background appeared reluctant to expose their hearts and viewed it as a sign of weakness. The fact that strong Israeli men could hug each other comfortably or freely cry in the presence of women made them appear manlier in my eyes. Alon's Sephardic culture made him a gracious and hospitable host, as well as a warm and friendly companion to lead me to discover Jerusalem. He was thrilled to be showing an American around his city. He had many war stories of his own experience in the recapture of Jerusalem by the Israelis. As he guided me to numerous historical sites of his city, it became evident that he was proud to be a citizen of Jerusalem. I was most excited to hear about his personal participation in the battle for the recapture of Jerusalem. Just listening to him made me feel like I was reliving history while it was happening!

Alon sprung a surprise on me. He wanted to share a special tour with me—a trip through King Hezekiah's ancient water tunnel! I had no idea exactly what was involved, as a guard handed him a flashlight and told me to roll up my pants legs. We stepped into a pitch black catacomb like tunnel, slightly taller than we were and almost touching both shoulders on each side. Suddenly I felt water rise to my knees and as we proceeded, then to my hips and my chest. Alon stopped and turned off the light. I was up to my neck in water, with my purse held tightly in my teeth! I began to feel panic. Alon laughed and told me it would be all right. After half a mile of this course, it appeared that no end was in sight. My head was almost touching the upper wall. "Alon", what have you gotten me into?" I cried.

He enjoyed keeping me in suspense as he promised I would not drown. Midway into the tunnel he decided that it would be great for both of us to sing "Jerusalem of Gold" in Hebrew while we pushed through the water. There we were a fine pair of soaking songbirds, sliding through the waters of an ancient tunnel, warbling "*Yerushalem shel shahav"!* We parted ways later when I went away to change my clothes in the car. It was a beautiful Independence Day celebration, and I thanked him for the tour.

Upon my return to the kibbutz, I knew which way I had to go. My destination was away from Yossi, away from the spiritual vacuum, and into the urban pulse of Israel. I wrote to the Jewish Agency office in Jerusalem asking them to guide me on my next step. I was especially interested in taking a course of Jewish and Israeli studies so I could gain a deeper understanding of the country and culture.

A few days later I received my answer. I was being transferred to a residence for immigrants in one of the oldest Israeli cities, Jaffe, which had now become a renowned slum of Tel Aviv. Its redeeming feature was that there was also an artist quarter there.

I said my last good-byes to the kibbutzniks in my very first home in Israel. I held Yossi's hand for the last time. As I drove past the grapefruit orchard I had helped to plant, I beamed with pride. I was going to spend the night in the home of two newly acquired American friends in Ashkelon and move to my new location the following day.

Inside the apartment of Jacob and Miriam, I re-entered the real world. The simplicity of cinderblocks and wood bookshelves, wild flowers and warm orange colors was soothing to me. The freedom to speak my heart with two new American Jewish Immigrants who were trying to order their lives made me feel really at home. The luxury of a tub bath with hot water was the perfect antidote for my sad separation. While I sat buried under a cloud of bubble bath, the melodic strains of Rodrigo's Concerto of *Aranjuez* floated over the stereo speakers into the bathroom. That was Yossi's and my song! He had played it often for me on the guitar. As I listened to the music, I felt the vibrant warmth of the Spanish heart inside of my Jewish friend, plucking the chords of his guitar. *Aranjuez* and the kibbutz—what worlds apart! The crass concrete reality of the cows, chickens, and the crops of a kibbutz and the romantic nostalgia of a lost era in Spain were diametrically opposed. Somehow, I associated the warm melody with the Sephardic Jews, and the cold rational work ethic with the Ashkenazi Jews. Whether there was any substance to my feelings, I needed to learn more about the two streams of Jewish culture before I drew any conclusions. What interested me most, though, was that I had lived and studied in both Spain and Germany. Both countries had made a strong impact on my life. The spirit of the Spanish and the Germanic cultures were the two central foundation blocks of historical Jewish culture and tradition in the Diaspora. I could hardly wait to find out what life was going to be like in Jaffe!

TRUMPET IN ZION

"Blow the trumpet in Zion; sound the alarm on my holy hill. Let all who live in the land tremble, for the day of the Lord is coming."
(Joel 2:1)

"*Milhama! Milhama!*" The swarthy youth ran down the street yelling. He was racing down the streets of Bat Yam crying "*War! War!*" His piercing pronouncement shredded the blanket of somber silence which was suspended over the neighborhood. It was *Yom Kippur*, the holiest day of the Jewish calendar, when most people were in their homes fasting for the atonement of sin or visiting the synagogue. Bat Yam, the bustling coastal resort city on the Mediterranean, had folded up its shop awnings and people secluded themselves behind the closed shutters in their homes or some had filled the synagogues for services. No one dared drive a car on this day. Not even the militantly anti-religious dared trespass against the reverence of the Day of Atonement. Even those who made no pretense of piety held this day with respect and awe.

No automobile could be seen moving in one of the most secular cities of the nation. For some, this cessation of activity was induced by intimidation from the religious extremists, for others it represented the one moment when all Israel secretly paused in national reflection and accountability before her God. The Israeli doctor who had treated me on the ship's crossing to Israel had told me his car had been stoned by irate religious zealots when he had to drive on an emergency call to assist a dying patient on *Yom Kippur!* Now, it was only two o'clock in the afternoon and the agitated youth dared to desecrate the sacred occasion by screaming in the streets. I jumped from my seat and peered over the balcony rail. Suddenly, doors flew open. Automobile engines were heard starting all around me. I had not understood exactly what word the youth was screaming. I leaned over the rail and yelled in English. "What's happening?"

"War!" We're at war!" The Sephardi yelled back as he rushed toward his car. Chills rushed down my spine. "Oh my Lord, what am I supposed to do now?" Maybe they are just overreacting. Perhaps some enemy plane had wandered into Israel's air space and had been shot down. Yet I heard others crying out "war," and the streets began filling with cars. Instant emotional paralysis overcame me when I tried to consider it. "Quick, get your radio," I ordered Barry, who was looking to me as an interpreter. Barry and Harriet had never overcome the hurdle of the language barrier as new American immigrants to Israel. We frantically flipped the radio dial back and forth looking for an English broadcast. It was the wrong time for English news. Surely there would be some special provision for tourists and immigrants in English for a national emergency. No luck.

We checked with all the surrounding neighbors for information. They were French, North African, and South American immigrants and they were all as uninformed as we were. Then, we tried to find some neighbors who had sons or husbands who were being called out to their military units who could give us further information. We could find no one. The events spinning around us were filled with an air of incredulity. War was a concept I had no way of relating to except from a television screen. Suddenly, I had been thrown into the periphery of its reality. What should I do?

Only half an hour before, Barry and Harriet, a couple of American immigrants, and Rachel, a young Jewish friend, and I had sat on a scenic balcony. We were fasting and supping on sun splashed whitecaps that slapped the shore of the rich blue Mediterranean. This view permeated the entire panorama. We had decided to fast and prayerfully commemorate the highest holy day of the nation of Israel together. After a visit to a local synagogue, we had slipped away to the silent shelter of the sea vista to meditate on the real meaning of the day. Barry was not a traditional Jew, and his wife, Harriet, was in complete ignorance, since she was a Gentile who had chosen not to convert. However, Rachel who was a Jew with distinct Messianic belief and I were taking the significance of the day to heart. We had been offering prayers for both national and personal repentance. War cries had interrupted us.

When my mental paralysis gradually began to subside and I realized that war was really occurring before my eyes, I began to question others I saw in the street who looked like old timers. "What are we supposed to do?" I asked one, then another. I assumed that there must be a plan of evacuation of certain areas, organized instructions, and assignments of activity to civilians. My helpless query was met with characteristic Israeli arrogance that I should even ask such a question. "Whatever you always do," responded the quick retort, obviously irritated by my ignorance.

I learned that there was no plan, no leader, no orders, or no instructions except for those assigned to the military. We would all be left to our own devices to cope with this national emergency and our own personal survival. At once, I felt very much alone as a stranger in a foreign culture. I had no immediate family to turn to. I picked up my Bible and began flipping pages looking for answers. My eyes fell on a passage "*Don't fear anything except the Lord of the armies of heaven. If you fear Him, you need fear nothi*ng *else*," I read. I heaved a sigh of relief and deliberated my next action.

First, I knew that I had to get Rachel back to her roommate, Lana, who would be worried about her. I hated to leave the two girls alone in their rickety old building with their Arab landlord. Their "hotel" was the last coastal stronghold of a crumbling Jaffe slum, standing proudly as a solitary historical monument next to the sea. The elderly Arab Christian matriarch who owned the property had held tenaciously to her possession while all the invading armies of the past had crossed the region. She had her battle scars to prove it. She had lost one eye in the last war. Her building had been shelled. Nothing melted her ironclad determination to hold on to her property. All of the opposing armies had only reinforced her resolve to lose her life if necessary before letting go of her land. It was for this reason her decrepit building alone stood in the path of progressive redevelopment of the coastal strip between Tel Aviv and Jaffe. She refused to sell at any price. Rachel and Lana had wandered upon the lonely hotel in search of cheap housing. There was something engaging about the suspicious old Arab woman with one eye, living with the sea at her doorstep. It had captured their romantic imagination. They had decided to stay.

I had barely moved into temporary housing provided for Russian and Romanian immigrants which was located not very far from my two new friends. Apparently the Jewish Agency was treating me no differently than a regular Jewish immigrant for absorption into Israeli society. The high rise building was a transitory center for those awaiting placement elsewhere in Israel. I felt both excited and scared in my new quarters. The culture shock I had initially experienced on the kibbutz was minute compared to life in the big building, bustling with new arrivals from Romania and Russia. There was only one other American there beside myself. The semi-modern hotel structure towered above the rest of the dirty, decaying Jaffe environs. The atmosphere was permeated with my favorite Hebrew word, "*balagan*", which means, "confusion". It was impossible to experience a dull moment, even if I longed for one! It was one more affirmation to the "headline" of my life's newspaper: "Hellen arrives. Action follows!" The center had already been the scene of questionable action before I ever arrived.

There were many Arabs and Jews living alongside each other in the Jaffe community. The latest event had been a violent feud between militant Arabs and Russian Zionists! The melee resulted in smashing the huge picture window in the lobby of the absorption center. The following day the newspapers announced that our hotel was the "last remaining slum of the Jewish Agency that is to be closed down." Besides the latest horror, the center was the location of various suicide attempts, overdoses of drugs, regular outbreaks of scuffles, and an earlier report of "missionary activity" which the press considered most dangerous of all. I was undecided whether the Jewish Agency was attempting to "help" me adjust to life in the Land of Promise, or discourage me from staying! The most redeeming factor of my new residence was that I was located only minutes by foot from the reconstructed artists' quarter, the "Greenwich Village", of old Jaffe. This quaint corner of the slum was one of the most breathtaking scenic spots in all Israel. I loved to slip away from the center and perch myself on jutting rocks on the deserted Jaffe beach nestled in the old port. I especially enjoyed watching the last fingers of twilight clutch the evening clouds in an attempt to prevent the day's escape. The lulling music of the breakers gently slurping through the rocky crevices of the shore soothed my frazzled nerves from daily survival.

It was my own special spot, where I could climb above the clamor, confusion and pungent aromas of the crowded Jaffe streets. High on my hill I could glimpse at Israel in a nutshell. Behind me a lofty minaret stretched its gaunt neck above the crumbling old neighborhood. It stood juxtaposed to a proud church tower reaching up to the sky in bold competition. If I turned my body just a bit, I could also view the round dome of an old synagogue ruin. That fascinating portrait of history was another face of Israel I loved. The rumblings of war now threatened its annihilation.

I safely deposited Rachel with Lana at their seaside resort and raced my little station wagon to the hostel. I noticed a frenzied pace in all the other vehicles on the road. I almost had a head-on collision with a soldier who was frantically leaving an intersection.

Once inside the center, the place was swarming with chatter in Russian and Romanian. A lonely pang struck again. I adored the warmth and vitality of these newcomers who surrounded me, but I could not talk to them. Our Hebrew was probably on an equal par, but I might have had a slight advantage over them, since I had spent more time in the land than most of them. When a pair of familiar warm eyes met mine, I immediately recognized Boris, a Russian immigrant dentist who spoke some English and who lived there.

Although Boris appeared to be about ten years my senior, his presence exuded fatherly protection. I latched on to him instantly for support. I had not considered that Boris might be looking for a wife, preferably an American one, if possible. I learned he had left a divorced wife behind in the Soviet Union. Boris would have made some woman a splendid husband. I knew I was not that woman, even though I was attracted to his soft spoken charm and the distinguished shocks of gray on both sides of his temple. I was much more cautious now after opening my heart to Yossi. I also felt a deep sense that God had a very specific individual for my life to marry. This was the only explanation that consoled me because of all the years of waiting I had endured. I felt a distinct sense of destiny and purpose for my life which I knew would involve my marriage partner. What God's script for my life entailed was unknown. I could be certain, though, that it was somehow tightly woven into the fabric of my relationship with Israel, her God, and her people.

It was actually humorous that I had received numerous offers of matchmaking in my first months at the absorption center. Ari, the Israeli assistant director, was determined to pair me off with a wealthy Sephardic diamond merchant. Even though I found the Sephardic Jews captivating, I had no intention of locking my life in with any hardnosed businessman. In fact, the business world had bored me until now. To me it was a necessary burden that must be endured for survival and completely unromantic. I was looking for a man of the spirit! Behind my back, every little old Russian matchmaker was carefully plotting just the right candidate to ensnare me. Some days, I even met with marriage proposals while walking down the street. Naturally, their seriousness was questionable, but a tall, blond American would be a nice ticket to the West. I could never go to the beach alone. On my latest visit, I was forced to vehemently repel the amorous advances of a warm blooded university student. In spite of the bother, this attention was flattering. Most of all I loved the intensity and zest for life that throbbed in the bloodstream of that people. *"L'chaim!* "To Life!" Life, vital and vibrant, always pulsating, was what Israel was all about!

The arrival of war brought the pall of death over the land. Boris carefully instructed me in the ordinances of the hostel. Everyone was to black out their windows with blankets, or not use the electricity after dark. There was a bomb shelter in the basement and we were required to report there instantly at the sound of the siren. Extra water should be stored in containers in our rooms, but supplies were also available in the shelter. Anyone who drove a vehicle at night was told to paint his headlights blue, so that no light would be visible from the air. I clung to Boris the rest of the evening with a dependency he enjoyed. Many of the occupants hovered around the available radios in the lobby, closely monitoring all the news we could get.

Around midnight I went to my room, still in the dark about the outcome. Alone in the shadows, I felt engulfed by the uncanny aura that hung over the land. The Israelis were still in a state of shock that their enemies dared to strike on the highest holy day of the Jews! Only the day before, the Israel I had discovered had felt herself to be invincible. After all, she had completely swallowed her enemies at the time of the previous Six-Day War in 1967. The glorious victory had become a source of national humor. Everyone said that Israel was bound to conquer in six days, since she was obliged to rest on the Sabbath! Since that time, all the Israelis I had conversed with concerning their national future were confident about their military superiority, even though the enemy forces and weaponry outnumbered them by gigantic proportions.

As I pulled up my sheet and leaned back on the pillow for the night, I begged the Lord to defend His Land. I was not aware of any immediate personal fear. I was confident that it had been the God of Israel Himself who had brought me to this nation for some purpose He had yet to fulfill. Although I held firmly to the promise of His abiding protection, I felt very alone. I thought about the words that had been spoken over me by another Christian before I left America, *"Like Abraham, I have called you out of your father's house and your land, to take you to a land that is not your own..."*

"How lonely it must have been for Abraham in his pioneering journey," I mused, "...and also for all those early Zionists who had to forsake all to come and build up their Land....but then they were Jews...people expected it of them....but what was a lonely Christian woman doing here in the Middle East all by herself?"

I began to doze and suddenly the sirens started whining. I jumped upright from the bed, grabbed my robe, and started for the door. "This is ridiculous," a voice inside announced, "Don't you know that God holds your life in His hands?"

I immediately remembered the words of the Ninety-first psalm, the psalm of protection. Someone had told me a true story of a Viet Nam veteran on the battlefield where all the men around him were being gunned down. He had prayed that psalm before going into battle and had chosen to put his trust in God. A bullet had whizzed straight for his heart. It stopped short of entering his body and lodged into a tiny Bible in his shirt pocket. When he removed the Bible, the bullet had stuck in the ninety-first psalm, next to the words "A thousand may fall at your side and ten thousand at your right hand, but it will not come near you."

I quickly decided I would get to the bomb shelter anyway because that was a house order. While I was heading down the stairs, an "all clear" signal sounded. Still in my nightgown and robe, I rushed back to bed. The following day we all learned that a missile was speeding toward the Tel Aviv coast, traveling straight on target. An alert Israeli airman had launched a weapon that intercepted it. How close we had come. Thank God for His help and for the skill of the Israeli military!

Overnight I decided that I was going to volunteer my automobile and my service as a driver for the Israeli army! How very paradoxical. I, of all people, had considered myself an ardent pacifist, and now I was willing to fight for this tiny land and even die if necessary, and I was not even a Jew!

Now, I had no idea of the severity of the crisis that had just over whelmed Israel. The enemy had struck her by surprise on her highest and most solemn holy day, and I could sense a heavy somberness overshadowing the country.

"OH ZION, ZION"

"Oh Zion, Zion, I long thy gates to see.
Oh lovely, Zion, Zion, when shall I dwell in thee?"
(Church Hymn)

The Six Day War of 1967 was not only a milestone in Israel's history; it was also the turning point of my own life in America. Till that time, the tiny nation of Israel had only represented the minute blob of the global navel in my mind. Of course, I had not been immune to the stories of its biblical history I discovered in Sunday school class as a child in Tennessee. All of the fascinating feats of Daniel in the lion's den, Jonah in the belly of a whale, and those three Hebrews whose names were impossible to pronounce, who were rescued from a fiery furnace, enticed my imagination about Israel. However, there was always a "universal" quality about the stories that never linked me to a modern day Israel.

They were biblical history and belonged to all believers everywhere. But what about the people who experienced them? I knew virtually nothing about them. My own Gentile parents were only nominal Christians, but they had roots from their own parents which encouraged me to find my own way as a little girl. Some rigid fundamentalist neighbors invited me to church, and I found myself enjoying the stories of all the Bible heroes, and their adventures and exploits. The love story of David and Bathsheba had been a favorite for my girlish fantasies. It gave me great hope as I learned that King David was "a man after God's heart" because God forgave him, even though he had committed adultery and murder. Recognizing the depth of God's forgiveness gave me more confidence to trust Him.

When I reached fifteen, although I really knew very little about him, I proceeded to follow in the zealous footsteps of the New Testament Jew, Saul of Tarsus. I had my own brand of conversion where I acknowledged belief in Jesus, as my savior. However, I had one of those adolescent religious experiences, where I was transformed from a timid introvert into a fiery zealot. I became a "guardian of the faith," intent on correcting the world, and more especially my own family from their excess of alcohol and worldly attractions. I had what the Bible called religious "zeal without knowledge". There was no question that I became obnoxious to my family. There was always one song I could sing in church with unrelenting fervency, "Oh, Zion, Zion". I had no idea what Zion was or whether it was heaven or earth. I knew I loved that song!

With all the gusto I could muster, I thrust myself into its words and I was elevated to another plain. "O Zion, Zion, I long thy gates to see. Oh lovely, Zion, Zion, when shall I dwell in thee?" Once I vocalized its harmony with an upward swing, I wanted to keep singing the chorus again and again. My inquisitive spirit began inquiring from everyone, "What is Zion? Where is it?" Nobody around me appeared to know or really be too concerned about the matter of its location or significance. I simply concluded that "Zion" must mean "heaven". I laid the issue aside and gave it no more attention.

Years passed and the intellectual attractions of academia cooled my religious fervor to a vanishing vapor. Moreover, my encounter with formal religion usually left me cold. The people around me in church seemed so caught up with their Creator that they appeared to have no time for His creatures. I always felt lonelier when I walked out of a church door than when I had entered. It appeared so much easier for all of these religious people to "love" a God that they had not seen, than to love their fellow humans which they could see. I deeply needed to be loved.

I sought other stimulation to satisfy the deep inner void which was crying out to be filled in my life. Travel, adventure and romance all offered the luster that was lacking in the academic world. Besides,

I thought that if I could only find the "perfect partner" my life would experience the fulfillment I was seeking.

At the height of my top academic achievements and enviable international escapades, which included all types of people from princesses to political extremists, I began to take a nosedive. Romantic disappointment, disillusionment with European intellectualism and snobbery all culminated with the shock of being arrested by the East German communists on an innocent visit to East Berlin. Whatever sage had stated that there are "no atheists in foxholes," certainly understood the theologian's words: "*man's extremity is God's opportunity.*" Suffering and survival can make a person bitter or better, but they never leave you indifferent. Suffering always accompanies birth, whether it is physical or spiritual. My spiritual awakening did not occur in the belly of a whale, but in the dark walls of a communist prison cell.

There I had a foretaste of how the power of the living God could enable a person to transcend one's circumstances and oneself and forgive and even love his or her persecutors. Years later, I heard that Anwar Sadat had experienced a similar revelation when he was a political prisoner. Consequently, just as in the Bible account of Joseph and his brothers who betrayed him, I could leave fourteen months of communist captivity with the conviction that *"although they meant it for evil, God meant it for good.!"*

Not everyone understood the newly found joy and hope that accompanied me upon my release. Some probably suspected that I might have been brainwashed by the ordeal. I returned to America with the solid conviction that God's love is the greatest power in the world! Enemies can be reconciled and men can become brothers! We can live in the Messianic age that Jews and Christians long for and pray for if we will open our hearts to God's Spirit. The key is a change of heart and repentance toward God. First, there must be recognition that radical change is impossible without the Spirit of God ruling within us human beings. That can only happen when we recognize our imperfection and sinfulness, which God has already atoned for, and receive the new heart and new spirit that the prophets Ezekiel and Jeremiah have spoken of. Forgiveness of the heart toward those who harm and abuse us is impossible without the power of God.

It is noteworthy to realize that the god of the Moslems is a god of revenge, not forgiveness, not love, and a god of vengeance, not mercy. Even though not all Moslems know this, they will never be able to live at peace with the rest of the world unless they have a change of heart. The God of Israel has commanded us to *love our enemies!*

At the same time Israel was fighting her spectacular war in 1967, I was engaged in my own personal battle. As Jacob had to wrestle with God before he became Israel, I had my own wrestling match with God before the vision of Zion was born in my heart.

One way of describing my own encounter would be imagining what it would be like standing behind Moses when he encountered the burning bush on the mountain. To touch the presence of the living God leaves an indelible mark etched on one's soul forever. The love of God that was revealed to me in my prison cell was the love He offered to the whole world. Later, I was able to receive that same love for myself! I could never doubt the reality of God again, and I knew that the God of the Jews is also the God of the Christians and the whole world.

Six years later, my life had been planted in Israel. I was stirred with excitement as I reported to the nearest Israeli army base to offer my service on behalf of Israel. For a moment I wondered if they would refuse me because I was not a Jew. No. A call had been issued to all civilians to report with their vehicles to the military installations. When my turn in a long line of volunteers arrived, a friendly sergeant gave me directions to the closest base hospital. I was still stumbling over my Hebrew vowels, but it seemed that some English speaker always popped up just when I needed one.

At the sprawling military complex, there were more lines, more people, more waiting, and more confusion. The public had not received any news from the front lines yet, but with every Israeli greeting came the favorite expression, "*yiheh tov*" ("It will be all right!"). Apparently, my job assignment was to help empty the hospitals of the ambulatory patients in order to make room for the wounded. My first task was to deliver three Arab babies to their villages. "*Oi weh!*" Like a good soldier I did not question the danger of such a mission at this time. I was sure that the soldiers would not have subjected me to the project with my limited knowledge of the language and landscape. I wondered how I was going to communicate with the Arabs if I could barely make myself understood with the Israelis.

About the same time, a guardian angel, in the form of a very tall handsome North African Israeli immigrant who had been quietly observing me, stepped up and offered to accompany me. I showered him with gratitude. Then I discovered that a local Israeli nurse would also accompany us on the expedition. With all the added assistance we were sure to succeed in our challenging mission.

My small vehicle was piled high with a motley crew of an Israeli nursing attendant, three sick Arab babies, a North African immigrant, and myself. I felt like a displaced person bouncing down the back roads of the countryside. None of the Arab villages where we were headed were even listed on my map. With typical Middle Eastern wrangling, our North African and nursing attendant launched into a heated discussion over the best possible route. After much circling around strange country roads, they had reached an impasse in their dispute over the best direction. Loud protests from a Bedouin baby rose up. We finally deposited two of our tiny passengers. The third tot was another matter.

We arrived at the address written on the baby's papers. No one in the house claimed to recognize the baby. Panic gripped me, as I noticed the woman pointing us to another direction. I dared not ask whether the village we were visiting belonged to friend or foe. The Israeli military was noted for anything but its efficiency, except in time of crisis. Because of Israel's size, she was considered a minor version of the American "melting pot" with all the varieties of nationalities that populated her land. Most Israelis called her the "the pressure cooker". A melting pot was big and had plenty of time to stir. The pressure cooker was enclosed by time and space and concentrated on the maximum pressure! Such was life in peace time. No one had the luxury or time for patience in his own struggle for survival. Israelis considered that their raw behavior in peace time was because Israel was still a fledgling nation. Give her time to grow up! Ironically, war brought her beauty and maturity to the surface.

War was another matter. A spirit of peace, love, brotherhood and cooperation blanketed the land. People pulled together. They were polite, helpful, generous and patient with each other. They forgot themselves as individuals and focused on how they might support one another when their nation was in jeopardy.

After crisscrossing the countryside and visiting all the Arab settlements, we found a mother who claimed the child as her own. I sighed in relief that both the child's mother and I were overjoyed to find the right home for the little one! After my first adventure on the "battlefield," I was ready for reassignment. Fortunately, the hospital received an excess of volunteers, and I could be reassigned. My next job was delivering packages for the military. My car looked official with a big sign on the front windshield, "In the Service of the Ministry of Security". I still had my Florida license plates on the rear, and a blue and white dove of peace on the front plate.

Israeli people are noted for their extraordinary capacity to accommodate and absorb the spectrum of cultural diversity in their midst. Nevertheless, almost without exception, people stopped and stared when the VW with the blue and white dove drove by. Later, I was grateful for my dove and my sign. They were responsible for getting me behind the lines to the Suez Canal zone after the ceasefire. Our military mission was short-lived. A ceasefire had been declared under pressure from America and the Soviet Union. Only after it was over, did the nation realize how close Israel had come to vast destruction, because of the surprise element of the attack. However, at the time of the ceasefire, Israel had penetrated the Egyptian territory, and could have also taken Damascus if they wanted to. The national pride had been humbled and high human carnage took its toll on the battlefield—for what gain? Israel could not afford the massive slaughter of her precious sons and mourned deeply over the many casualties. I grieved with the nation. The tiny Land had taught me much about the value of *one life*.

I had a unique opportunity to drive to the front lines soon after the ceasefire. A soldier friend of Lana and Rachel, my two Jewish friends, needed transportation to return to duty at the Suez Canal after his leave. Driving through the Sinai once more was pure delight. The spectacular shades and variations on a desert theme of sand, rocks and mountains blending and contrasting with each other left me breathless. The Sinai desert possessed an awesome drama like the sea, swelling and falling with great power. I was accompanied by Vladimir, a Russian Jew, and three other soldier hitchhikers I had just met. We rolled past El Arish and the last signs of Western civilization—including gas stations! I had not reckoned with the fact that no civilian gas stations were located where I was going and I had a long drive back that same night. I uttered one of my SOS prayers quietly under my breath. As soon as I spotted an Israeli military convoy truck making a rest stop along the shoulder of the highway, I pulled over behind him. The group of soldiers seemed to be shocked that a live female was standing before them in the desert in a long denim maxi skirt! I asked where I could find fuel, and their leader said, "Wait a minute" and brought out a huge jerry can and filled my gas tank! I could have kissed them all! There was absolutely no civilian gas in the Sinai at that time!

Wide dark sheets of smoky clouds were spreading over the evening sky as I reached the first camps of the Canal Zone. There was a stark contrast between rolling mounds of sand as far as the eye could see and innumerable tanks, tents and troops scattered over them. I considered it a privilege to be in an area where civilians were not supposed to be. I had crossed the checkpoint, and I had been motioned on through because of my big sign and white dove on the front of the station wagon.

I deposited my precious cargo, said my "good-byes" and turned to go. Some of the troops rushed over to me and asked me whether I had food for the long drive back. When I nodded negatively, they offered me their rations. I was deeply touched. I felt bad taking them, but they insisted. Oh how I loved those Israelis! In spite of their "sticky" cactus like arrogance on the outside, they were truly sweet and tender in their hearts, just like their namesake, the "*sabra*". The exterior was only their defense mechanism.

As I drove through the Sinai alone in the dark, a huge moon lighted my way and majestic mountains made me feel safe. I would never forget the sights, smells, sounds, and sensations I experienced in that one day driving through the desert with four Israeli soldiers, and the back of the station wagon filled with their uzi machine guns.

Another agenda was already taking shape for the hour of my return. Through the efforts of the Jewish Agency, I had become enrolled in a course to study Judaism under the auspices of the Chief Rabbi. This came about after I had told the Jewish Agency I wanted to learn about Israel. I had mixed emotions anticipating what this would involve. Again, there was irony in the entire situation. The very Israeli who had told me that it was impossible to be a Jew and believe in Yeshua at the same time, had sent me an assistant from the Jewish Agency to take me to the rabbinate in order to sign up for instruction to become Jewish! I was apprehensive about what all this might entail!

TO BE OR NOT TO BE—A JEW

"A man is neither a Jew
if he is only one outwardly,
nor is circumcision merely outward or physical.
No, a man is a Jew if he is one inwardly;
and circumcision is circumcision of the heart,
by the Spirit, not written by code.
"Circumcise yourselves to the Lord,
Circumcise your hearts, you men of
Judah and people of Jerusalem,"
(Ro. 2:29; Jer.4:4)

Like Abraham, I've called you..." continued to ring in my ears as I sped down Interstate 40. "....to leave your father's house.... and your country." The band of believers who had spoken prophetically over my life knew nothing about me. I had walked into their small fellowship for the first time in my life. Their leader called me to the front of the assembly and spoke those words over me. She said much more than I could remember, but she also uttered something about "writing books."

The group happened to be one of the many spiritual gatherings of Christian believers who assembled all over the country in the Seventies. These were people of all ages and backgrounds who had experienced the empowering of the *Ruach Ha Kodesh, the Holy Spirit* in their lives in a new dimension. Such events are described in the Book of Acts in the New Testament, and the book of Joel in the Old Testament. The Spirit of God had come upon many individuals in the Old Testament, leading them to speak prophetic utterances or have faith for miraculous acts. Ezekiel, Joel, and Isaiah had all spoken of this event. Elijah, Elisha, Moses and others had all experienced the miracle working power of the Holy Spirit for God's purposes. God's Spirit had come upon Sampson, Saul, David and others in prophetic utterance at a time of God's purposes in history. However, for me it was a miraculous discovery and a spiritual awakening to find out that men and women in the Twentieth Century could experience this same kind of relationship and intervention of God's Spirit in supernatural ways, as God directed. I was convinced that this same Spirit of God was the breath that breathed upon the Jews of Eastern Europe and many other countries to return to their homeland in Israel. The Spirit of God both birthed and inspired many Jews to return to the land of their fathers. They called it Zionism or the return and restoration of Zion. It had been foretold numerous times all throughout the Bible, especially by the prophets. For that reason I could not view this as a political event, but as God's Spirit fulfilling God's Word. There was also a definite link between the outpouring of God's Spirit on the Day of Pentecost in the New Testament and the restoration of Israel. When Yeshua had told his disciples about the empowering of the Spirit, they had asked him, "Are you going to restore the kingdom to Israel"? He said that it was not for them to know the time.

The prophetic pronouncement concerning Israel that had been spoken to me at a time when I had decided to leave my job as a clinical social worker in the prisons of New York City, was also such an event. It had confirmed my way and empowered me to take a "step of faith" into a new direction with my life! The word had been spoken to me at an intersection of my life to reinforce and confirm the direction I personally felt I should go. It was the second event of its kind that occurred to me immediately after I turned my back to the skyline of Manhattan. The first had been even more dramatic.

The night I decided to leave New York City, three friends dropped by to pray with me. While in prayer, the Spirit spoke through them, saying, "This trip is of God. Do not worry about anything. I will take care of your every need." One of the women then concluded the prayer with the words, "*I wrap you in Psalm 121*." As quickly as they came, they departed.No one had ever prayed that way with me, nor had anyone spoken a prophetic utterance over my life. I needed to have confirmation and reassurance for my decision, since I knew that my destination was Israel for some purpose God had for my life. I was leaving my family, my country, my source of income. If God was guiding me, I would have to trust Him for everything. I had no savings, and like the early disciples of the Bible, I had disposed of everything to follow His leading. "But why Israel?" my friend Sandra questioned, as she sat beside me in the car, traveling south on the Pennsylvania Turnpike. I was on the way to say good-bye to my family in Tennessee, and Sandra was going to go north to her family from there.

A couple of years earlier, a friend had told me, "*If you want to be in the center of the heart of God, you'll be in Israel.*" I deeply wanted to be in the center of God's will for my life and discover His purpose for creating me. I did know that Israel was the center stage of God's great drama with the world, and I wanted to be one of the players instead of a spectator. I diligently sought Him in prayer for further confirmation before I stepped out into this uncharted territory. A love for Israel and her people began to grow within my heart. I told a rabbi's wife that the reason I loved Israel so much was because I was in love with a Jew. She immediately answered, "And his name is Jesus!" She was not one of his followers, but she understood what drew me to the nation and people who had brought him to me. At that time, I had never set foot on Israeli soil, nor had I ever met an Israeli!

While Sandra and I were cruising along the Turnpike, I asked her to read Psalm 121 aloud to me. I did not remember its contents. She began. "*If I lift up my eyes to the hills...where does my help come from? My help comes from the Lord, the Maker of heaven and earth. He will not let your foot slip...He who watches over you will not slumber; indeed, He who watches over Israel will neither slumber nor sleep....*"

As Sandra read, the car filled with the sweetest presence imaginable. It seemed like God's Spirit was joining with us in hearing the words. She continued, "*The Lord will keep you from all harm... He will watch over your life; the Lord will watch over your going and coming both now and forever more."* As soon as she finished speaking, I watched a pickup truck slowly enter the Turnpike from the left, heading straight in front of my path. I was driving 65 miles an hour. I noticed that there was no shoulder on the right side. To avoid hitting the vehicle broadside I would have to aim for the right side where there was a ditch. I pulled the car to the right instantly, bouncing up into the air with such impact that I felt we would flip over many times. Momentarily we were suspended in mid air and I heard Sandra shout. *"Praise the Lord!"* At once a force which felt like a huge hand caught the car and placed it directly into the ditch with a heavy thud, alongside the highway.

We sat dazed and motionless for some minutes. My body felt weightless, as if I could instantly float heavenward with no effort. The car was saturated with the presence of God's Spirit. Finally, Sandra shouted, "I'm free! I'm free!" Sandra explained to me that her life had been ruled by fear after she had suffered weeks of unconsciousness from an automobile accident as a teenager. While we were suspended in the air, the power of fear was broken from her life. "I know that God is in control of my life, now," she exclaimed, "and nothing can happen without His permission." And I was freed from the fear of death while I was up in the air!

I climbed out to inspect for damage. There was none. The worst obstacle was that our tires were sunk in about a foot of muddy water. I had no idea how we would get a wrecker out in the countryside of Pennsylvania. For some unexplainable reason, I sat back down in the driver's seat, started the engine, touched the accelerator, and immediately glided back onto the Turnpike like a 747 on takeoff.

As I caught my breath, a still small voice inside spoke, "*See, I have shown you my WORD. I will watch over your coming and going forever! I wanted to show you that my WORD is true!"* Then, I remembered the Ninety-first psalm which said "For He will command His angels concerning you, to guard you in all your ways; *they will lift you up in their hands…*" I had no doubt that we had been lifted up into the hands of angels! What greater assurance could the God of Israel give me than the truth that His hand was guiding my path? And he had demonstrated the truth and power of His word!Later, I disengaged myself from outside activity in what I would call a wilderness of prayer and contemplation. I determined that it was indeed God's plan to send me to Israel and allow me to identify with His covenant people as an "intercessor" in prayer for the Land and people of Israel. I would go like the biblical Moabite, Ruth, and make His people, my people. My mission was prayer and loving service to their needs through social work, and to become one of the "watchmen on the walls" that the prophet Isaiah speaks about. *"I have posted watchmen on your walls, O Jerusalem; they will never be silent day or night. You, who call on the Lord, give yourselves no rest and give him no rest till he establishes Jerusalem and makes her the praise of the earth."* (Isaiah 62:6,7)

Later, I began wondering whether the Almighty might also have a Boaz there, awaiting my arrival, in order to plant me more firmly in the Land. I would simply have to trust His plan. Whether my identification with the Jewish people was synonymous with becoming Jewish in the religious sense, I had no way of knowing. I had known a few other Christians who had undergone a ritual conversion because of marriage. In fact, one of my cousins had done so.

The Yom Kippur War dealt a painful blow to Israel's national self confidence. Not until the fragile ceasefire had been completed and the last rumblings of war were muffled into national introspection, did most people really know how close our little Land had stood on the precipice of severe disaster. Once again, those who really did trust in Israel's God could sigh in relief at His sovereignty in sparing His Promised Land. The aftermath thrust me into a difficult decision making process about the path I was to travel for Israel's destiny to become my own.

To be or not to be a Jew was no easy decision for a person who had experienced as much revelation concerning Yeshua as I had. The Jewish Agency, who had given me their moral support in my effort to immigrate to the Land, also knew where I stood in my faith. This presented no real issue at the time. I was well aware that for many others, especially religious extremists, the adamant rejection of Jesus was a major cohesive factor that linked them together in their Jewish identity. I had learned this the hard way, by listing as references two people whom I barely knew, who were Messianic Jewish believers. Only when I arrived in Israel did I learn from

General Narkiss' assistant that each of these references had experienced unusual incidents in their lives in the time following my listing them. One had innocently shared her Messianic views with a well known rabbi's relative. This ignited the fury of fanatics. The other had shared his beliefs privately at an absorption center and was secretly falsely accused by a disgruntled new immigrant, who accused him of being a "missionary"! Even though he was a new Jewish immigrant, he had to leave.

I was quickly learning that "missionary" was one of the ugliest words in existence to the Jews who had suffered persecution, especially going all the way back to the Spanish Inquisition. The word evoked images of forced conversions in the Crusades or Spanish Inquisition, pogroms or violent pillaging in Eastern Europe, and ultimately annihilation through the German nation, which the Jews erroneously believed was a "Christian" nation. In any case, to those people who had suffered any form of anti-Semitism, Christians were viewed as their enemies and dangerous. Moreover, since 1956, allowing missionaries into Israel for extended stays was illegal. Mini waves of hysteria would briefly sweep through the Israeli papers any time some incident involving what merely looked like it was missionary related occurred. Therefore, there were often undeserved accusations flying around if a Jew was discovered believing in the Messiah of the New Testament, or a Gentile Christian shared his faith openly with a stranger.

I discovered that there really *was not true religious freedom* in the only democratic country of the Middle East. In theory, there was, but in actuality there was not if you wanted to stay longer than a tourist visit of three months. Some of Israel's most extreme religious parties had held power in the Interior Ministry of the country since the inception of modern statehood. Because every election resulted in a coalition government, extreme religious parties who won a minority always sought seats in the Interior Ministry. These parties appeared to be the most accommodating on the outside in order to maintain a religious grip over the people. The Interior Ministry monitored those who entered the country, and visas were issued through their decisions. Anyone with an outspoken faith in Yeshua as Messiah was a *persona non grata to them at that time.*

This could be determined from the paper work one had to fill out. This person was automatically labeled "missionary" by the extremists and denied a visa beyond ordinary tourist time. The exception was only for students, or needed professionals of the work force. *I also learned that most Israelis knew nothing about this.* Moreover, most did not know the difference between an Evangelical Christian and a missionary. I had been learning about this from different Jews I met who had immigrated to Israel.

In all fairness to Israel, she was more democratic than most nations of the world except in the area of religion! Even though she was founded as a Jewish State, she allowed Arabs in her Knesset. Unfortunately, the religious parties were intent on coercing a "theocracy" through their rule over the State, and the Law of Return protected Jews but not the stranger in the land, or Jews who believed in Yeshua as the Messiah. If I had known this before, I would not have listed the Messianic Jewish references I did and would have graciously proceeded to enter the land and comply with the task I felt I was to do—pray for the Land and serve through my profession of social work! So, merely on the basis of my references, I received rejection from the Interior Ministry before I ever set foot on Israeli soil!

I was shocked and appalled, but so was the local Jewish Agency in Miami. I had been caught in the middle of an Israeli culture war. Once I became the "underdog" they rushed to my defense. *"Don't worry; we'll get you there through some other way,"* the local *shaliach* had announced that my papers were transferred to the kibbutz desk and I was caught in the middle of an Israeli cultural war which I knew nothing about, between the religionists and the secularists. I had gotten a glimpse of that war in the temple in Miami Beach the night I met General Narkiss. His spirit appeared open and magnanimous in contrast to the angry rabbi who was prejudiced against non-Jews helping Israel.

The scene appeared to me no different than in the days of the New Testament. The common people were open to the love and mercy that Yeshua sought to bring to them, but the fear, obstinacy and self righteousness of some of their religious leaders stood in the way. It was no different in the Christian church, either. The power and control of religious leadership often blocked the simple and spontaneous interaction of the people with their God. Indeed, all of the first followers of Yeshua himself were Jews—most of them from the ordinary people and not from the religious rulers. All of the writers of the New Testament were Jews; the guidebook of the Christian faith was Jewish! The roots of Christianity are distinctly Jewish, and I had not really understood this significance before.

I thought about this word, "missionary". The Hebrew word for it was "*shaliach"*. The emissary of the Jewish Agency, one who had a mission to fulfill for others, was called by the same name. It was a "noble" word for Christians, meaning "one entrusted with a mission". The "mission" that every Bible believing Christian had was to "bring God's love and good news to others." It was the love of God, burning in the hearts of His people that compelled them to share the good news with others. There was not a mandate to force another to believe or accept it. Many Jews felt that a missionary was a paid professional church employee, or a religious thief, moved by anti-Semitism who wanted to steal the souls of their religion. In view of the past history of anti-Semitism, one could understand their fears and suspicions of all Christian missionaries, especially after the Spanish Inquisition when Jews were forced to convert or be put to death.

Even though I had received a "rejection" from the Interior Ministry, God informed me that he had the last word in the affair. Who was in charge of Israel, anyway? The Jews or their God? Somewhere I had heard a little proverb that said "One man with God is a majority!" The Miami *shaliach* had sent me off to Israel with his blessing! I considered it "divine intervention" in spite of the cultural war in Israel.

The second "miracle" had preceded my departure. I had only thirty-two dollars pocket money to my name and was due to report to a kibbutz in Israel in four weeks time! It looked impossible. I was gripped by a verse in the Bible which stated, "*Give and it shall be given to you.*" I gave away all the money I had to others at a time when I most needed it. Initially, nothing was coming back in return. I nervously continued to hold fast to God's promise. Finally, after two weeks, people began to come to me and offer me money for my trip. Each person said that they felt God had wanted them to do that. On the last night before I was to pay for my ticket on the ship for myself and the car, the total amount came in with two hundred dollars left over! God does provide!

Uri, the first Jewish Agency representative I met in Jerusalem after my arrival, took me aside into his office. He was the assistant to General Narkiss. He cautiously closed the door. "*Here, read this!*" he ordered emphatically as he thrust a paper into my hand. I scanned the letter in front of me. It was a hate-filled tirade against Christians in Israel, outpourings of bitterness and malice. My stomach churned with anxiety as I once again encountered the acrimony of rejection. I wondered why he was showing me the letter.

As if he read my thoughts, he declared "*We have some crazy people in this country*! *We are willing to help you, but you must be straight with us if you want us to be straight with you*!" His eyes hit mine head-on. "Are you here as a *missionary* or not?"

"No, I'm not a missionary." Certainly not the kind he was implying. "I have come here as a social worker," I declared once more. "In fact, I am even considering becoming Jewish!" I announced.

"That's impossible," he replied like a friendly foe, "you can't be a Jew and believe in Jesus."

"Oh yes you can!" I graciously contradicted. "Some of my friends are. And what about all the writers of the New Testament? Aren't they Jews?"

Like his boss, Uri was open-minded and even open-hearted. He appeared to enjoy our amicable argument. I felt free to continue to express my views to him, but I was afraid he might interpret my views as an attempt to "convert" him. "*Oi weh!*" It was becoming obvious that I was not going to have freedom of speech in Israel if I wanted to stay there. We had finally arrived full circle when I requested a reassignment from the kibbutz and a desire to enter some form of Israeli or Jewish studies to learn about the country and people. Uri quickly assigned a young woman to take me to the Rabbinate and take out papers to enroll me in classes to become Jewish! That was the last thing I ever expected after our little discussion. Israel was such a land of *paradoxes!* I had *not* knocked on this door of "conversion" to Judaism, but it was suddenly opened to me.

Was this really what I was supposed to do? I had been instructed to write down my reasons for such a step to accompany my application. I addressed it to the Chief Rabbi of Israel and did my deepest soul searching before I wrote the letter. I agonized before God in order to make sure I was doing the right thing.

Dear Rabbi

For some time now, I have been examining the question of identification with the Jewish people—both in my personal study of the Tanach and in conversation with members of the Jewish faith. I have come to the definite conclusion that my personal identity is to join with the Jewish people.

When I stepped onto the Israeli ship that would bring me to this country from the United States, I experienced a distinct feeling that I was home, and that I belonged in Eretz Israel with her people. However, I had already arrived at this conclusion before I left America. Earlier, I had approached an American with the question of what being Jewish meant to him. He had responded with the words: "It is a feeling." Later, I asked a representative of the Jewish Agency. Again, he expressed that being Jewish is a distinct feeling. I am confident that I possess this feeling of becoming identified with the Jewish nation and people.

Of course, I know that being Jewish is much more than a feeling. I understand in its concrete expression it is the relationship of a people, bound together by a common tradition based on the Book, the Spirit and the Law that unite its destiny, despite physical dispersion into every nation of the world. However, since I already possess this subjective feeling of identification with the Jewish people, I am now ready to commit myself to the Jewish people in a concrete manner. The Jewish religion is at the foundation of Israel's history. I became aware of this fact through studying the Tanach. There, I discovered the reality, spoken of by the ancient prophets, being fulfilled today—the homecoming of the Diaspora and the restoration of Eretz Israel. I also read that when that took place, "foreigners would join themselves to Israel" in that day. (Isaiah 14:1; Isaiah 56:3-8). In that day, the God of Israel promised to gather to His Land others, in addition to those of the House of Jacob (Isaiah 56:8), and they would be joined to His people. I feel that I am one of these who want to join this Land and people.

I desire to commit my talent, skill and abilities to the service and best interest of the people of Israel. My training in social work is presently greatly needed in this country and I believe I can make a contribution through it. I am convinced that all of the events of my life have been a preparation for taking this step. I am confident that the direction of my life is to join with the Jewish people. I have already chosen a new name that I wish to be called by: "Ruth Yael". "Yael" is the animal that ascends to mountain heights with sure footing. I was informed by a linguist that the name is derived from "to ascend", the same root as "oleh", which means an "immigrant". Consequently, I desire to "ascend" along with all the rest. The name "Ruth", of course, I have chosen because of the precedent of the Moabite who joined herself to the Jewish people as the first "convert". Like Abraham, she left behind her father's house and tradition to choose the people of God. Ruth expressed my desire with her words: "THY PEOPLE SHALL BE MY PEOPLE AND THY GOD, MY GOD."

SHE LOOKS JUST LIKE A *SHIKSE*

"The Sovereign Lord declares— He who gathers the exiles of Israel: I will gather still others to them besides those already gathered."
(Isaiah 56:8)

From the beginning of my loving relationship with Israel, life became bittersweet. Like a bottle of vintage champagne, life gurgled and sparkled with the effervescence of that unlimited vitality that characterizes the Jewish soul. However, almost from the first moment that I determined to cross over the bridge and enter into the world of the Jew, I felt an inhuman conspiracy arise to keep me out! I had enemies. I had not done anything consciously to provoke them. It became difficult to determine who my enemy really was and who my friend was, now that I was a solitary stranger in a culture that I desired to embrace.

Never did the scare of a sudden surprise attack from terrorist guerrillas or their bombs seriously cross my mind during the hostilities of war. Even when there was no outright confrontation in combat, potentially death was daily at the doorstep of every Israeli, if he was fearless enough to face its reality in his thoughts. Most, however, shoved this reality into the recess of their minds and accelerated the pace of their vitality, so that they would not have to stop and think about the possibility.

When the supermarket where I shopped suffered the shock of an explosion by terrorists, or the hotel within a mile of my residence was seized and held for some time, I still remained untouched by their threat of destruction. The words, "THE GOD OF ISRAEL WILL GUARD YOUR GOING OUT AND COMING IN" continually rang in my consciousness. There was another terror, though, that began to pursue me.

Somewhere in Israel there was an invisible underground army that worked for the Interior Ministry. It was a religious militia that secretly spied out those who deviated from their doctrine of Jewish belief. By accident, first here and then there I had met a steady stream of individuals who had become the target of their intimidation. Some Messianic Jews in Jerusalem I had met had received letters threatening that "they would be crucified" if they did not leave Israel. I would not have believed it if I had not seen the letter with my own eyes. Because of their belief in Yeshua as the Jewish Messiah, they were considered "traitors" to their own people by these underground extremists. The Jewish Defense League, imported from America, was one group of self proclaimed defenders of the Jewishness of Israel. Although many Israelis did not welcome them, they undertook violent acts of "self defense", of which they were very proud. They had even claimed credit for setting fire to three churches in Jerusalem.

I found myself sometimes feeling paranoid about the extremist forces that surrounded me. I kept remembering what my friend, Uri, from the Jewish Agency had warned me: "*We have some crazy people in this country.*" The terror of this unseen army began to haunt my imagination. I knew that my initial references must have called my name to the attention of foes, when the first extension to my three month visa was not renewed to stay on the kibbutz! All of the others were. This kibbutz had to fight for me, and I finally got the extension. At the same time, one of my references had become the target of paint bombs, threatening phone calls and other harassment. I had only spoken to her once since being in Israel. I was greatly disturbed that the extremist religious militia had the support of part of the government. Whether the rest of the government was ignorant or merely tolerated their intolerance I was uncertain. I began to feel like a "marked" person!

Initially I had been innocently convinced of the authenticity of Israel's democratic principles, and even the statement of religious freedom in her founding charter. This made it difficult to believe the facts which were unfolding before my very eyes. *How could the Jews, of all people, who had suffered the most persecution of any one people secretly oppress and intimidate or deny freedoms to others which they had been denied throughout the world?* I could understand that many people were scarred with bitterness, hatred and fear from their suffering. I, too, had experienced some persecution in my own experience of being a prisoner in a communist prison—under the East Germans. What I could not understand was that the government of the Jewish people could possibly engage in any such subterfuge. I knew I had to examine this matter more deeply to penetrate the roots of this reality. It appeared to me that the Jewish people in America enjoyed greater freedoms than in the Jewish State!

I learned that my little Messianic friend, Rachel, had become just one more victim of political and religious intimidation. I had met Rachel at a gathering of believers in a Tel Aviv home one evening. Everything about her evoked a positive aura of her Jewish identity. Her long, thick, dark hair, which was twisted modestly at the nape of her neck and her oval face with big, warm, sad eyes drew me to her instantly. She was a newcomer to her faith and understanding of her Messiah, and a recent Jewish immigrant from the States. Rachel appeared to be in great need of a friend, so I offered myself to be her "big" sister if she so desired. At the suggestion of an older couple, I "adopted" her under my spiritual wing, since she was several years younger than I.

Although Rachel was reticent about revealing all of her recent past to me, she did divulge that since she had come to her newly found faith in Messiah, she had been very outspoken with others. This had created problems for her. She confided that she had also lived in the same immigrants' hostel as I, but had ultimately been "thrown out" because of her beliefs and warned never to set foot inside again! I was appalled at all this information. I became apprehensive when I realized that she had deliberately defied these orders by visiting me in the center when she told me her story. Visions of the horror of "guilt by association" loomed over my mind.

With this kind of backdrop to my drama already from the moment of entry into Israel, I became very fearful about my upcoming encounter with the Chief Rabbi, who would either approve or deny my application for identification with the Jewish people. Would he, too, prove to be one of the religious extremists? Or, as highest representative of the religion of his people, would he be a man of compassion and understanding, as some Israelis I knew hinted he might be? I was scheduled to meet with him for an interview the following week to be screened as an applicant to his class.

I felt like a tiny lost cork bobbing about in the midst of a sea of belligerent bewilderment. Was my heartfelt sincerity and sense of divine calling to identify with and serve this nation enough to stand against the stormy winds of suspicion that two thousand years of anti-Semitism, tradition, and a perverted mockery of Christianity had generated? Clearly, there existed a very high and thick wall of separation between the world of the Jew and the Christian. My Bible had enlightened me to the fact that this "wall of partition" had been broken down and dissolved in the Spirit of the sacrificial love of Messiah. The question was whether or not the Chief Rabbi could receive me in that Spirit.

In the midst of all the tempestuous sea of intrigue, I did have one anchor of support in Israel. Naomi was given to me by God as my dearest friend and companion. She was the Jewish mother in Israel who entered my life just as I was departing the kibbutz. The Almighty could not have given me a more beautiful gift than her trusted friendship. In so many ways we were outward opposites. I was the tall, square shouldered blond Gentile with long hair. She was the tiny, round shouldered brunette with closely cropped hair. She was timid and retiring. I was bold and outspoken. Naomi provided all the warmth and unconditional love I had not received from my own mother. Her loyal friendship gave me a true sense of belonging in a foreign land. Our trust in each other was unwavering, but it was not born overnight. First, I had to "lay down my life as a bridge", which she later intimated to me, so that she could "walk across to the other side." She dared not cross the dangerous chasm that separated Jew and Christian for fear, until I bestowed her with the gift of unconditional love and acceptance. My last night on the kibbutz, as I was packing in my barren room, she came for her only visit to my quarters. There we sat for a couple of hours together while I bore my entire life to her. That was the real beginning of a deep friendship and sisterly love that lasted until her death.

I confided in her the love story I had experienced with her God and Messiah, who had ignited me with great love and compassion for her people. I recounted my long, lonely search to find genuine love in this life. She listened intently, seated in the middle of half packed suitcases. I also learned that she was a survivor of the Holocaust having hidden in the bottom of a boat in Northern Europe for three years. Our encounter was the kind that psychologists call "door-step discovery," because our real meeting of minds and hearts began only at the time of my departure from the kibbutz. Our two worlds of such hostile and diverse histories found it safer that way!

Beginning that night, we were knit together with a beautiful spiritual friendship, and every weekend I had available I began to visit her and her husband, Asher, on the kibbutz. Initially Asher seemed to welcome me into his heart just as Naomi did. After some time, though, fear and jealousy began to sprout up like thorns in his heart and marred the harmony of the three of us together. Naomi then took to sharing her heart with me when we were alone.

One evening I could never forget, Naomi gave me a glorious gift. Naomi and I sat quietly for some time outside on a weather-beaten wooden bench. The chipping paint revealed the telltale signs of longstanding neglect. Behind us eucalyptus leaves applauded gently in the evening breeze, while the shadows and hues of dusk began to embrace our solitary kibbutz corner. It was the hour when all of the kibbutzniks had returned to their quarters for the evening rest after dinner. Although we said nothing, I felt it was a sublime moment for Naomi and me. She was usually so diffident that she reminded me of a graceful, gun-shy doe in the forest, always listening for the footsteps of the hunter. When no hunter was visible she spoke. Naomi's eyes danced with elation and awe as she dared confide her most sacred secret. Soon after I had shared my own personal encounter with her Messiah and God's Spirit, she said that she had begun to experience "nightly revelations" from God's Spirit. As she told me details, I marveled that she was experiencing deep and intimate communion with God. She learned about holiness, justice, mercy, and above all, of His personal love for herself. She had begun to record the accounts of this spiritual encounter in daily diaries, which she offered me both to read and keep for her. As I read through the pages, God began to teach me through her revelations as He did her.

From the time Naomi began confiding these heavenly experiences in me, I saw that they all bore a true witness to my own spirit that this dear woman was truly in touch with the same God I knew and loved. Each night He would awaken her to reveal His attributes and ways. Yet, anytime I would mention anything whatsoever about "Jesus", Naomi would immediately withdraw and state emphatically, "I am a Jew! Jesus is for the Gentiles!" This response so baffled me that I had to take the matter to prayer for myself. What was this all about? If Naomi was really in touch with God's Spirit, how could she possibly reject His Messiah? Naomi was resistant to the name of Jesus, but very open to his reality and characteristics as I knew them. I concluded that perhaps some evil spirit was counterfeiting God in her nightly visitations. Naomi herself produced the answer to my enigma.

For the first time, Naomi dared to trust me enough to give me one of the diaries that she had started after her spiritual revelations. She handed it to me like a little child who had prepared a birthday surprise for her mother. One night as I was reading it alone in my room, I leapt from my bed with a burst of enthusiasm. I had just read the words, "What your friend (meaning myself) is telling you is true, but you are not able to understand it. However, you will be able to understand it one day!" Hallelujah! We were both in touch with the same God! We were coming from different places of knowing Him. A verse of Proverbs from the *Tanach* burst into my thoughts. "There is a friend that sticks closer than a brother." Such was the gift God had given me in Naomi!

Naomi never failed to support me when I was weathering my fears and doubts in my steps toward Judaism. While I did not understand the way God was working with her; neither did she understand the way He was working with me. Nor did I myself understand my own spiritual path. I merely walked in the faith I possessed at the time, always reminding myself of the verse in Proverbs which exhorted me: "Trust in the Lord with all your heart and lean not to your own understanding. In all your ways acknowledge Him and He will direct your paths."

Naomi was continually asking me, "Why on earth do you possibly want to undergo such steps of becoming Jewish? You already have a relationship with the God of Israel." "But not with His people," I answered. The very roots of Christianity are Jewish, and I wanted to understand the significance of the Jewish roots of my own faith in depth by walking through the world of the Jew. I had an inner passion to deeply know the Jewish people and this seemed to be my particular path to this end. I also felt that *I had a debt of love to the Jews for my own faith.* There were practical considerations, as well. First, if I was going to be working with them through my profession of social work, it behooved me to know them more deeply. Also, it was almost impossible for non Jews, especially Christians, to remain in Israel for an extended time unless they became "Jewish". In fact, this door had been opened up to me without even knocking, and I felt I had to walk through it until it closed.

The day finally arrived for my initial screening with the Chief Rabbi. As I rode up in the elevator to the rabbi 's office, it felt as if I had left my stomach on the ground floor. My emotions were filled with anxiety about the encounter. I entered a large room where many people were sitting around a long table. The Rabbi scrutinized me intensely. He was sitting next to the woman who would be the class instructor. She was another rabbi 's wife.

Before I entered into that interrogation room, I agonized in prayer. No matter how strong my desire for identification with Israel was or how powerful the opposition might be, I was determined to respond honestly. If I was rejected, then I knew that this was not the route I was to travel. Straight as an arrow the Chief Rabbi's first question flew at me, striking me in the heart. "What do you think about Jesus?" Spontaneously unexpected words popped out of my mouth. "I think he is a Jew *par excellence!*"

The Rabbi's eyebrows flew up to his hairline. "A Jew *par excellence?*" Shock and disbelief erupted in his features. He exchanged amazed expressions with the other members of the Board of Inquiry. "Why, he wanted to destroy the Jewish religion!" The learned man corrected me. "That is not my understanding of him," I calmly replied.

I had no intention of entering into an argument there on the spot. It would have been futile. I had already done much research myself. Jesus himself had said "Do not think that I have come to *abolish* the Law or the Prophets; I have not come to abolish them but to fulfill them. I tell you the truth, until heaven and earth disappear, not the smallest letter, not the least stroke of a pen, will by any means disappear from the Law until everything is accomplished."

"Well," the Rabbi insisted emphatically, "he allegedly performed certain *miracles*." His intonation expressed his doubt of their validity. "Didn't Elijah and Moses perform miracles?" I quickly retorted. "Oh! So you think he is like Elijah and Moses?" he interjected, again trading surprised glances with the others in the room.

I made no reply to this question. He hurriedly asked, "Well, do you think he was the Messiah?" Someone had already alerted me to the fact that this rabbi did not believe in the coming of a "personal" Messiah, but of an age in history which would be a "Messianic period" for all men. I thought about the time Jesus had asked his disciple, Peter, the Jewish fisherman, the same question. When Peter answered in the affirmative, Jesus said that "flesh and blood" had not revealed that to him, but only God. I felt it was unnecessary to dispute with anyone who had not had a *revelation to his spirit*. I answered a question with a question. "What do you mean by Messiah?" Abruptly, the Rabbi shot back. "Do you think he was the son of God?" "What do you mean by 'son of God?" I questioned. In the Jewish Bible, the *Tanach*, Psalm 2 spoke of "son of God", as well as Proverbs 4:30, Psalms 80 and 82. I knew that it seemed "blasphemous" to many religious Jews to consider the fact that God had a "son"; however, it was a matter of understanding exactly what this meant. This was not the time for a dialogue, but I did hope the opportunity would arise later. The rabbi mumbled a few more questions about my personal interest in Judaism, noting that I had already chosen a Hebrew name for myself and excused me to leave.

I sat on pins and needles for a week, wondering whether I would be a candidate or not. Finally, the answer came. The receptionist at the hostel entrance announced with an assuring twinkle that the Rabbi's office had called and not to worry. Everything was all right! My heart was bursting with joy. I felt free to take my Hebrew name, which was already what most of my friends called me. "Yael" was truly marching upward to Zion at last!

A Japanese friend in New York City had advised me to take the Hebrew name, "Yael", when I immigrated to Israel. He was a leader of the *Makuyah* in Japan which was an indigenous Japanese Christian movement that embraced the Jewish roots of Christianity. They annually sent many Japanese to Israel to work on kibbutzim.

I liked the sound of the name, Yael. In the book of Judges in the Bible Yael was a non Jew who had fought for Israel's liberation from her enemies at the time of the Judges. God had used this Kenite woman to destroy the leader of Israel's opposition. I tended to be a "fighter for justice" by temperament, and with a family name of "Battle", I determined that it was probably my destiny. Since the name was derived from the same root word as "immigrant", I chose the name. Most new immigrants to Israel take a Hebrew name upon arrival if they do not already have one. This practice is symbolic of beginning a new life in the renewed nation.

When they heard the news, most of the Russian immigrants at our center rejoiced with me. Ari, the assistant manager of the hostel, took special delight in my acceptance of his people. This redheaded sabra usually strutted about the premises with a scowl, but I always seemed to be able to evoke a smile. He had some very religious relatives and maneuvered me a Sabbath invitation to get a foretaste of what life was really going to be like for me "on the other side". First, though, Ari had another task he wanted to assign me. A group from the American Jewish Congress was visiting Israel and wanted to see our center for new immigrants. Ari asked me to be the tour guide and the spokesperson for them!

I loved it! Showing a group of American Jews around an immigrant's hotel in Jaffe was the last thing I ever thought I would be doing in my lifetime. I openly shared with them both the pleasures and pains of "giving up the American way of life in order to come and live in Israel." I had no doubt it was worth it. Values were worth far more than dollars, although the latter was necessary. I truly believed in the Land and its future. America also had been a pioneering nation at one time.

After my little talk, many of the people confided how inspiring they felt my words had been. While I was walking around the room among the people, I could not help but overhear two older Jewish women conversing. "I think it is wonderful what she has done.... and, you know...."she looks just like a *shikse." (female Gentile)* I ran into the bathroom to squelch my laughter. I was uncertain how they would have responded if I had told them they were receiving an inspirational lecture on Zionism from a bona fide *shikse!* I did not have the heart to tell them. Not just yet, anyway. I was a *shikse* with a *Yiddish* heart!

Later, I was contemplating my upcoming visit with Ari's relatives for the Sabbath. I had every intention of taking those 613 laws to heart and attempting to observe the little I knew the best I could, if that was the only way I would be identified with the Jewish people. The only problem was that I was a beginner in learning about them. I was still very ambivalent about the value of that expression of Jewishness. I felt that being a true Jew was more of a heart and spirit matter than just mere externals, although the expression of their Jewish religious tradition had served to maintain their integrity as a nation through more than two thousand years.

The steps I was taking I was choosing as an act of my free will, but I knew that it would require great sacrifice. That was the price of my servanthood and I would take my responsibility very seriously. I felt like a pioneer about ready to be initiated into a religious order. I was planning to get two sets of dishes in order to keep kosher practices, dividing my dairy and meat into separate sections. I firmly decided I would not drive my car on *Shabbat*. Although I usually wore a head covering, I realized that only married women were required to do so, but it kept some of the excessive male attention away from me! I also made a point to avoid sleeveless dresses, and I wore skirts that did not expose too much of my legs. I was amused that this was taking place at a time when Israeli female soldiers were wearing mini-skirts and carrying machine guns on their shoulders! I was being willing to step backwards through tradition into the past! I wondered whether that was really relevant in some of the ways the rules were observed, because Israel had now returned to her homeland. Many of the 613 laws that observant Jews had to follow were rabbinical interpretations and extensions to actual Biblical mandates, which appeared to be more related to life in the Diaspora.

On the Friday afternoon preceding my Sabbath visit to Ari's relatives, I rushed my preparations in order to arrive before sundown. They were prepared for my arrival. Devorah, the lady of the house, was plump and congenial. She welcomed me into the wholesome home life of the Orthodox family to learn more about Jewish customs. She wasted no time in warning me that the rites, rituals, and privileges of Jewish practice were really for the men's world, but she offered this information as a matter of fact. "You'll soon see," she announced with a hint of condescension, "that most of what these men are involved with is really political." Her words struck me with a sudden revelation of many things that had transpired since dealing with the government in Israel. I had already had another glimpse into the world of ritual as I visited a synagogue on Yom Kippur.

Unlike the American synagogues I had attended, this Orthodox one was strictly sectioned off for men and women separately. The ladies were secluded behind the back stairway in the balcony. This was not to be construed that women were inferior. My instructor in Judaism class had informed us that the practice was in order that the men might give themselves totally to concentration of their religious duties and not suffer any distraction from the ladies around them. Frankly speaking, it was easier to keep your mind on God when the women were not around.

The synagogue visit also enlightened me to Paul's admonition in the New Testament for the "women to keep silent in the churches." While I sat upstairs in the circle of these religious ladies, it seemed that they sometimes got sidetracked from their prayer books and caught away in current news in the neighborhood. No doubt, in biblical times, the women's section could have been the clucking corner of the hen house, instead of the house of worship!

I saw a distinctive beauty in sharing the Sabbath's arrival together with the family at sunset. Devorah covered her eyes and inaugurated the evening with the ritual prayer upon lighting the candles. Warm assembly of joy around the dinner table followed. The table was dressed in a crisp, clean white cloth. The father's blessing was spoken upon the bread as it was broken. Everyone partook of the cup of wine following the prayer. Then, songs of joy and celebration about "Queen Sabbath" and the goodness of God followed.

The inner beauty of rest and familial cohesion, and the proclaimed awareness of the Almighty were the intangibles that provided the warmth of the Sabbath's inner light. After the last rays of the sun had slipped over the horizon and the roar of traffic died, the Sabbath candle lights flickered their warm welcome. I could truly feel a restful peace descending over the city like an awesome veil. How consoling to realize that all Israel was remembering their heritage and their God together. While I was their guest, I tried my best to honor every regulation that I was aware of. Devorah's eight year old son watched me carefully everywhere I went. Young Moti walked in on me unexpectedly while I was writing down my impressions on this new experience. He spun on his heels and ran out to his mother aghast. I immediately knew I must have "desecrated" the Sabbath. I had no foreknowledge that writing was considered "working" on the Sabbath. When I heard the children snickering in the other room I knew I had done something terribly wrong. Nor did I realize that I had really almost ruined the whole evening when I touched the wine bottle on the table. I was quickly informed that when a Gentile touches the wine bottle, it is defiled. *Oi weh!*

Indeed, the time the men were not in the synagogue, rocking back and forth in prayer *(davening)* reciting their ritual, they all sat in the house around a long table and discussed all their local political aspirations of bringing their particular religious faction to power. I noticed not the slightest trace of activity or interaction I would consider "spiritual".

Devorah and David were warm and loving people, and I was determined that I would be able to adopt their lifestyle, without the politics, of course. Even if it meant regressing an entire century in my American freedom, I was willing to try. The Jewish Paul of the

New Testament—whom many Orthodox did not like—had tried to become "all things to all men" in order to express the love of God to them. If this was the cost, I was willing to pay, because I did not even notice the price because of the love I felt welling up within me for these people.

I noted in my diary on that date: *"I discussed Judaism with Devorah. She told me how difficult it is to keep the laws—long sleeves, no mixed swimming, keeping kosher, keeping the Sabbath. So far, nothing that she said really bothered me that much. I keep thinking about Moses. The Torah says that he gave up his privileges at the head of the Egyptians to serve the people of God*—for divine love. I am ready to enter into this world for the sake of love—in identification with the Jewish people—if this is my calling. I pray that you will show me and direct my steps."

The following Sabbath, after my lovely introduction to a traditional Jewish day of rest, I was sorely tested. I was back at the residence where I stayed. Four *Yeshiva* students were assembled in their black religious garb, conversing at the sidewalk café outside the center. I had received an earlier invitation to go meet some friends in Bat Yam some miles away for ice cream. When time came to go, I realized that according to religious orthodoxy, I would be desecrating the Sabbath if I drove my car. I wrestled within myself. Did I really want to go through with all this? Finally, I decided to sneak out the back of the building where the ultra observant Jews could not see me and drive away. Another voice admonished me not to go. I must not become a "hypocrite"! After some moments of inner debate, I looked down and saw I was carrying my pocketbook. Law 5, paragraph 14, or something of the sort, stated that "thou shalt not carry money on the Sabbath!" "Oh rats," I thought. This was the one free day of the week in Israel, and I am not allowed to drive my car or carry my money! I peeked out front again, to see if those ultra religious Jews were still there. They were. "Oh well", I finally concluded, "I am not going to put myself in slavery." I sneaked out the back door of the building, jumped into the car, and zoomed off. Suddenly, I felt free again! "It's impossible to be a religious Jew!" I told my friends when I met them for ice cream.

I really knew that God would not be mad at me if I drove. But what about the religious Jews who surrounded me, who knew of my intentions of becoming Jewish? Would they condemn me for such action? I decided I was *afraid* of them and their reactions! What was I doing to myself? I had already discovered such freedom to soar through life on the beautiful wings of God's Spirit, and suddenly I was no longer free. The yoke of 613 laws was a heavy weight to put upon the back of that gentle and gracious dove! Did God really want me to go through with all this? Or was there some other way that I could express my love and commitment to Israel and willingness to identify with her, without wearing the ancestral robes of tradition and at the same time without being rejected by the religious faction of the government? It ultimately boiled down to the answer of whether or not they would let me remain in Israel without going through all of this!

WHO IS A JEW?

"Not everyone who is born into a Jewish family is truly a Jew." (Romans 9:6)

The Chief Rabbi's approval for me to participate in his class had helped me surmount a great hurdle. Still I had tiptoed into the classroom with trepidation on my first day of instruction. The instructor was the wife of another rabbi, and from all outward indication sincerely enjoyed the privilege of practicing her religious heritage. The Chief Rabbi had hinted to me in our interview that she was stricter in her observance than he was! When I studied her shaky gestures and her clipped movement, I felt compassion for her. Her body suffered from constant trembling, as if she might have a nervous tic or even a mild touch of Parkinson's disease. I wondered whether her shaking might have been generated from the stress of the religious system under which she tried to live.

Three classes for converts were offered at the same time in Hebrew, German, and English. Our English class consisted mainly of non-Jews who were either married to or in the process of marrying Jews. Civil wedding ceremonies were nonexistent in Israel. Nor were ceremonies performed for those of differing religions.

I carefully scrutinized each candidate in the class to determine just how many of this small number were there on the basis of genuine conviction. As we interacted, I was saddened to observe that most of the motivations revolved around pleasing a mate, the in-laws, or the religious authorities of Israel. Very little had to do with faith in God. There was Tommy from Australia. He and I had met on the same kibbutz. He had impregnated a Yemenite girl living there, and after much inner debate had decided to tie the knot. He declared to me openly that he was an avowed atheist, but he was merely complying with all the religious "nonsense" in order to have a legal ceremony in Israel. I was probably the only candidate with any genuine belief in what I was undertaking, and even then, nagging doubts began to gnaw at my decision. Apparently, no one on either side of the cultural chasm I was crossing understood why I wanted to walk across that bridge to the other side. Neither did I understand, but a burning fire compelled me onward. The waters below the bridge were murky and turbulent. I was enveloped in a loneliness of knowing that those on either side were viewing me with fear, suspicion, doubt, and even rejection. Was I being naïve to think that just maybe I was "building" a bridge—one of reconciliation and peace between two ancient enemies? "Like a bridge over troubled waters" the song by that name reverberated through my soul. I had no influence over those who did not know me. But those who cared about me, I begged not to judge me. I sought their prayers and encouraged them not to trust my judgment, but rely on God to guide me. His ways are not man's ways and an inner voice continued to coax me to "lean not unto my own understanding."

The few Gentile Christian friends I had acquired in Israel saw no need for such an extreme. A couple of them did pray for me without even understanding. Most of the Gentile Christians exhibited a latent hostility toward such an action. Inside, I criticized them for their lack of understanding the people or culture with which they shared the same national roof. Then, the first blow struck.

Some of my believing Christian friends in America who had supported me in my decision spiritually before I left suddenly cut me off without any explanation after I told them about the step I wanted to take. I wrote numerous letters to activate dialogue between us, but all I received was silence. The rejection hurt, especially at a time when I was so vulnerable. It drove me into a deeper conviction that I really did belong with the Jewish people and I was experiencing some of the rejection they had received for generations from so-called Christians. The Jewish people had been forced to stand together with each other throughout history. I had seen little of this standing in the Christian world. A second blow struck. In my second class on Judaism, the instructor blasted Jesus in no uncertain terms. She elaborated to a great extent on why one could not be a Jew and believe in him. She said it was difficult to erase him from the hearts of Christians, but it must be done if they became Jews. "One key reason," she iterated, was "that it is impossible to be a Jew and believe in Jesus because the authorities 'fear that you might try to influence other Jews.' "

Jesus was called Rabbi by the Jews who followed his teachings. Those Jews did not question his Jewishness. History was filled with many Jews who followed Jesus. The early disciples, for example, the writers of the New Testament, and all of the original believers of his message were Jews.

One of the most famous was Saul of Tarsus, who killed the early Christians in his desire to fight against what he had considered blasphemy. However, when Saul had a personal revelation in his own encounter with Jesus, he became a leader of the early Christian community, which was all Jewish. Indeed, that belief in Jesus could only come through *personal revelation and commitment.* Jews do not stop being ethnically Jewish when they have this revelation. All of the ones I have known become more committed to God and to loving their fellow man. I saw a true Jewish spirit that has nothing to do with religious ritual. I found it typified in an Israeli pilot who had been shot down on the battlefield in the Golan Heights during the Yom Kippur War. As he lay wounded on the ground, he spotted an injured Syrian pilot, lying across from him, whose plane had also crashed. He crawled over to him and saved his life! Jesus had commanded his disciples to "love their enemies". This Jewish man did that spontaneously. It was a decision that was born from his heart and not ritual propriety.

I left the classroom that day greatly concerned with many questions about the appropriateness of the direction I was contemplating. I rushed back to my room as quickly as I could maneuver the clogged Tel Aviv traffic and began wrestling with my own thoughts. I was determined to leave the class at once if that was appropriate. I knew many Jews who were believers in Jesus as their Messiah. It had made them more committed to their identity and heritage than they had previously been. Some of the demands placed upon a convert had nothing to do with the Judaism the *Torah* and *Tanach* described. Yeshua typified a mercy and compassion that was the essence of the true Jewish spirit. He grew up in a Jewish home, was circumcised, kept the Law, and attended synagogue and taught in the Temple!

Why were some so afraid of him? Jews were not easily influenced about anything. They possessed strong minds and opinions of their own. Not even Moses was able to influence some of the people to follow God. The Jewish prophets also got more than their share of rejection.

I concluded that Judaism certainly was a religion that contained a structured body of commandments and duties, but there was also a heart attitude and spirit that were part of Jewish identity which God required over and over. At one time the prophet Jeremiah said to the people that the "House of Israel is uncircumcised in their hearts." (Jeremiah 9:26)

Indeed, there was a true Jewish spirit that had more to do with faith in God and one's heart attitude toward his fellow man in compassion. Wherever I had met it, I found it to be very beautiful. To me that spirit was incorporated in that Israeli pilot who had been shot down on the battlefield. I also had another encounter with the same spiritual reality while I lived on the kibbutz. A Libyan airplane which strayed into Israel's air space was shot down, only to discover that it was a passenger plane that had mistakenly deviated off course. All passengers were killed. Many of the kibbutzniks who surrounded me cried genuine tears of grief for those Libyans—their enemies! The Libyans hated the Israelis as much as the Syrians did.

It sounded as if the instructor was saying that the only mutual definition that many Jews could agree upon concerning Jewish identity appeared to be the rejection of Yeshua. There were atheist Jews, Bahai Jews, secular Jews and many other categories with much tolerance. However, Messianic Jews, who acknowledged Jesus as Jewish were rejected as Jews. Golda Meir's government had just collapsed because they could not reach agreement on this very matter. *Who is a Jew?*

I returned to my next class ready to hand in my notebook. The instructor did not even mention the matter of Jesus again and began to assure us that Judaism was based on "deeds" rather than "creeds." In other words, "actions are more important than one's beliefs. Little time was spent in class with the Bible at all, but with rules and regulations of behavior. There was a prescription for every act of behavior imaginable, including all those activities one usually practiced in the privacy of one's bathroom or bedroom. Men were instructed how to urinate. I felt overwhelmed when I learned that it was not appropriate to "tear" toilet paper on the Sabbath or to use solid toothpaste in some circles of Jewish observance.

To be observant on the Sabbath, Jews were required to use mechanical timers to turn on and off their electricity. Such direct behavior with light switches was interpreted as a violation of the law which forbade the building of a fire. This mentality was completely alien to the freedom I had known and enjoyed with a relationship with God through His Word and Spirit. Slowly, I was becoming burdened by the route through the wilderness of this spiritual journey. Then another blow struck.

In my spare time between Hebrew classes and Jewish instruction I slipped in visits with my friends Lana and Rachel. They both questioned my behavior. They were assimilated American Jews who had never observed the Law in their own lives. I wanted to encourage them to get more deeply connected to their Jewish roots. I felt they had lost something beautiful in their lives by forsaking relatedness to their own people. A small family group began to be developed in the little "hotel by the sea". One of the members was a fiery South American immigrant who passionately pursed me for the purpose of marriage. I reassured him that I really did care for him as a person, but I did not believe that I was to marry him. When I rejected his marriage proposal, he erupted in a volcanic rage. He struck out like a cornered rattlesnake! "You're a *traitor*, and I am going to denounce you!" He was referring to my belief in Yeshua along with my friends. He no more doubted my loyalty to Israel and the Jewish people than he did his own Jewishness. I feared what he might try to conjure against me!

The past horrors of my communist imprisonment loomed before me once again. I spent the night wrestling with fear of the damage one angry malcontent could initiate against me. At the same time I was reminded of the words of the prophet, Isaiah, "*No weapon formed against you will prosper!*"

The following day, I was shocked to hear that his father had unexpectedly died in the night, and he had to urgently leave the country for the funeral. I sighed in relief. As soon as one storm subsided, another seemed to be brewing on the horizon. Again, it was a jealous and bitter man. It happened because I failed to keep my guard up and fell into a "trap"of being too friendly to an unstable person.

Jacob was a tall, clean-cut American man around my age who resided at the hostel. He and I were the only Americans who lived in the temporary housing in Jaffe. The rest of the occupants were Russian and Romanian. We stood out as novelties to the others, who constantly interrogated us about all aspects of life in the States. For many, they had met with bitter disappointment in Israel.

The Russians had come expecting to be welcomed with open arms into the "Promised Land flowing with milk and honey." They had been rejected in their own land prior to their departure, some suffering captivity behind the Iron Curtain. Upon their arrival they were met with housing shortage, Israelis who resented their economic benefits, culture shock, and great difficulty with the new language and Middle Eastern culture. They had entered the steaming caldron of the pressure cooker!

My own love affair with the Promise Land was also undergoing a mellowing and maturing process. It was rather painful to swing from a starry-eyed sentimentality to the sober, divine unconditional "Israel, I promise to love you for better or worse." Currently, it seemed to continue getting worse. Most American and Russian Jews who had never been to Israel pictured the country with a beautiful mystique, as a glorious place suspended between heaven and earth. The heavenly Zion ruled their imagination, until there was a crashing confrontation with the earthly reality.

Even in her raw, gutsy condition earthly Israel held a special charm for me. The clash between the vision and her reality unfortunately embittered many Jews who came from abroad. Most people took one of two routes when this happened. They either chose to engage in more rigid forms of nationalistic rationalization or carefully reevaluate what their Jewishness was about.

Jacob sat outside the hostel in the sidewalk café. He appeared depressed. We had engaged in some friendly conversations in the lobby in the past on a few occasions. When he saw me stroll past, he leapt up like a frog and invited me to join him. It was a balmy night in Tel Aviv and I had nothing else to do, so I agreed to chat with him a while before retreating to my little cubicle above.

"I'm so discouraged," he announced, "I'm simply fed up with life here!" With my most enthusiastic voice, I attempted to share my latest revelation with him about what "mature love of the Land" was all about. It was about loving Israel, no matter what.

"Why Jacob, it's like marriage...you know, for better or worse..." Neither of us had ever been married. Jacob half listened and after some conversation about trusting God, he confided that I had inspired him to continue trying to make a go of it in Israel. When I told him "good night", I left feeling that I had encouraged one sinking immigrant to resurface with power both in his relationship with the Almighty and Israel. After that short visit Jacob and I had a few other sessions of warm open sharing together. I could sense his strong attraction to me and how keenly he needed to be loved, but I knew I must carefully guard the boundary of our relationship. It was obvious that Jacob would not. It was evident that life on foreign soil could become more intensely lonely than in one's own country, especially in Israel. The entire nation was like a young woman, filled with the vitality and intensity of the lust for life itself!

Naomi was far away and seldom available, but I knew she stood with me under all circumstances. Lana and Rachel were close by but limited by their work and their own fears. Boris continued to pursue me patiently from time to time, but his interest was waning because of a lack of fuel on my part. I really did desire a relationship in marriage but for some unknown reason, the right person had not come along. In the past the wrong ones had come across my path from time to time. The disappointment of experience had been a hard schoolmaster for me. I had stubbornly refused to learn quickly, insisting on my own way until I "wrestled with God", like the patriarch Jacob, whom God renamed Israel. In such a wrestling match, I was destined to lose. I finally succumbed to entrust myself to God's keeping and choosing. He alone knew who could best comfort and encourage me. First, I had to learn to allow Him to do so and not make an idol out of a human relationship. "Can two walk together unless they are agreed?" asked Israel's prophet, Amos. The Almighty knew that the only partner who could provide contentment for me would be the one who wanted to live life in God's Spirit as passionately as I did. Whatever the price, I was willing to pay it. Otherwise, there was greater peace in remaining alone.

As loving consolation, my heavenly Father did manage to send me a warm, cuddly, canine companion to live with me. My furry friend slept snuggled tightly up against my side in bed, and loved me with deep devotion unlike anything I had ever experienced from a human. She had entered my life as a stray on the kibbutz. My Hebrew class voted on a name, and we came up with *"Efes"*, which means "zero" in Hebrew. The name described her condition when we found her. Efes was much like new immigrants—lost, lonely, disoriented, and extremely hungry for love and affection. Yossi had found her out in the pear orchard on the kibbutz. Her long, blond shaggy hair was matted with burrs, and her tangled coat was laden with ticks, but it was still love at first sight when I saw her. She rushed into my arms as if she had finally found her mother and showered me with exuberant kisses on my cheeks.

I initially felt bad about a name like "Efes", but I quickly discovered that there was great wisdom and even humility in first becoming "nothing". Zero was significant in that every newcomer to Israel began at that point—at the bottom. The adorable little creature taught me many lessons of trust and humility when no one was around. She loved me faithfully when no one seemed to notice my needs. She taught me one of my most greatly needed attributes, gentleness. When my frustration had reached the boiling point and I ordered her immediate obedience with a ferocity, a still small voice inside said, "Now I don't talk to you that way, do I?"

"Yes, Lord, I hear you." I knew His Spirit was speaking to my heart. "I'm sorry." Then, I would gently call my little Terrier and she instantly obeyed. When I screamed at her, she would always stop dead in her tracks, refuse to budge, and shiver in fear. How much like us mortals with the Almighty was this marvelous animal! Sometimes the fear of God's wrath immobilized our obedience, but the certainty of His loving acceptance enabled us to trust Him and elicit our cooperation. How important it was to possess assurance that we had truly been accepted by Him!

Efes was no stranger to miracles. When I had moved into the center, I had been informed in no uncertain terms that "dogs are not allowed!" I had begged Yossi to leave Efes in his care on the kibbutz until something could be worked out. I really pleaded with the Lord to change the director's mind. I truly believed that "all things are possible to those who believe." I began to pray fervently for permission for Efes to move into the hostel with me.

While on the kibbutz, Efes had slipped off with one of the neighbor dogs. The aftermath was that she had become pregnant. If we had only known, we could have prevented it, since the kibbutz gave birth control pills to all the female dogs! Even with God on my side I was certain that there was no way I could possibly get permission for an entire litter to be accommodated in a residence of Eastern European immigrants! Zero added to my chagrin when I learned that she and some of her kibbutz cohorts had gotten into a feeding station set up for local rats. They all devoured the poison, but Efes was the lone survivor. Yossi had doused her throat with milk, and she and all of her babies except one survived the ordeal. Then I received the news that Yossi was returning to the States and an immediate solution for Efes' living quarters had to be found.

I trudged into the center with a heavy heart. I did not want to stop for superficial chatter in the large lobby. When I headed straight for my room I failed to notice Jacob sitting in the lobby. Later, I learned that I had committed an unforgivable sin, especially since I was a shikse. When I reached the elevator, Avraham, the director of the center, cornered me at the door. "Why so sad?" he asked with genuine concern."Oh, I have just learned that the fellow who is keeping my little dog on the kibbutz is returning to America, and I have no place for her." "Well, maybe we can work out something here," he reassured me. "You know that one of the Russian ladies brought her dog with her from Russia, and we've allowed it to stay as an exception."

"Oh really?" I inquired with excitement. "You know I have a Russian roommate, but she is terrified of dogs…but I applied for a single room a long time ago!" I quickly added.

"I think we can work it out," the manager announced with a sense of pride in his compassionate accomplishment. "*Yiheh tov,*" "It will be all right" was the favorite expression of most Israelis. It showed me that they always lived with hope for the future. Only weeks before, this man had lost his only son in the War. Now he was comforting me.

"Oh, I could give you a big kiss!" I exclaimed.

He beamed brightly, but he was not the type of man to be frivolous with his affection. He received my gratitude with the sisterly affection it represented. How was he to know that he had provided the answer to my prayer! This was a time when I was learning to pray for *everything!* From electric heaters in the winter to warm my feet, to private rooms in the "Grand Central Station" for world immigrants, and ultimately for a place for my adopted dog to live! It was scary and exhilarating at the same time—this life of faith! Truly in Israel everything is possible because it is God's Land.

I was often surprised to see just how some things were resolved. For example, whenever Israelis said, "It's impossible," I would interrupt them and say, "No, wait a minute and I'll show you. The impossible only takes a little longer—with God!"

My new room was a tiny cubicle, but it still offered the luxury of being a single room, just large enough for Efes and me to turn around. All of her babies had been safely distributed to kibbutz families. It looked as if we might live happily ever after, but as soon as one issue was resolved another cropped up.

Quite by accident one afternoon, I learned that Jacob had been enraged by my overt rejection of him when I entered the building with Efes. Ari, the assistant, pulled me aside and warned me to "watch out for Jacob." "For some reason, he has it in for you," Ari admonished with fatherly protectiveness. Heeding his admonition, I cornered Jacob the next time I saw him. "What's the matter?" I prodded. When he pleaded ignorance, I continued to challenge him. "I've already heard that you have been talking about me..."

Jacob appeared stunned that I knew. He quickly confessed. "Well, no Gentile is going to treat me that way! No sir! I'm no scum...I did it because you ignored me when you came into the building...I guess...I'm sorry...you see, when I was a boy in Paris, a gang of Gentile boys grabbed me one day..." He hesitated, cringing. "They pulled down my pants. Then, they laughed and pointed at me...see, the dirty Jew...he's circumcised!"

"Oh dear God! Jacob, I'm so sorry! You've been deeply hurt! I would never treat you that way! I did not even see you when I walked into the building!" I moaned in disbelief.

Jacob hung his head. "Have they contacted you, yet?" he inquired sheepishly. "Who?" I asked bewildered.

"The Israeli Intelligence."

"What?" I cried aghast.

"The *Shin Bet*, the Israeli Intelligence. You see, when you ignored me, I determined that no Gentile was going to get away with that! I was a paid informer for the FBI in the States before I came over here. I went down to the American Embassy and told them all about your East German imprisonment..."

"Jacob!" I cried, incredulous, "I've already written a book about that. It is no secret! I've done nothing that would warrant their suspicion of me!"

"But I thought you already knew what I had done...you implied..."

"I was referring to something else." I interrupted. "I had no idea that you had done such a thing"

"Well, I am sorry. I really thought you had rejected me!"

"Oh Jacob, what is the name of the man you spoke with? I will immediately go to the Embassy and correct this!"

Jacob cooperated willingly. As soon as the American Embassy doors were opened the following day, I sat in the office of the FBI representative. I informed him of my presence in Israel and announced adamantly that I was a victim of a vindictive and jealous admirer. There was absolutely nothing that warranted any suspicion concerning my activity, and even if he felt there was, I was more than willing to cooperate by answering any questions or concerns. Whether he believed me or not, the sedate gentleman calmly assured me that my report had also been his own conclusion about the matter. I returned to the center with deep gratitude to God for allowing Jacob to divulge his own story to me, through a "divine" misunderstanding. It enabled me to dispel any danger that was being devised against me. I was also startled to discover just how unstable Jacob really was. At the same time I was learning that when God's love comes too close to a wounded heart, it can drive the demons to the surface! Wounded people wound others. Moreover, I was also grateful that only a few weeks before the incident, I had registered at the US Embassy in Tel Aviv. At that time I had asked an attaché for advice concerning the best possible way of maintaining permanent residence in Israel for a non-Jew. His recommendation had been "conversion", which he recorded on the back of my card at the time. I took his advice as another confirmation that I was on the right path. I sighed in relief once again.

One of my sunny afternoons with reprieve from opposition, I strolled into the building with optimism. The future looked bright and hopeful. The Russian immigrant manning the reception desk reached into my mail box compartment behind him and handed me my mail. One envelope caught my eye. The address read "The Gospel Association" or some other similar title with the local street address. "Oh, this one isn't for me," I said, feeling confused. "How did such a letter get into my box?"

"But you know these people, don't you?" he questioned suspiciously. "Of course not!" I shot back. "I don't have the slightest idea who this is!" I handed him the letter, noting the strangeness of it all. Later the event completely escaped my mind because I gave it no import.

Outwardly, my life seemed to be on a smoother course. I was beginning to be able to relax and drop my guard. Still I kept feeling a heaviness which I could not explain. It took the awareness of an outsider to wake me up. Eli was a Messianic Jew I had met in Ashdod on a visit to a friend's house. He and his wife were new American immigrants. While he was visiting in Tel Aviv, he decided to stop by and greet me. After walking through the lobby of the center where

I lived, he led me outside. "I sense there is some kind of danger or darkness hanging over you. I have a sense of foreboding about you that I do not understand."

I needed to hear more. We re-entered the building and chose a secluded nook of the lounge to talk. Eli confided that he could actually feel a great cloud of hostility that was directed against me when he walked in the door. I had not noticed, but when I gave it some thought, I could trace a growing coldness toward me from some of the residents. I supposed that Jacob might have stirred it up because he had not completely forgiven or forgotten. I also noticed that Ari had been scowling at me of late. I really had no time or energy to bother about others' petty moods or gossip. I was too busy with my Hebrew and Judaism classes to think about such things.

Some days later, just as the sun was disappearing on the horizon with ribbons of smoky gray, I ambled into the hostel alone. The same Russian who had handed me the mistaken mail was seated at the desk. He greeted me with an unusual gusto, so much so that his voice smacked of syrupy deception. I was not on the lookout for trouble, so I ignored his behavior. I should have recognized this sign as a signal of warning.

"You speak English, don't you?" The Russian inquired. I found the question strange, since he knew I was an American. He also spoke fluent English. "Why yes," I replied, "what can I do for you?"

"See that lady sitting over there," he pointed to the sofa near the entrance. "She needs some help."

"Of course I'd be glad to help her," I answered, eager to be of assistance. The stunning Eastern European Jewish lady arose, as if awaiting her cue and strode toward me. "Can you tell me where Mr. Kreisky lives?" she asked. Mr. Kreisky was a Russian immigrant who had lived in Israel many years. He had a Bible bookstore a few doors away from our location in the same building complex. He was the leader of a congregation of Messianic believers which met on the premises. I had never met the man, but others had told me about him. Many Messianic Jews in the area knew him. I only knew of his presence, his name and the location of his store. That was the sum total of the knowledge I possessed.

"Yes," I responded. When she requested me to show her, I opened the door and pointed to the Bible store. I felt very stupid, because the entrance was visible from the place where we were standing. The bookstore was dark and obviously closed. I had no idea that Mr. Kreisky also lived in the apartment building next door. I left the woman and returned to my room. Under all the increasing mounting pressures around me, I was beginning to feel tired all the time. I did not have the mental strength to scrutinize the events which were occurring.

The following day on my way to the Jewish class, the gas tank on my car sprang a leak and the entire contents spilled out on Ben Yehuda Street. I pulled over to the side and opened the door to step out. As I stepped on the street, a car instantly sped up on the left and smashed my front door. I could have been killed if I had not jumped back. I was too tired to think about it. A huge cloud of heaviness hung over the day, both in the sky and atmosphere. I felt evil all around, but I could not pinpoint its source. I had no idea how I was going to pay for the car repair. I skipped my class in order to take care of the car. "Somebody has tried to harm me!" I suddenly thought.

The next day in class one of the students whispered to me that the instructor had lashed out in a rage against Jesus again. I felt it was significant that it happened while I was absent. The young American said he found the religious exercise of the class a "big game". He had one goal in mind and that was getting his marriage legalized before his baby was born by the woman he had impregnated. He acknowledged that he was really an agnostic at heart. Several of the other students had confided their qualms to each other about going through the process of conversion. We were approaching the end of our formal instruction. Two big hurdles remained to finalize our acceptance as Jews. The first was the final examination of all the information we had assimilated. The second was another interview with the Chief Rabbi!

I felt great confidence about the final exam. I was certain I would soar through the academics with flying colors because I was sincere in my motivation and sure I had mastered the content. All of my periodic test scores had been at the top of the class. The second challenge was much more serious. The fact that the instructor had gone out of her way to malign Jesus was a hint that I might meet more of the same from the Chief Rabbi. From what I learned in class, Judaism was about *"deeds and not creeds*". Those were the very words our instructor had given. I was willing to observe the deeds, and I concluded that what I believed did not really matter. My private personal belief system was irrelevant.

While I waited the decisive moment I felt as if the jaws of a vise were closing in on me. I could not diagnose the problem. The anxiety of the unknown gnawed away at my inner peace. I decided I would discuss my struggle with Uri from the Jewish Agency. After all, he had been the one who had sent me to the class in the first place. I trusted Uri, and felt I could be completely candid with him about my dilemma.

As Uri and I met together, I confided that I was uncertain whether they would ever accept me because of the strength of my faith in Yeshua. Uri smiled. "Didn't you go to the university?" he asked. "Don't you know how to give the professor the answer he *wants to hear?"* His eyes twinkled. It was a very simple matter for him. "Once you have given them the answers they want to hear and they have given you their stamp of approval as a Jew, then you are free to believe anything you want to!"

There it was again. "Judaism is based on deeds and not creeds." His offer to compromise my true conviction was tempting. "Yes, I know what you are talking about," I stated firmly, "in this matter I cannot compromise. For me it is dishonest!"

"Well, you have to suit yourself," he advised. He seemed to feel no duality within himself in offering me this alternative.

The more I thought about his response, the more I realized that Israel functioned in this way. One part had to accommodate the extremism of the other, especially in the political and religious arena. Deeper issues were at stake. Israel could not afford a cultural war between the secular and the religious as long as there was a threat of invasion from the outside. A fragile coalition was maintained for their own survival. Many segments of society were hurt because of this arrangement. Conservative, Reform, and Messianic Jews were all discriminated against because of the political hold of the extremists among the Ultra Orthodox. To engage in an internal struggle was a luxury that this young nation could not afford. “Divide and conquer” was a watchword that must be heeded. Like every other nation, Israel’s youth were suffering under the perceived hypocrisy of their elders. I had heard many Israeli young people say “I am not a *Jew, but* an *Israeli!” They did not want to identify with the hypocrisy of the religious extremists.*

I left the Jewish Agency in confusion, mingled with hope. I was confused because I hated the kind of hypocritical compromise I was advised to exercise. I was hopeful, because I realized that the man who advised me saw through some of the sham of a political system that he was somehow forced to perpetuate. The problem was rooted in the cultural battle between the Jews who were born and had lived in the Diaspora and those who had been born and raised in Israel. Longstanding tradition could not be changed overnight. That night I recorded in my diary the words of Jeremiah the prophet: “*For I know the plans I have for you, plans to give you hope and a future.*”

This act in the drama between “Ruth Yael” and Israel was coming to a quicker climax than anticipated. The day after I received the top grade on a preliminary examination in my Judaism class, I received an invitation to an audience with the Chief Rabbi. No one had expected to receive the appointment so soon. I was scheduled to meet with him at the end of the week in the Tel Aviv office.

My emotions immediately became a violent battleground of opposing forces. Fear and love fought viciously to take control. If I were to be rejected by the Chief Rabbi, I would have to give up my beloved Israel. Yet, I wondered how he could possibly accept me after two thousand years of enmity between traditional rabbinical Judaism and Christianity. At the inception of Christianity, all the early believers were Jewish—the early church was composed of Jews who chose to follow Yeshua as their Messiah. Many in the Jewish religious establishment severely opposed them because of disputes over the Law and practice; however, the early church was definitely Jewish and remained so until the destruction of the Temple in 70 A.D. by the Romans. Of course Gentile believers had also begun to join with them. Initially, there had been disputes about what degree of Jewish practices were required from the Gentiles. The dispersion of all Jews into the *Diaspora* followed. Without a

Temple, Jewish ritual and practice had to be restructured and rabbinical Judaism was born. The rabbis of the time met together and instituted a system to maintain a cohesive religious community in order to teach their people. At this time there was a distinct break and separation between the Messianic followers of Jesus and those of rabbinical Judaism. Some of the Jews who opposed Yeshua did so on the grounds of their expectation of a Messiah who would restore political power to their nation. When this did not occur, they rejected Jesus' authority.

From the time of Jesus death in 30 A.D. until the dispersion in 70 A.D. many Jews became followers of Jesus of Nazareth, who had been born in Bethlehem according to Messianic prophecy in the Tanach. These Jews believed him to be their Messiah, not just for the Jewish people, but for the world. Consequently, they brought many Gentiles into the congregations of believers as they spread the good news of spiritual rebirth for all mankind. As they shared their faith, they often received rejection and persecution from both Jews and Gentiles. Their faith began to spread throughout the Middle East and continued to expand throughout the greater region. The Roman Emperor Constantine became a follower of Christianity in 300 A.D. and institutionalized Christianity. The political power of Rome and many of the pagan practices of the day began to compromise the teachings of Jesus and the Bible. This was the beginning of a greater apostasy of belief in the original teachings of Jesus and the Bible.

I was willing to try to become observant to those 613 laws of rabbinical adaptation of contemporary Judaism, if that was the condition of my loving identification with the Jewish people. This whole drama had begun after my life had been touched and revolutionized by the Spirit of one Jew, named Yeshua. His suffering and love made me willing to follow in his footsteps. In his great love he had become a human bridge across that horrid chasm of a history of division and hate between Jew and Gentile, light and darkness, God and man! Through that same Spirit, he wanted all mankind to be reconciled to God and one another!

While preparing for my examination, I experienced a burst of inspiration which I was looking forward to share with the Chief Rabbi. I was delighted to discover that through the Jew, Yeshua, I had come to faith in the God of Israel. It was His law, His prophets, and His Messiah that had captured my heart and brought faith, hope, rebirth, purpose and direction for my life! I wanted to tell the Rabbi how grateful I was for his nation, their suffering, and faithfulness to bring the Word of God to all nations. I wanted to tell him that I loved his people and his nation because of his God, and I was willing to stand with them at any price. I did not know if my fear would allow me to say those things. Therefore, I decided to put my thoughts on paper and offer them to him if the opportunity permitted. How would he receive me?

THE BETRAYAL

"No servant is greater than his master. If they persecuted me, they will persecute you." (John 15:20)

As the time closed in on the day of decision, my heart grew heavier and heavier. Eli had invited me to visit with him and some friends in Jerusalem. Eli, who was my very first Messianic Jewish friend in Israel, was a warm, fatherly man who was twenty years my superior. He seriously looked out for my welfare. He could not understand the horrid weight I felt on my heart before meeting with the Chief Rabbi. Neither could I. I imagined how Yeshua might have felt before he was called to face national accusation and rejection before the Sanhedrin. While he had been in the Garden of Gethsemane, the man of sorrows had longed for those closest to him to stand with him in his agony, but they were not able. He had to walk the last difficult stretch alone.

I cried out to God in prayer, asking that whatever awaited me, His presence would be there with me. I asked Him to show me that the steps I was taking were led by Him and not my own doing, whatever the outcome.

The morning of my appointment with my destiny in Israel, the weather scowled with the blackest, stormiest outpouring of hysteria I had seen. My life ran parallel with the weather in monumental moments. The weather was a portent of what lay ahead. I prayed *"whatever I have to face, whether it is good or evil, please give me a sign of your favor with me."* Then, I waited. What kind of sign should I ask for? *"Lord, even if it is bleak outside, let the sunshine of your presence be upon me…and, yes…let the sun* shine outside between 1p.m. and 4 p.m. I did not know why I prayed that way. My appointment was at 1p.m.

When I climbed into my station wagon to go, black wet gusts thrashed across the car window and fierce winds blew through the air, angrily assaulting my path. It was stormy! The moment I pulled into the parking lot of the Chief Rabbi's office in Tel Aviv, before I could get out of the car, the storm reached a crescendo and subsided. A bright splash of sunlight burst through the sky. My tiny gold watch ticked at exactly 1p.m. I deliberately left my umbrella on the car seat. I felt I would have undermined my own faith to carry it.

I entered the tall building. I was in the waiting room only a few seconds when a male assistant politely ordered me into the Chief Rabbi's office. He seated himself at my right, and I faced the Rabbi head on. My most extravagant imagination could not have prepared me for what awaited me!

As soon as I was seated, both men viewed me with intense hostile suspicion. The Rabbi leaned way back in his swivel chair in studied silence. His assistant, to the contrary, leaned far forward in my direction and proceeded to pounce upon me verbally with the most scathing attack I had met since the communists interrogated me in East German captivity.

The assistant's eyes were glaring as he announced that he had a statement signed by two "witnesses" that I was a "missionary" who worked for Mr. Kreisky! He went on to inform me that it was known to these authorities that I had said that "the Holocaust came upon the Jewish people because they refused to believe in Jesus." He continued with a long string of other preposterous accusations, lies, and allegations, all railing slander, hurling them at me with machine gun rapidity and in such hatred and viciousness that my brain could not absorb them!

"*This is just like the Nazis!"* I gasped and then burst out in shock. The Rabbi was stunned, as if I had slapped him in the face. This is *outrageous lies!"* I continued in disbelief. I don't even know Mr.

Kreisky! I've heard of him, but I have never even met him! This is absolutely preposterous!" I exclaimed.

"Have you ever been in his store?" The Rabbi questioned cautiously.

"Why...I believe...once, when a friend wanted to purchase a Bible." I answered. "And, those other things I never even said! *I don't even believe that way! I insist that these 'so-called witnesses' say these things to me in your presence so that I can confront them openly. Then we can establish who is telling the truth!*"

"That's impossible," the Rabbi calmly replied.

"Why this is unjust!" I cried in indignation. "I love and identify with the Jewish people. I am willing to fight for them and even die for them if necessary! My life has been parallel to theirs in so many ways...I've suffered political persecution, too, in a communist prison...so I understand some of the suffering they have endured."

"Why didn't you tell us that in the beginning?" The Rabbi seized upon my East German imprisonment as if it were some item of significance which would have altered the situation if he had he known in advance.

"No one asked me. Besides, I have written a book about it!" I retorted. This fact appeared to alarm him even more.

His assistant must have had a long list of trumped up charges and accusations against me, which he quickly stopped reading when I exploded. Yet, with fire and violence blazing in his eyes, he attempted to stuff words into my mouth that I had never even thought, much less muttered! I was appalled and had no idea where all this false information had come from.

The horror of my communist imprisonment suddenly took shape before my eyes once again—interrogation, lies, intimidation, false accusations. I distinctly felt the same spiritual forces of hatred and control projected against me as I had in East Germany. Whether they knew it or not, these Jewish men were presently being used in the same manner as the Nazis or Communists as instruments of evil. It was perhaps not yet to the same degree of degradation and depravity. The power of their hatred was unexpected and too much to bear. I had only felt love for their people. I was totally disarmed for any kind of attack of this sort. A flood of tears broke through my fragile self control and began to spill ceaselessly upon the Rabbi's desk.

Suddenly, with machine gun rapidity, questions about my convictions poured forth. Instead of allowing myself to be verbally mangled and mauled by the assistant, who could have easily been a Spanish inquisitor, I handed the Rabbi the paper I had written up for our meeting. He wanted to know exactly what I believed about Jesus. I had put together sources that were strictly from a Jewish and rabbinical perspective.

He began to read what I had written as an academic response, with information from the Talmud:

> "According to my personal understanding of the New Testament, Jesus desired to point the way to the God of Israel and enable man to establish an existential relationship with His reality. He did not seek to undermine or detract one iota from Judaism, but enlighten man to the Spirit of its content, which for some had been lost in the rote performance of externals, "the letter of the Law," alone. This conclusion is based on the statement that:
>
> The rabbis tell us: "Jerusalem was destroyed because the rabbis at that time insisted on fulfilling the letter of the Law found in the Torah (Baba Metzia 30b). What did the rabbis mean by that statement?
>
> Answer:
>
> This statement is based on the following Midrash: The Torah was asked, "How can a person who has sinned obtain forgiveness?"
>
> "Answered the Torah: Let him offer a sacrifice!" They next put the question to
>
> G-d, who replied, 'Let him *repent first* and then offer a sacrifice!' The L-rd desires that man repent before offering his sacrifice. A sacrifice without repentance will be of no avail because it will not bring the sinner forgiveness. This is

> the meaning of the words of the rabbis, who said: Jerusalem was destroyed because they fulfilled the letter of the law of Torah." They followed the strict letter of the Torah which states that we must offer sacrifice when we transgress the law. But, they did not follow the spirit of the law as expressed in G-d's own reply "that the sacrifice must be preceded by *repentance*."
>
> Had the Jews followed the spirit of the law and repented first, Jerusalem would not have been destroyed.
> (HASDE AVOTH)

This was the spiritual atmosphere in certain segments of Judaism at the time of Jesus' teachings. Hence, he was a teacher whose authority was not accepted by some of the rabbis of his day.

It appears that all of the original followers of the teachings of Jesus and even those who recorded the accounts of his life were Jews, living in Palestine. It was not until after the destruction of the Temple in 70 C.E. and the subsequent Dispersion, that the severance between these Jews and the rest of Judaism took place.

Unfortunately, for the reality and spirit of the biblical record, the powerful Roman culture paganized Jesus and his teachings. The subsequent history of organized, institutional Christianity is the result. The paganism and political power of Rome engulfed this branch of Judaism with its own traditions and annihilated its genuine spiritual content, reaching a pinnacle under the power of Constantine. Thus, Jesus became a "Gentile", and western Christendom became a political power which was divorced from its Jewish roots and content, and which persecuted Jews. Hence, I cannot or do not identify with such traditional, historical institutional Christianity. Nor do I possess any religious affiliation creed, or dogma that formally links me with such a Christian institution.

> However, I have been inspired by the person of Jesus as depicted by the Bible, as historically many Jews have been. The historical distortion and even caricature of Jesus that was propagated by western Christendom and which led to the persecution and rejection of Jewish people has too often

been accepted at face value in the Jewish religious world. This Jesus has been rightly rejected by Jewish leaders, who have suffered as a consequence of its propagation.

In so far as I can see from the biblical account, Jesus did not undermine Torah, but commanded man to obey its authority and the authority of the religious leaders. His sharp criticisms appear to be directed at those who had substituted "the letter of the Law" for the absolute performance of letter and spirit.

(In other words, they were doing their duty, but their heart was not repentant.)

After the Rabbi's shrewd eyes carefully examined the contents of my paper, he quietly looked up. "Would you sign this for me?" he questioned.

Aghast, I announced "No!" I recoiled in horror. The months of Communist interrogations swarmed before my face again. All the statements against myself I was psychologically forced to sign. I was reliving the nightmare of one totalitarian regime in the midst of another. The Chief Rabbi suddenly became the Chief Rabbi interrogator, who was snatching any evidence he could to convict me of some unknown crime. Was it a crime to believe in a Jew named Yeshua?

"Have you told others of your beliefs in Israel?" He probed cautiously. "Yes, I have. Though I certainly don't go around the streets talking about my beliefs. When I get to know someone, well, I share my convictions with them where appropriate."

"Well, you should not tell anyone else in Israel what you believe about Jesus!" The Rabbi ordered severely.

"I cannot agree to that!" I responded. I was utterly appalled that this scene was taking place in the Twentieth Century in one of the most enlightened nations in the world! What a repetition of history! How the early disciples had been forbidden to speak about Jesus with the threat of imprisonment! When that happened, they answered "*We must obey God rather than men!*" The Chief Rabbi of the Jewish State was attempting to deny my freedom of speech and I was not Jewish!

"My beliefs are a part of myself, which I share with others when I get to know them. I am not a 'so-called missionary' according to your definition and one which horrifies the Jews. But neither am I willing to stifle my personal freedom of speech to any kind of religious totalitarian control," which I felt he was attempting to exercise over me and his nation! His eyes flashed in anger that he was unable to coerce me, and he had maintained a quiet study of me while I erupted all over his office under the provocation and intimidation of his assistant. I knew I must have sounded defiant to the leading religious authority of the nation, but like the Jewish fisherman, Peter, I knew I must "obey God rather than man." Part of God's will for every believer is to share His love and good news with others!

"Well, your *thinking* is not Jewish! It is impossible for you to become a Jew!" He declared with the finality of having pulled out the trump card from the deck. His words were crushing, but I still leapt to my defense. "...But I love the God of Israel, identify with the Jewish people, and I am willing to do my best to follow in the traditions of this heritage. My instructor taught us that Judaism is based on *deeds* rather than *creeds*. Why does it matter what I really believe in my heart?"

"Your *thinking* is not Jewish," the Rabbi again announced in an air of finality. "Are Jews really so monolithic?" I asked. This stood in complete contradiction to what I had learned in class. If what he was saying was near the truth, then Jews suffered from national religious mind control, and I refused to believe that! Why even the Talmud was loaded with differing views of the proper interpretation of Judaism! The schools of Hillel and Shammai stood on the opposing poles of Biblical interpretation. Jews even differed on whether the Messiah was an "era," a person or both!

"I think that it is *tragic*," I emphasized the last word with all the emotion I could, "that you are willing to make Jews out of people who proclaim themselves to be atheists, and even others who have no further purpose than marriage. Yet, you deny me, one who believes in the God of Israel and I am willing to attempt to comply with your laws and traditions, when many of these other people will not continue to do so after they complete their conversion procedure! "Yes, it *is* tragic." He offered no defense for the system that appeared to adopt liars and reject believers. "But, your *thinking* is not Jewish." I was too upset to think about asking him what he considered to be "Jewish thinking". For history's sake, it would have been quite significant to record his answer. Then, all of the Jews of the world could be polled, and we could determine what "Jewish thinking" really is. From what I could determine, everything hung merely on the rejection of Yeshua as Messiah to determine how Jewish thinking was defined. I was certain that all Jews did not think or believe that way. All of the writers of the New Testament (Covenant) were Jews. Moreover, neither did Reform, Conservative, Orthodox or Hassidic Jews all think alike. Who gave him the power to decide who is a Jew? I wondered whether he thought Jews were a monolithic society in their rejection of Yeshua. History had proven that this was not true. Hundreds of European and American Jews had encountered personal faith in Yeshua as their Messiah along the way, including a cardinal of the Catholic Church in France who was considered Jewish.

"Well, I will appeal," I stated. "I am sure that there are other rabbis in Israel who have different views." (I even knew of some I had heard about.) I would fight. I would not give up on the basis of this one man's opinion, even though I knew what his office represented.

"I will personally see to it that no other rabbi in Israel will accept you!" He announced with the absolute power of a dictator who had a confident grip over his people. "You might inform your instructor that you will no longer be able to participate in the class!" He arose from his chair, as if he had tolerated this indignation long enough, and with his smoldering assistant, still breathing fire down my neck, directed me to the exit.

Tears were streaming down my face as I strode toward the car. I almost did not notice that brilliant sunshine splashed its rays on me in waves of comfort. "*I am still with you,*" an inner voice said in consolation. With the shafts of sunlight still sparkling off the hood of my car, I climbed inside, closed the door and stared at the petite hands of my watch. It was 4 p.m. exactly. As I started the engine, the brilliant opening in the sky collapsed, and wind and rain lashed out upon the city once more. God had answered my prayer and given me a *sign*! I had been in the office exactly three hours. The rain had stopped during this time. When it returned, it was more furious than before! I was determined to fight.

I had one thought in my mind—to drive straight to my class and announce my termination, which the Rabbi had summoned me to do. I would proclaim the deceit and injustice of what was occurring to me. I pressed the accelerator to the floor and darted through the erratic traffic. Those people in my class had no idea what they were getting into. Already I knew that a couple of my classmates were experiencing deep soul searching about whether to continue with the conversion process.

I knew that most of them did not have any real relationship with God in their lives. They were merely adherents to whatever culture they had grown up under. Faith or a personal relationship with God had never occurred to them. There was one exception. Tommy the Australian.

We had spoken with each other many times about the class and Yeshua. He confided that as a boy, he had been a believer, too. However, he had become bitter when God did not do anything about freeing his father from alcoholism. Now, he concluded there was no God. He had played the "religious game" better than anyone in the class. He knew exactly what the instructor wanted to hear and loved to pump her ears with the right answers. Tommy enjoyed the game. The only pain it caused him was the final circumcision ceremony he had to undergo! I feared that Tommy might have been an accomplice in the betrayal that had just occurred in my life.

When I arrived at the classroom, instead of standing up and pontificating on the great evil, deception, and injustice of the system these naïve people were about to embrace, I broke down and wept. I walked into the classroom with tears streaming down my face and announced I have been rejected because I believe in Yeshua. Then, I turned around and left.

God did to me what He had done to Ezekiel. "I will make your tongue stick to the roof of your mouth so that you can't reprove them; for they are rebels!" God said to the prophet. Outside in the hallway, my weeping broke through like a flood pouring out through my voice. It was a crescendo of heartbreak there in the hall for all of the candidates and instructors to hear.

The Chief Rabbi had cut me off from his people! No where else had I so deeply felt the sense of commitment and belonging as I had among the Israelis. I realized that the ultra religious lived in a world of their own and often very isolated from the rest of the population. That environment I could have adapted to, but it was probably better that the door was closing. My only concern from that point forward was that I was labeled in some underground of religious darkness. They would never leave me alone if I chose to try to remain in Israel. The vile and malicious accusations I had met in the Rabbi's office were like a cancer eating at the core of the nation's health. I was convinced that most Israelis knew nothing about it. If they had no reason to be involved with the people behind it, they could ignore its existence and move on. Perhaps, those behind such a religious tyranny over their nation and people were more dangerous to Israel's welfare than the Arab terrorists who threatened their nation. They knew the terrorists from the outside were there and knew how to deal with them. Those religious terrorists who used words to slander and divide their people were far more dangerous, especially when no one was courageous enough to stand up to their power.

According to a Jewish rabbi in America, the God of Judaism always wanted His children to become creative partners with Him. Moreover, God wanted a whole people, a nation that would reflect His reality to the world. That was my view of Israel as well. This was the promise of her future. For God had truly chosen Israel for Himself, had revealed His oracles to the Jews, had promised Abraham that all nations would be blessed through him, and that Israel should carry God's message to the world. Consequently, it was a privilege to be born a Jew, as well as a great responsibility. I was grieved that some were willing to allow liars and hypocrites to rule in the seats of religious power, and reject many people in their midst— Jews and non-Jews who loved their God and their Land! A wonderful Jew, named Yeshua had given me a new heart and a new spirit and a love for Israel and the Jewish people. Why was he so hated?

Back in my tiny cubicle room, I picked up a copy of the Christmas message I had written for some of my friends in America. I had stood upon the hills of Jerusalem with a group of Jews, some Messianic and some not. My heart ached over the City. The message I had written had been prophetic. "Christmas has come and passed. Across the land life continues with the same oblivion to the world shaking event that was birthed from her own womb. In the distant sky there is a lonely reminder—a glowing comet, a star larger and brighter than the rest. It appears to be centered over Bethlehem. From the distance the muffled cries of a baby break the stillness. Somewhere in the lonely stable of the Bethlehem of our hearts a choir of rejoicing is heard. "*A king has been born! His reality has been born in us! Our lives can begin again!*"

> I wanted to rush to the balcony and shout to the walls of Jerusalem: "Behold, your king is coming! You will see him when you are ready to say *"Blessed is he who comes in the Name of the Lord."* (Matt. 23:39)

OUTSIDE THE CAMP

**"Let us then go to him outside the camp,
bearing the disgrace he bore.
For here we do not have an enduring city,
but we are looking for a city to come."
(Hebrews 13:13)**

Overnight, I felt like *persona non grata* in Israel. I had already begun to seek out other living quarters, when I received the notice from the Jewish Agency that I was no longer eligible for my living accommodations. Moreover, Naomi had informed me by mail that religious "investigators" came to the kibbutz and had attempted to secure a copy of the book I had written about my East German prison experience. The kibbutzniks, who had no love for the religious establishment in the first place, informed the "investigators" that more than likely I had used other names in the book. These religious police displayed little professional expertise, according to Naomi.

Underground religious police in Israel—like Saudi Arabia! I could believe such a thing now that I had walked through a dark side of the nation. It was evident that they were going to try and cast suspicion upon me and make me look like a security risk for Israel. I would have laughed, if it had not made me cry! No matter how rotten they were, it was not legal to throw someone out of the land because of their beliefs. So they probably thought they would have to make me out to be a threat. I would gladly give them a copy of the book I wrote about my imprisonment under the Communist East Germans.

The East Germans had considered me a threat, too. My belief in personal freedom was not compatible with their system. They had to trump up charges against me, too. They made me sound like "Public Enemy Number One", a lone woman who was a "threat to their system" because I told a young man how someone had escaped from the massive prison camp of East Germany. He did not even try. I had felt that my imprisonment by Nazi-like Germans gave me a much deeper understanding of what many Jews had endured in the Holocaust. How ironic that the religious extremists of Israel were attempting to turn it all against me! Those who had suffered most had a choice of becoming bitter or better.

My imagination began to play havoc with me. I began to suspect Jacob or Ari for being a part of the plot. I realized that the Russian immigrant who worked at the desk was a part of the set up when he put the wrong letter in my mail box, and directed me to the tall lady in the trench coat.

As I lay down on the bed, Efes smothered me with reassuring kisses. She always rolled over into ecstasy every time I returned to the room after any absence. She was as enthralled with her new quarters as I was. I remembered when I picked her up at the kibbutz to bring her to the city. She carried herself like a show dog when I put her on the leash. She did not take well to the confusion of the noisy streets of Jaffe, though. On the kibbutz she had been her own boss, with a free run of the place, and everyone adored her. In the urban world she was overwhelmed by the aggressive self assertiveness of the people around her. She shied, cowered, ducked and buried her tail between her legs as we walked the streets together. When the tough canine city slickers snarled at her on the sidewalk, she did not fight back. Usually she grabbed my leg and wanted me to pick her up. Lately, she had allowed one big dog to jump her without resisting. I saw myself in little Efes.

My scared little Terrier showed me how fear could paralyze my creative energies. Then, I began to discover just how one fear after another could tyrannize my life. In the face of an uncertain future, fear was always lurking just around the next corner, waiting to launch a surprise attack. Much of my energy began to be invested in warding off imagined enemies, as well as the real ones. Now I had to contend with both.

If my enemies desired to devise a story against me to throw me out of Israel, I was defenseless against them. I was convinced that no Jewish person would stand up for me after the Chief Rabbi had rejected and slandered me. I felt a dark conspiracy trying to push me out. Some of it was very real. I became very paranoid about religious Jews. If I saw someone dressed in their garb or even wearing a yarmulke, I would cross over to the other side of the street. That "*kipa*" became a symbol of all those right wing extremists who wanted to destroy me. I felt helpless with them. If they would openly deal with truth, then I could stand up to them. I did not know where I could even turn for justice. Of course I knew that all religious Jews were not the same, but how could I know whom to trust?

It never dawned on me at the time that my feelings and fears were identical with those that many Jews had experienced in the Diaspora in all the Gentile cultures where they lived. I was experiencing the exact *reverse sense of discrimination in their culture.* In spite of the paralysis of fear, deep down within me was an urge that prompted me to keep on fighting against this hostile wall that divided us and gain their acceptance—because I loved them!

One day I reached out to Rachel for reassurance, since she had already experienced her own brand of war against the extremists, and she was born Jewish! "Rachel, will you stand with me?" I pleaded. "It seems as if I have been betrayed by everyone else."

Instantly, her big brown eyes darkened with fear. Shamefully, she lowered her head. If I am truthful," she mumbled, "I'm afraid that I cannot promise you I will."

"Oh God, is all this betrayal because I am not a Jew? Or is it because I am determined to stand with You?" The question was rhetorical. I believed that if a person was an honest believer in God, he should be able to make a commitment to stand with other believers. I wanted to be that kind of person. I knew of only one person in Israel I could be sure I could count on, my dear faithful Naomi.

Naomi rescued my faith in mankind, and more especially the Jewish people, from being shattered in the devilish onslaught that surrounded me. She was a Holocaust survivor, and caring Gentiles had saved her life. She was a gentle doe of a woman, gracious and loyal, yet shy and retreating. She had avowed her allegiance to stand with me no matter what. I recognized that she lacked the human strength and courage to stand against the powerful forces I had once faced with the communists and now in the religious extremists in Israel. Yet I did believe that God was faithful and would impart the power for her to stand if necessary. Naomi was willing to pay any price to remain loyal to me with the deep bond of our friendship which had been welded by the Hand of God Himself! I had never had a friend as loyal as Naomi. Our friendship was a priceless gift from God.

My experience with powerful rejection began to carry me more deeply into the wounds and bruises of those who had been persecuted. I was especially sensitive to this heartache, born of generations of oppression, in the Russian immigrants who came to Israel. I had empathy for the pain I sensed in many I met. Again I learned that it is a terrifying thing to be loved unconditionally by another when one has never experienced it. All of the darkness of one's soul is driven to the surface. What would the other person do with it? I thought about the words of John, the disciple of Yeshua, "Perfect love casts out fear." I was learning that each time I was hurt and fearful of more pain, I had to reach upward to receive more *love* to overcome.

I began to question myself. Had I done the right thing with my decision to join with the Jewish people? I was instantly reminded of a prophetic word that had been spoken into my life before I left America. Someone in New York had prayed for me and said, *"Where you are after the kibbutz, you will think you got there by deception, but it was God's will for your life!* That memory gave me great consolation and strength. What was my role now with Israel? Should I pack my bags and depart?

I was unsure which way to turn. Naomi suggested that I sneak away for a few days retreat to some secluded spot. It sounded like the ideal solution. I had always wanted to visit the location of the Mary Sisters, German Christians who had a retreat center for Holocaust survivors. These women of God had begun as a community in Germany after the War. God had directed them to build a chapel in His honor under impossible conditions. Their story was wrought with miracles. I had read many of the books of the founder, Mother Basilea, and I was drawn to their depth of devotion to God, and their love for the people of Israel. They took responsibility for reparation of their nation's war crimes against the Jewish people. It was almost impossible to find an opening to go to their retreat center in Israel because their schedule was always filled. Miraculously they had a space for me when I called!

My experience at the Retreat House was a re-entry into the Christian world. Like an astronaut who had just returned from the moon, I needed the time to unwind and recondition my thinking back to earthly reality. I had certainly had some contact with Christians in Israel, but most of my experience was with Jews, and my mind had been geared to identification and assimilation with them. The quiet peace of God's presence among the Sisters transcended all cultures. I asked Him to meet me in that place and He did!

The perfect tonic for my weary soul was their spacious dwelling with a generous garden in a quiet suburb of Jerusalem. Each room had a name of a Jewish biblical leader on the door. My door read "Moses". As I stepped over the threshold, the big, bold words on a wall plaque met me head on. They were Moses' prayer in Exodus:

> *"If I have found favor in your eyes, teach me your ways so I may know you and continue to find favor with you. Remember that this nation is your people." The Lord replied, "My Presence will go with you, and I will give you rest." (Exodus 33:13-14)*

I felt the tender presence of God's Spirit come over me as I read the words. Moses' prayer was my prayer. His answer was my answer. I took it as confirmation. I turned and saw another plaque in the room. This time I read the words: *Now, the Lord had said to Abram, "Leave your country, your people and your father's household and go to the land I will show you." (Genesis 12:1)*

The crowning gem of this warm welcome was the little bud vase with a rose at my bedside. It had a card that read "God, the Almighty, enjoys doing great deeds, even for the least of His children."

My heart leapt for joy. I was not there by accident or mistaken direction. It was the Creator's plan that brought me there!

I had a lovely meeting with one of the sisters in the evening. As gracious and spiritual as she was, she did not understand the unusual path I was led to walk. I had to exercise a "stubborn faith" when it disagreed with my own understanding. Many of the prophetic paths that God had led through his people had been questioned and misunderstood by many.

This time it was Shakespeare's words that encouraged me. *"Above all to your own self be true and you cannot be false to any man!"*

My heart declared "bend yourself more toward the Jewish people."

I dearly loved the Christians I met in Israel, all of the flavors, versions and varieties; however, I sensed that so few had really transcended their own cultures in order to climb inside of the hearts of the people they were serving. It was a scary thing to drop one's denominational and cultural walls and expose oneself to a stranger.

Actually, before I left America, my deepest prayer was that God would make me an "intercessor" for the nation of Israel. An intercessor is a person who stands before God on behalf of another. In Ezekiel I had read that God told him that "He was looking for someone to 'stand in the gap' on behalf of the Land and intercede for it as Moses had for Israel. I was willing to stand before God and pray for the needs of that nation. In fact there were prayers of many Christians gathered in Jerusalem, as well as Jews, in the Yom Kippur War who "stood the gap" in prayer together to protect Israel. There were multitudes of Christians in America, too, who were continually praying for Israel.

At that time God's Spirit had shown many believers to pray specifically that the country of Jordan *would not enter* the war. Israel had been surprised by the attack from two sides, Egypt and Syria, and would have initially had difficulty handling the three nations at one time. As many believers prayed, King Hussein of Jordan wavered back and forth, finally deciding not to enter the war. In learning to be an intercessor, I had to "wear" the shoes of those I was praying for, so I could pray with understanding for them. I had not known what I was asking to do. Now, I had no choice. God's love had already decided the issue for me.

As I left the Mary Sisters, I was peacefully confused. I had great peace that I was in God's plan. I was confused about where, how, and when I really fitted in. Then I had an insight. Maybe there were also many Jews who felt the same way I did—especially those who wanted to embrace Yeshua as their Messiah! Now, all I needed to do was turn at the correct intersection. It was clear that I had to persevere. Once I recognized this challenge I received encouragement from both Christians and Jews alike.

At the same time I learned that my little friend Rachel had just been denied an extension to her visa because of her belief in Yeshua. Her heritage was as Jewish as they come. Her grandfather was buried on the Mount of Olives, and her blood was as Jewish as the best Jew in Israel. The Law of Return promised any Jew the privilege of homeland in Israel. Yet, an arbitrary committee of the Interior Ministry decided to deny her the privilege of Jewishness and order her out of the country. That even went against *Halacha*, Jewish religious law itself, which stated that once born a Jew, then always a Jew. I decided I would help her fight for her rights in her homeland. *The whole world would rise up in indignation if a Jew was refused entry to America for merely being a Jew.* How much greater was the injustice because Rachel was a pure blooded American Jewess, who happened to believe in another Jew, called Yeshua. Her faith had thrust her more deeply into the investigation of her Jewish roots and belonging to her people. For that very reason she had come to Israel. Now, the Interior Ministry on behalf of the Jewish State was going to throw her out of the country and ban her from re-entry. What hypocrisy!

I sat down at my typewriter and began to write. I decided the first letter would go to one of the most objective men I knew of in the Israeli Knesset. This member of Parliament had been responsible for handling famous cases in Israel in previous years, and he was respected in Israel on all sides of the political spectrum.

Dear X,

In the course of my contact with Israel, I have had the opportunity to follow some of your outstanding work in handling difficult cases. I have come to the conclusion that there is no one is Israel who is more of an authority in executing objective judgment in matters of controversy than you. Therefore, I have a matter of urgent concern to bring to your attention. It concerns the present problem of legislation about "WHO IS A JEW?" and religious discrimination in Israel. It is not only an issue of interest to you, but I greatly desire you advice or assistance in resolving it.

I came to Israel from America a year ago with a deep desire for living out my sense of calling of identification with the Jewish people—with the intention of making this my people and offering my professional skills and experience in social work to the service of the Land. I sought to take this step with full commitment, just as the biblical Moabite, Ruth: "Let your people by my people and your God, my God."

Through the direction of the Jewish Agency I was led into instruction in Judaism under the auspices of the Chief Rabbi's office. I attended classes daily from mid-September until mid-January and received excellent scores on my examinations. I was even willing to attempt to live by observing all the religious duties and responsibilities to the best of my ability—if this was the only way I could become identified with the Jewish people and become a legal resident of Israel.

However, in the meantime, individuals unknown to me, appeared at the Chief Rabbi's office with false accusations, charging me with being a so-called "missionary," connected with individuals I have never even met. Moreover, slanderous statements I never made nor even believe were attributed to me. Even though I protested against the unreliability of the information, I was dismissed from my course and told I could not take the final examination. I was informed that my "thinking" is not Jewish.

This conclusion was evidently based on my understanding about Jesus—which I felt in no way went against what I had learned in class about the practice of Judaism. Indeed, I had learned in class that Judaism is based on "deeds", rather than "creeds"—in other words, what you do, instead of what you "believe". I accept this concept and feel that my own particular ideas or views concerning Jesus (as an individual in the context and continuity of Jewish culture) were not even relevant to the *practice* of Judaism or my identification with the Jewish people.

Moreover, subversive methods to "frame me" for these false charges—such as planting letters in my mail box, which were not addressed to me, were used against me. I was "set up" in other ways. Then, I was not even given the opportunity to face my accusers. All of this not only violates the principles of genuine democracy, but the very essence of the TORAH. One of the Ten Commandments was broken to bear false witness against me; in addition, the command to "exercise justice to the stranger in the land" was also violated in ignoring my plea to face my accusers.

Now, these events are perhaps incidental, except for the fact that I still very much desire to become identified with the people of Israel with the full acceptance and assurance of democratic rights that every other individual is guaranteed. I have been excluded from this privilege on the basis of false accusations and personal private convictions. There is no legal way for a non Jew to remain in Israel, except by becoming Jewish through Orthodox Judaism—which has rejected me. Moreover, I was told that the Chief Rabbi would personally advise Jewish rabbinical courts not to accept my case. Is there no place in the land that I might turn to for justice?

Earlier I consulted the American Embassy for advice on becoming an Israeli citizen. At that time I was advised to become Jewish. Now, I desire to do so, but I have been prevented because of the slander from some unknown religious extremists. In light of these events, and the present issue concerning WHO IS A JEW, is it not time to re-evaluate WHO IS A JEW? I have Jewish friends—born to both Jewish parents—who have been told by some religious authorities that they are "no longer Jews" because of their particular understanding about the Jew, Jesus, and in some cases intimidated into leaving the country. They have in no way converted to another religion or renounced their heritage or Jewishness. They were not even proselytes, nor were their parents.

Finally, I think it is a deep tragedy for Israel and the Jewish people, if those who are willing to lie and be hypocritical are more readily acceptable to religious authorities than those who stand on truth. I personally know of cases, including individuals in my own class, who acknowledged their preparation to lie to rabbinical authorities for the sake of convenience in conversion. If rabbinical authorities are willing to accept false witness without question or examination and totally dismiss an individual on that basis, to whom shall one turn for the truth?

I turn to you with the sincere hope that you might advise me on an appropriate course of action.

As I dropped the letter into the mailbox, my heart fluttered with hope. This was the one man in Israel who could help me if anyone could. I also sent a copy to another member of Knesset who was a champion for human rights in the country, and strongly opposed to religious coercion and control.

The Israeli leader from the Ministry of Justice upon whom I had hung great hope wrote the following:

"I wish I could help you. It appears from your letter that you have been disqualified from conversion into Judaism because of your belief in Jesus in the context of the Jewish culture.

As you know, as a result of the horrible persecutions suffered throughout the ages, The Jewish religion dissociated itself from Jesus and from his disciples. This is not necessarily the view taken today by many Jewish circles, including historians and writers like Professor Klausner and Kabak. Conversion into Judaism is, however, entirely within the hands of the Rabbinate. For them, conversion involves a complete dissociation from the previous belief.

Did you attempt to air your problem with the Chief Rabbi himself? Do you want me to transfer to him a copy of your letter?

My heart sank. This man was not able to help. I was dejected to read what he had written about "Jesus and his disciples." He did not even know that some of the religious leaders of Jesus' time had persecuted Jesus and his disciples. Those Jewish disciples lived with great fear of their Jewish religious leaders even at that time in history.

I had much difficulty understanding how such a gifted and educated nation of people could continue to deny and reject one of the most beautiful Jews who ever lived on the earth. Could they not see the light that this one Jew had brought to the nations of the earth? How freedom, democracy, brotherhood, and the equality of women had come to the world through one Jew. It was even more greatly significant that this one Jew was responsible for bringing millions of people around the world to believe in the God of Israel, the one true God. Unfortunately, I had not yet discovered how almost two thousand years of anti-Semitism from the world that is called "Christendom" had blinded both Christians and Jews.

The pain, rejection, torment and torture the Jews had suffered at the hands of those they thought were Christians had simply reinforced any blindness their own religious leaders carried. Sadly, they did not know that those who hated and harmed the Jewish people were not true Christians, which the Bible defined according to their deeds as well as their creeds.

Unfortunately, they had not met men and women who had experienced true life changing repentance toward the God of Israel and His Messiah who were commanded to love their neighbors, as well as their enemies. Perhaps many of the Israeli Jews had lived in lands where so-called Christianity was a compromised worldly political power not based on the truth of the Bible, but on the traditions of men. The horrors that these Jews experienced had come from the power of evil, *just as those same lies I had experienced at the Rabbinate.* The wound of history culminating in the Holocaust was still filled with deep pain in the hearts of the survivors who made up the land of Israel. I could understand their fears.

I was grieved by this recognition. There were millions of Christians worldwide who loved and wanted to serve the Jewish people. They were grateful for the Jews who had brought the light of salvation and a relationship with the Living God into their lives! Their desire was to bless the people and nation that had done so. Anything else was not the true Christianity of the God of the Bible. The more I thought about this the more small seeds of reconciliation were being born in my heart. *All Christians everywhere owed* the *Jews a deep heartfelt apology for all the sins that were committed against them in the name of Christianity*, whether they were of discrimination, neglect, hatred, harm or abuse. Even then it would be difficult to heal many of the Jewish hearts that had been wounded. A Christian was only genuine if the Spirit of God was the one leading his or her life and not merely religious tradition! A deep work of repentance in many Christians had to take place before there could ever be any genuine reconciliation between Christians and Jews, who both believed in the same God. Yeshua himself had said, "By their fruits you will know them!"

Three weeks later I received another letter, this time it was from the other Knesset member I had written. It read:

As expressed in the Party Platform..."Knesset Member X's" views are that in order to identify with the State of Israel, there is no need to go through with conversion. The situation in the Religious Courts is tragic and well known to us. The Rabbinate refuses to admit that religion is a personal matter and therefore official ceremony is redundant.

You have certainly addressed your case to the proper authority on the matter, and we very much hope that you will receive speedy attention and ultimate satisfaction.

I had traveled full circle, arriving back at the same starting point. There were scores of people out there among both Jews and Christians that believed in honest and truthful behavior. Articles were appearing daily in the newspapers describing similar plights because of the "Who Is a Jew" issue which the government was in the process of debating. I was exhausted from combat fatigue. Giving up the battle also meant giving up Israel. The Interior Ministry was not willing to grant me an unlimited visa for any reason because of the string of associations that had attached themselves to my name.

While in the midst of the political and religious flurry, I had to find new housing and continue to fight the powers that prevailed. One day I wandered into the office of Canadians and Americans in Israel. I thought that they might have a good lead for employment which would make my next visa possible. A job that offered significant contribution to the country would be a valid reason for granting extension to stay. My Hebrew was not yet adequate for the demands of social work, so another field would be required. Receiving a visa to stay longer than the three month minimum was the subject of sweat, tears, prayers, and often wrangling with the authorities for every Christian and even Messianic Jew I had met.

At the office of the Americans and Canadians in Israel, I got into conversation with an American lady. I had mentioned something about difficulty getting a visa. She snatched hold of my statement with excessive curiosity. I think the word "discrimination" must have caught her attention. Her eyes lit up and she invited me to dinner that evening. I spontaneously said "yes" without thinking.

Driving home that evening I began to feel great fear. I realized that I had already promised my friends Barry and Harriet I would come over for a mini celebration for my anniversary of my liberation from prison. I tried to call the lady I had met in the office to cancel my visit, but I learned she had no telephone. She was not to be reached at work. I jumped into the car and drove to Bat Yam to discuss the change of plans with Barry and Harriet. I felt very uneasy about going to the house of the stranger I had just met.

"I am convinced," I said as I presented my problem to Barry, "that I very much need to be there or I definitely should not go at all. I have some great apprehension. Since I cannot reach her by phone I believe I should go in order to keep my word. What if they start asking me a lot of questions after what I have been through in the country, I don't know who it is I am talking with."

"Well, then, you need to practice an old Jewish trick," Barry exhorted gently. "You just answer a question with a question. Or even better, you keep asking them questions!"

"Hey, that's a great idea. I think Yeshua was a master of that technique. He used it with the corrupt religious leaders who were trying to trick him." Barry nodded in agreement.

I left the seaside apartment, still astir with anxiety. Hurriedly I stopped by the home of a Christian friend where we also had prayer together asking God to take over the evening.

When I arrived at the Goldberg's apartment, Mrs. Goldberg instantly informed me that her husband was at the synagogue, but would join us soon. I sighed deeply. What have I gotten myself into? It was midweek and not a Jewish holiday. That meant her husband was either devout or devoutly extreme.

I quickly began asking her about her life. In a few minutes I learned she was an ardent and militant Zionist. They were members of the Anti-Defamation League and were "extreme rightists in the religion". All of which could be very innocent and loving, but I sensed that I had fallen into another trap! I was going to have dinner with some of those people who deeply distrusted Christians, and maybe even hated them.

I was very grateful that I had prayed with others before going. I was also glad to hear that they had invited another young woman to come over for dinner. I was counting on her to shift the conversation away from me and "my story". I decided that Barry's strategy of asking questions would be my modus operandi for the evening.

At the dinner table the family brought up the subject of another young woman in the country who was a believer in Yeshua and had undergone conversion to Judaism. They expressed their disdain of her, claiming that it was a poorly *disguised mission effort* "to draw people away from their own religion." My stomach was churning while I listened. I said nothing, but I was thinking that another poor person was probably being slandered. I was normally outspoken and transparent. but I was certain that this was no place to be myself. The discussion suddenly turned into an argument between the husband and wife.

Like all the other Israelis who read the newspapers, the couple was preoccupied with the current national war in Israel over the question "*Who is a Jew?*" Everywhere I went such discussions would break forth! The pair began to verbally fight with each other over the issue of whether "once a Jew, always a Jew" was valid. Their positions were diametrically opposed to each other. They became so absorbed with the concept of "creed" versus "deed" regarding the definition of Jewishness that they forgot I was there. The wife concluded that even though Judaism was based on deeds, Spinoza, DaKosta, and others were "excommunicated" on the basis of "creed". A lively debate presided over the entire evening, and they hardly noticed when I graciously thanked them for their hospitality and slipped away into the night!

Outside in the winter air, I exhaled a great sigh of relief. "Thank you Father for taking over the evening...." When I took a deep breath of the crisp fresh air, I had a beautiful revelation about the evening. I had caught a glimpse into the lives of those severely rigid religious people who sat across the table from me. They appeared to be extremely hard on others, especially Christians, because their minds had been brainwashed by what they thought a Christian is. Or perhaps their hearts had become embittered because of the history of Christendom in its failure and betrayal of the Jews. I knew that no words I could have uttered would have ever penetrated the steel wall that had enclosed their hearts and minds. To them it had been Christians who conducted the pogroms, the Holocaust, the hate attacks on the Jews, the job discrimination, and an endless chain of abuses and injustices Jews had suffered throughout history. Of course, real Christians could have been involved. However, these were evil acts which would be condemned by genuine believing and practicing Christians. Nor did they realize that thousands of Christians had died in the Nazi camps as well as Jews. If I had said to them "Do you know the Jesus I have met really loves you so much that he chose to give his life and suffer just for you?" I suspect that it would have been the same as telling them that Hitler loved them! Their minds were bitter and poisoned. Oh God help us!" I cried out in my heart. Jesus had said that "the truth would set men free!" (John 8:32). There was a deep work of reconciliation that had yet to be done between Christians and Jews.

This experience provided a great revelation for me to see how twisted and distorted the Jesus in their minds was from the Jesus of the Bible. Some of his so-called followers later in history were probably guilty for part of this, as well as *the people's own willingness to believe slander*. I was stricken and smitten by the defamation of Jesus and his true followers that darkened their Jewish minds. At the same time I was completely set free! Inside I felt the pangs of a deep sorrow that perhaps I had been trying to give birth to a phenomenon before its time. I would only have hurt these people by sharing my understanding of the Jew, Jesus, with them. They were so spiritually blinded by past deception, heartache and abuse of their people that words alone could not suffice to heal, or reconcile. I knew that only patient, loving action from those who truly knew Jesus could prove that he and his true followers really loved them. I suddenly felt a need to apologize to the Chief Rabbi and my instructor. I had no conception of the depth of the distortion against Jesus that the very people I had sought to serve lived under. Those in deepest darkness *are not able to see*...they must first be healed by the reality of God's genuine love in His people!

Once again, on February 3, the date I was released from a Communist prison, I was liberated! *And, the husband and wife I was visiting did not even agree on the definition of who a Jew really is*! Moreover, I recognized that *Christians have a great debt of love and mercy to grant to the Jewish people for their hearts to be healed!*

IN YOUR GATES, O JERUSALEM

"I rejoiced with those who said to me,
'Let us go to the house of the Lord.'
Our feet are standing in your gates,
O Jerusalem."
(Psalm 122:1-2)

The steep winding ascent upward from Tel Aviv to Jerusalem reminded me of one gigantic, majestic cork screw. Every time I wound my way around the mountains, I was reminded of the psalmist's strong reassurance which had become my anchor of hope: "*As the mountains surround Jerusalem, so the Lord surrounds his people both now and forevermore.*" Every twist in the corkscrew surprised me with another huge mound of soil sprinkled with trees, and sparkling sunlit settlements scattered throughout the hills. Along the road lay wreckages from the War of Independence, scattered as lonely monuments reminding all that the blood of her sons had been spilled to redeem her land. When the last twist of the spiral road was achieved, the magnificent City glistened like a golden crown upon the pinnacle of the heights.

I always held my breath in suspense as I circled the last bend and arrived at Jerusalem's outskirts with a burst of joy. Jerusalem was filled with mystique and charm which captivated me every time I touched her. Jerusalem was also a strange symphony composed of contrasts. The extremes of earthly and spiritual, ancient and modern, simplicity and splendor both merged and clashed with magnetic intensity. Her multicolored personality boasted an entire parade of humanity and culture in her streets—a Moslem peasant woman covered in veils; black-coated Hassidic Jews with dangling side curls and wide brimmed hats trimmed in mink; long, brown robed Catholic monks with beaded rosaries; studious looking scholars with their arms loaded with books; zany and sophisticated artists who assembled their crafts; oriental artisans who peddled their wares in the streets; soldiers scattered everywhere in military olive with their machine guns slung over their shoulders, and always an international array of tourists, decked in cameras and dispersed among pedestrians.

Unlike many visitors who exulted in meeting the great City in the Holy Land for the first time, I was moved with a sense of reverent awe and fear. At the same time a golden glow shimmered brilliantly from her walls and soul, another eerie darkness could be felt hiding in her spirit—spiritual wickedness and religious deception. It was anything but holy. A sensitive observer could feel the world conflict that surrounded this city. Wars had been fought to possess her, to control her, to rule, and she was no stranger to conflict. I could also sense a great hope for her future. Now, I was to relocate closer to the Hebrew University, where I would engage in Israeli Studies.

I was moving to the outskirts of Jerusalem into the middle of the environs of East Jerusalem which was a nicer portion of the Arab sector. A very accommodating Christian lady who had lived in the land for years had offered to rent me a room at the foot of Mount Scopus where I would be attending classes at the Hebrew University.

My introduction into an Arab neighborhood was fascinating and frightening at the same time. I loved to visit the Old City, including the Arab quarter, which was kaleidoscope of pungent, musty and exotic smells of spices and fruits I had never seen before. There were native costumes and shop stalls filled with items from another era and world. The Arab children tended to close in on anyone who looked like a foreigner and beg for alms. The most difficult smell was the half rotting raw meat covered with flies, hung out on flesh hooks in the open market. I always felt nauseous as I passed it. I never ceased to be enchanted though, with the narrow stone passageways with low slung arches and multiple strange nooks and crannies where tiny apartments were tucked away in the walls.

Relating to the Arab men required a great adjustment for a Western woman. They outwardly effused friendly smiles and warmth. At the same time, their hot-blooded temperament and rigid cultural barriers between the sexes made Western women a special prey for amorous advances and manipulation. Some of the foreign women I met were very naïve concerning their culture. Jerusalem was filled with stories of seduction and intrigue. I learned this on my first encounter in the Old City where an Arab tour guide tried to persuade me to go with him. In my American friendliness to all people, I nicely refused the young man's offer to see the City. He stubbornly persisted. I maintained kind respect in refusing his offer. My kindness seemed to fuel his determination even more, and he would not leave me alone until I abruptly dismissed him.

Later, I had to take my car for repairs, and since there was a shop at the end of the street where I lived, I thought I would give the Arab business a try. It was a modest looking garage with a VW sign out front. I felt safe to leave it there. At the end of the day I walked down the street to pick up the car. Upon driving my car home, I learned that I had been rooked! I was 120 shekels poorer, without the promised spark plugs, and tricked by placing it in the wrong shop.

Twilight was spreading on the horizon as I set out on foot through the valley to get help for my car for a second time. The spiraling road descended deeply into the outskirts of an Arab village. I questioned the wisdom of a lone female silhouette on the roadside. Most of the other garages that aligned this road were closed by this time. When the VW garage sprang up over the square roofs of the neighborhood, I saw light inside the building.

An enthusiastic young Arab youth welcomed me with smiles. As soon as he heard my plight in my broken Hebrew, he made no explanation. He reached for a screwdriver and gave some announcement to his associates in Arabic. Instantly two other Arab mechanics climbed into the back seat of a paneled station wagon without any explanation. The young man motioned for me to take a seat next to the driver. Without questioning I obeyed. My trust in these strangers immediately evaporated as I watched the direction they were driving. It was away from the city! Glancing at me quickly, the driver mumbled something to me in Hebrew about "two kilometers."

Before I had time to think, I was seated with three strange Arab young men, driving to a mysterious destination. My emotions were becoming volcanic. How could I ever have been so foolish as to fall into this situation? Suddenly the car stopped. I held my breath in suspense.

The threat of abduction turned out to be nothing more than a free ride home from work to Bethlehem for two buddies! I sighed in relief. Mohammed himself, a kind and polite youth, knew exactly what was wrong with my car when we returned to repair it. In a couple of minutes the silver wagon's engine was purring again. He instructed me to bring the car to him the following day and he would check it over free of charge. All he sought in return was a cup of coffee. He kept his word, and Mohammed had no idea of just how much he had restored my confidence in his people!

My new home was in an Arab neighborhood, but I spent my free time with western Christians, and lived in the world of the Jews at the university. I had enrolled in a special course in Israeli Studies for English speakers. I had a ravenous appetite to devour all the knowledge I could about the Land and its people. This time I would be studying it from the secular side, where I felt safer.

One of my courses was on the Holocaust, the tragic massacre of six million Jews by the German Nazis in World War II. Each evening I would leave the classroom very upset from hearing about the horrors of human abuse. Although I knew what the Holocaust was about, I was appalled by the depth of human depravity I was discovering. One evening a survivor of one of the camps related the terrible experiences she had suffered. Grief and agony contorted her face and burning hatred pierced through her words. "I don't trust anybody anymore—only ourselves! *Only the Jews!*"

I felt the intense sting of rejection. When she finished I rushed out of the room, choking back the tears. My heart felt as if it were going to explode. I wanted to reach out to her and reassure her that not every non Jew was her enemy. However, her hatred and bitterness were so powerful that I was terrified of her.

As I walked across the dark campus of Mount Scopus, I reflected on the incident. Her words kept circling through my mind. "We *trusted* when they selected us for the camps....and we *believed* again....and we *trusted* again...and we *believed we were really going to the showers*....when they turned on the gas....No! We will *never trust again!* Not anyone else. Only *ourselves...only the Jews!"* That woman mirrored the broken heart of Israel to me. I felt incredible pain when I heard her words. But, I also felt alienated. I could visualize a wall around her and her culture, built with the bricks of a common heritage and held together with generational pain and suffering. She sounded as if she spit the word "*goy*" with great venom when she spoke about the Gentiles which she considered despicable. I cringed as I wondered how many people felt the way she did. I not only felt like a second class person, but an "enemy"!

Inside my heart I longed to be a reconciler to her, to be a healing bridge for her to escape the destruction of the hatred and rejection of her broken heart. My eyes were opened to see that her pain was too deep ever to accept me into her world. I felt helpless by being labeled by all her hurt and wrath, and yes, even assaulted by her words...but I did understand her pain.

Outside, I crossed the campus through the silent night amid a maze of construction piles. I was briefly transported in my memory to Berlin—the charcoal scars the bombs had etched on the city's face....my own trauma with the Germans....with so much love and naiveté that had made me want to identify with the smitten Jew. Yet, it seemed that everywhere I tried I was closed out. There was a veil of enmity toward the outsider that enshrouded the culture. It said to me, "We don't want your love!"

As my footsteps wove in and out of the stacks of construction material that stood waiting to rebuild Israel's future, I was seized with deep pangs of loneliness. Even the survivor had been given a new family with the restoration of her nation. I was alone and an outsider. The hollow clicking of my heels echoed from the stone walls. The sounds continued until my thoughts were badgered with scenes of atrocities in death camps.

Suddenly, I recalled the words of hope she had timidly chosen to conclude her talk. "Yes...." after much hesitation, it was a whisper that rang with shame, "yes...I have known *some righteous Gentiles.*"

That night I held a dialogue with her in my heart. "Would you be willing to meet the one person in the world who would never let you down? The Jew, Yeshua? No, not the king of the *goyim*....but another Jew, just like yourself....who suffered more than anyone ever has without deserving it and could yet say, 'Father, *forgive them, for they know not what they do!'* This same Jew bore your pain and mine and carried our sorrows...He's the one who inspired me to leave all and follow him...to this very place...yes, all—father, mother, a dynamic profession, the prospects of a comfortable American home and family...." I especially wanted to tell her that Yeshua was no friend of the Nazis. They were the antithesis of all that he represented. Anyone who professed to follow Yeshua and deliberately hurt the Jews was a liar!

I also wanted to tell her, "Yes, you are right....don't put your trust in the nations—the *goyim*! They will let you down! They did in your darkest hour! They closed your door of hope. You lay broken, bruised, and bleeding—the last drops of your blood were being spilled for your dream of your homeland, and they dared shut you out of the Land of your Fathers, the Land that God promised to your people! No do not put your trust in *them!* Your calling is to put your trust in the Lord, your God!" Then you will enlighten those nations..."

While devouring all the contents of my courses with a greedy appetite for all I could absorb about the Land I loved so much, a giant question mark hung over my future. After all that had transpired in some secret vendetta against me, would I finally be thrown out of the country on some kind of trumped up charges? Time would tell. Unfortunately, time was running out! I had submitted my papers for another visa to the Interior Ministry, but I suspected they had something to do with those who maligned me.

There was a hidden leaven in the country. I was convinced that most Israelis knew nothing about it. The extremist clandestine control over the stranger in the land, as well as multitudes of Jews, had nothing to do with national security but everything to do with religious and political control. In this regard, Israel failed to live up to her reputation of being a democratic nation. Like all the surrounding Moslem nations, there was religious tyranny being exercised over her people. I was certain that short of a miracle, my visa would be rejected. In spite of all that, I took a "leap of faith" and relocated in Jerusalem without any funds to survive.

The miracle did occur! I received a scholarship from the estate of the old Arab lady in Jaffe who had suddenly died. I helped Lana and Rachel move, and we even inherited the furniture as well. I used the scholarship to enroll in Israeli Studies at the Hebrew University but I was still awaiting a visa.

While all my personal campaign for human rights was being conducted with the Israeli Ministry of Interior, Israel was fighting her own international standing with the U.N. The United Nations was in the process of applauding Yassir Arafat, an act which rattled the national spine and set off sudden chills of paranoia throughout the Land. A terrorist, responsible for murdering scores of Israelis was being honored by the world body. It reminded me of the Holocaust survivor's statement that she could never trust the Gentiles. I did not blame her one iota when I heard the news that a murderer and anti-Semite was being exalted in the world community.

One afternoon after class, I opened the mail box at my apartment. I looked at the official government stationery that bore my name and address. My emotions did a nosedive. The letterhead, "Prime Minister's Office," meant I was receiving very good news or very bad news. I ripped open the envelope and read that I was "invited" to a meeting. I examined the top of the page. There were two words I could not read in Hebrew. I raced to my dictionary and plowed through its frayed pages. "Ah, yes!" It was the *Office of State Security*.

Instinctively, I expected the worst. My mind traveled back to my secret conspirators. They had left me alone for a good six months of quiet rest. I figured that they were finally getting around to interrogating me, since I knew the Chief Rabbi's Office had made such a fuss about the fact that I had been a political prisoner in East Germany.

The terror of my Communist interrogations flashed before me once again. I decided I did not fear the secular Israelis as much as the *religious* ones. My knowledge of Israelis at that time left me with greater confidence that the secular ones had been more open and honest and trustworthy. I guessed that the religious extremists had portrayed me as some sort of security risk in order to get me out of the country. With these thoughts in mind, I took along a copy of the book I had written about my imprisonment to answer any questions they might have in order to dispel any lies.

It was a dark, stormy morning when I reached the Israeli "Pentagon" in Tel Aviv. The streets were flooded from heavy sheets of rain which continued to beat the city unmercifully. My emotions were ambivalent. On the one hand, I felt it was a questionable "honor" to be called to the attention of the Prime Minister's office. I had always wanted to meet Prime Minister Rabin. On the other hand, I feared that further slander from religious extremists may have sought to bring about my demise.

I was not given a diplomatic reception when I arrived. Two young Israeli men appeared rather surprised as I walked into a very modest government office. We mutually studied each other hurriedly. After each one spoke about their purpose of calling me in for an "interview," I knew I was in for the "good guy-bad guy" interrogation I had under the Communists. One struck me as being somewhat hostile and militant; while the other was kind and accommodating.

The glaring interrogator shot off a question with hostile suspicion. His counterpart was soft spoken and gentle in his question. Naturally, I took instantly to the nice one and trusted him readily. In fact, even before I had come I had shared with Naomi that even if my "invitation" consisted of an investigation, I trusted the Israeli's ability to be objective—even if they did not agree with me. I had already discovered that this trait was truly woven into the country's multifaceted democracy if one excluded the religious extremists.

Sly remarks slipped from the lips of the militant interrogator. His intonations and glares frightened me. His attitudes came across as fascist. Fortunately, I was drawn to his companion and the two of us carried on most of the conversation. Their first question was "We have heard that you were in East Germany? Can you tell us about it?"

Communist East Germany was one of Israel's worst enemies, and mine as well. While incarcerated I heard that East Germans were "more Russian than the Russians." It was true. They were fanatic in their political administration and control of their population. I readily volunteered my own story and experience to eager ears. I immediately handed them a copy of my book, and informed them that all the details they wanted were inside. I would also be happy to answer any questions they had.

After they had extracted enough information to form an impression of me, the friendly interrogator inquired, "Why is a woman like you in Israel by yourself? What are your goals?"

I readily told him that I believed in the God of Israel and the Bible promises to His land. I felt that I had been brought there by Divine Providence for some purpose—especially to serve in my field of social work. Concerning my goals, I acknowledged that most of all, I would like to get married and settle down, but only with the right person. So far, I admitted that I had not met anyone who loved both God and Israel in the way that I did.

"Oh," my warm hearted intruder interjected, "So you think you are going to find a Jew who really believes in Jesus here?"

I noted that I had only said "God", and he brought up the issue of "Jesus". I paused, took a deep breath, and replied.

"Why yes," I answered with assurance. "There are many Jews in this country who believe. You even have members of your Knesset who do."

"What are their names?" he asked as he grabbed his notepad and smiled.

"Fortunately, I don't know," I responded. "Others have told me this." I was glad I was ignorant in this case, because I did not want to jeopardize their careers in the service of their country. I knew of several cases of people who had been fired from their jobs when it was discovered that they believed in Jesus."

When the two men had finished probing my life and my motives, I was told I could leave. Then, a remarkable event took place. Israeli men were not noted for being endowed with any type of "chivalry". The raw frontier of this rugged pioneer society dictated that it was every man and woman for oneself! Nevertheless, the gentle, sensitive interrogator hopped up from his chair, leapt over to where I stood, and proceeded to help me with my coat. He accompanied me to the door, and spoke. "Thank you very much for coming out in weather like this....and ....God bless you!"

I closed the door behind me. I loved him! He represented the true heart of Israel to me! He reminded me of Uri from the Jewish Agency, who one day said to me "I might not agree with what you believe, but I sure do admire your spirit!" That was the right stuff of a real democracy!

As I pressed through the lashing storm outside, once more I wondered whether I would be denied a visa. As I closed the car door, I mused "Never a dull moment!" I was getting weary. Adventure apparently loved to latch on to me like an old sorority sister. If a visa was denied, I felt I had no more fight in me at this point....especially since I had committed the matter to the "Highest Court" for a decision. I was willing to accept any verdict and even eager to get away from it all to replenish my strength. God certainly knew what He was doing even if I did not!

While I was awaiting the outcome of my next visa, a new front of attack was opened against me. This time it was the Christians! I had met a handful of sincere and dedicated Christians in Israel; I also met some who had come there with questionable motivations. Some suffered from delusions of grandeur that they were supposed to come to Israel to "set the Jew straight". Others spilled over with a heartfelt zeal, but knew absolutely nothing of the ancient culture and heritage of the people they wanted to serve. There was also a great number who were there not with any special concern for the Jews or the Jewish state, but with their own sentimental need to walk where Jesus walked. There were numerous misfits from many cultures, who often were Christian in name only.

In my experience with evangelical Christians in Israel at that time, I had found much fear, great jealousy and competition, and little genuine community with one another. In essence, it was the absence of the radiant light they were supposed to reflect. I had also found a handful of trusted and faithful believers who could be relied on as friends. Today there are probably many more mature and solid believers than there were before. Through a crisis, I ended up having to move in with one of the wrong ones!

I was forced to relocate through circumstance. My current landlady was expecting multiple guests and needed to move me aside for a season. Overnight I found an extra room in the house of a middle aged American divorcee from the South. This lady had religious delusions based on ignorance and a distorted background in her church training. This was not immediately apparent or I would have searched elsewhere.

One afternoon I arrived home unexpectedly, only to find that she had literally thrown all my belongings into the middle of my bed. There was no visible reason for the upheaval or any explanation. I was being thrown out! It was one day before Christmas Eve. She refused to tell me why, and I had no earthly idea. Nor did I have money or another place to go.

That Christmas in Jerusalem became one of my more memorable ones. I was allowed to experience a bit of it through the eyes of two Jews, named Mary and Joseph who found no room in Bethlehem, which was nestled just outside Jerusalem. I sat down and wrote in my diary.

> There was no room available to them. It was the most significant moment in their lives, because at any moment, the babe in Mary's womb was ready to enter the world. Was there no one in the city who would be willing to make a place available to this young woman, already pressed with the pains of labor? Now, almost 2000 years later, here I am a stranger in Jerusalem, and I am homeless.

I walked outside among the star speckled hills of Jerusalem. I could even see some distant shepherds wandering on a lonely hillside. In my mind's eye, I envisioned the curtains of heaven being withdrawn. Messengers appeared to announce the entrance of God's long awaited Messiah, God's ultimate plan of redemption for the whole world. Good news and good will had been brought into the world as a gift of love and hope for all humanity. Mankind had found favor in God's eyes! God had chosen to exalt man in His great mercy! God, the Great Judge of the sins of humanity, had stooped to lift the fallen race of mankind to His level!

That night I was invited to share a temporary place on the floor of a Christian pastor's home. Two other believers were homeless at the same time. The three of us found great fellowship together in our trials. Later, my original landlady was able to accommodate me with a room once again.

Just when it appeared that I really belonged no where in this land of paradoxes, my mailbox met me with an official notification. I held my breath as I was ready to open up my ultimatum. As I ripped open the envelope, I had to blink several times before I could comprehend the words. *The Interior Ministry had awarded me a new visa!*

Hallelujah! The God of Israel reigns! The God of Israel had proven His faithfulness to me time and time again. I agonized how much longer I was to endure the incredible loneliness I felt. I was certain that somewhere there was a companion that God had prepared me for…a man of faith….who was waiting until the time was right. My heart was encouraged as I read one of the psalms that night:

"The Lord raises up the poor out of the dust, and lifts up the needy from the ash heap and dung hill, that He may set them with princes, even with the princes of His people. He makes the barren woman to be a homemaker, and a joyful mother of children." (Psalm 113:7-9)

BRIDGE OVER TROUBLED WATERS

"Your time has come to shine. All your dreams are on their way. See how they shine. If you need a friend, I'm sailing right behind. Like a bridge over troubled waters, I will ease your mind."
(Simon and Garfunkel)

Although every day life in Israel could be compared to hundreds of kernels of corn popped in a giant hot cauldron, it was interspersed with moments of bliss that surfaced like bubbles of joy and life bursting in the air. Even in the midst of my own fiery furnace, time and again my lifelong romantic fantasies found their way to fulfillment. For example, once I found myself plunked down in the rubble of a Crusader castle, camping out in the Golan Heights. The silent deserted area, garrisoned by steep mountain peaks, was disputed between Syria and Israel at the time. It stood as a majestic monument of the past towering from the highest summit. There I camped out with a friend from the kibbutz. Moonlight was my only electricity and my dear friend, Efes, stood guard over my sleeping bag. I was thrilled be tucked away in ancient ruins that held the secrets of ages!

I had another special thrill the time I slept out on the bald rocky mount overlooking the light studded Gulf of Aqaba, which was canopied with the brilliance of a star studded sky. The Jordanian settlements on the other side were visible at night and glistened like jewels across the water.

There was no doubt that the Creator of Israel must have had romance on His heart when He went about His handiwork with His Land. The more I pored over the great stories of the Book, such as Jacob and Rachel, David and Bathsheba, Sampson and Delilah, and Ruth and Boaz, the more evident it became that the God of Israel was the world's greatest Romantic. After all, it was His idea to create a woman for man. It was a welcomed contrast when modern day Israelis, strained from daily confrontations with wars, terrorism, inflation, threats of invasion and recurring traffic jams fed their hearts with a good love story. One day as I was reading The Jerusalem Post, I was greatly amused to discover the story of a female Israeli soldier who had been reprimanded by the military authorities for entering a zone which was off-limits in the Golan Heights. A national scandal rocked the press, and every bustling pedestrian huffed about the streets in indignation as they bought their newspapers. Such reckless behavior could bring international repercussions upon the nation. Everyone was angry with this young soldier until it was learned that she was only sneaking behind the lines into forbidden territory to meet with her beloved boy friend. He was one of the U.N. soldiers stationed there from Austria.

Upon learning the reason for the woman's conduct, there was a national sigh of relief, and all charges against her were dropped. Everyone began to root for a favorable outcome for these two lovers to come together. In their hearts, all of the Israelis loved a love story. Moreover, there was an inborn matchmaker living in almost every woman who had aged. I had not expected it of Naomi, my kibbutz mother, though. She was timid, retiring, and never even tiptoed into the affairs of another. It was easy to imagine the shock I felt when Naomi pulled me aside one day. "I find myself praying for you a husband," she confided cautiously.

My heart felt as if it skipped a beat when I heard the news. Naomi almost never *asked* God for anything! She graciously received all that He wanted to impart to her, but she would not dare to intrude upon Him. I concluded that it must have been a divinely inspired prayer that God had given her for me. She had no inkling that a new actor had just walked onto the stage of my life, and I had asked God about just what role he was to play. Perhaps it was finally God's time to meet that deep longing of my life.

I was unsure when our story had really begun. I had entered the cozy lounge of a beautiful old church in Jerusalem, when David appeared before me. He was an impressive handsome man with warm and penetrating brown eyes. He was sitting and having tea with Clara, a lovely middle aged deaconess from England. I quickly snuffed a tiny spark of curious attraction. I concluded a man his age was probably married, and that was strictly taboo for me. Secondly, he was a sabra—a native born Israeli. I was also living under an unwritten law against fraternization between Christian believers like myself and the "very worldly sabras". Christian believers in the Land warned about such a liaison with Israelis. It could only end in nothing good. The Jews were also wary of the religious influence of such a relationship, and they certainly did not want to lose their sons to Gentile women.

Clara introduced me to this man who appeared larger than life when I spoke with him. He seemed to be different from many other Israelis I had met along the way. Of course, it was impossible to stereotype any sabra because they came in every size, version, and variety as the people of other nations. Their ancestral roots from the Diaspora had molded them into a unique international array of Middle Easterners. Every native born Israeli brought a little of the old country of his forefathers along in his genes and customs, which made for exciting cocktails of the human species. Light skin, jet hair, olive tanned, yellow blond curls, blue or green eyes, Nordic height or Oriental stature all found their way into the modern Israeli people. Israel merely proved that there was no pattern or blueprint for being a Jew!

When David left the room for an appointment in the city, Clara wasted no time to hit me with a warning that I was to make a covenant with my eyes, like Job, never to look upon this one with any delight or favor again! "Watch out!" Clara warned in emphatic terms. "He's the kind who is always chasing women!" Clara, an attractive single woman in her forties and probably some years his elder, proceeded to imply that she herself had been the object of his conniving intentions. Although Clara had never married, she by no means reflected the air of a stodgy spinster. However, the stuffy pious propriety she sometimes projected left me wondering just how much of her inference was truly reality. She clearly depicted him as an Israeli "playboy."

I greatly took her admonition to heart. I had expended much energy in guarding my affections from all possible candidates since I had arrived in Israel. There had been those who tried hard to capture them, but I carefully screened any male attention directed at me to determine whether it was safe or even significant. Until I really felt a "go" sign, I knew I had to hold the brakes tightly, or be swept up into the boiling cauldron of all sorts of passion which appeared volatile in the Middle East.

Clara's warning was adequate to restrain any potential fantasies from exercising their crazy acrobatics in my mind. Moreover, any normal feminine warmth I might have offered this stranger as a friend was quickly suppressed by the "danger" signal Clara had given me. After experiencing such a deep heart attachment to Yossi on the kibbutz, I was determined to guard my heart. I had to admit to myself that I saw something special in this man. A natural charm oozed from his demeanor without making one dent in my suspicious armor. I could handle him.

Everything about Clara was proper, and she had been a church worker in the country for several years. I figured that I could trust her judgment. Still I thought I detected a ray of maternalistic condescension from her and other Christians I had met in the congregation that Clara served.

I gave no more thought to the charming sabra I had met in the church lounge. On another visit to the congregation lounge, where anyone was welcome to come for refreshment, I often dropped by to visit with Clara. She and I were chatting about the church's desire to establish a Messianic *yeshiva* in the area. There was a local building up for lease or sale which appeared ideal for the project. David felt no discomfort in walking in and joining in our conversation. When he heard the topic of our conversation, he asked to see the paper I had written about such a proposal.

When he finished reading, he handed me the paper with a wide grin. "*I'm a believer, too,*" he announced. He then proceeded to inform me just what he had discovered about me by reading my paper.

"I see that you are very sensitive and diplomatic," he stated with assurance. Suddenly, I felt very transparent in front of this bold, towering man. I had difficulty believing his comments about being a believer because of Clara's previous warning. He watched while I recoiled in fear. My reaction incited a greater initiative on his part to continue his candid analysis. I felt more vulnerable when Clara disappeared into another room to answer the telephone.

With a twinkle in his eye, he informed me he had to leave for an appointment, but made sure to let me know that he frequented the place often. Clara returned and fed me more details about his life. He was a gifted musician who led musical concerts and events regularly in the church. He liked the atmosphere of the old church as a backdrop for programs of musical artists from around the country and sometimes abroad. I began to understand his highly developed sensitivity because of his artistic temperament. He played several instruments himself.

After he had gone, I confided in Clara that David said he was a believer. She immediately uttered a loud "hummmmpf! Some believer!" she contested. It was obvious she disagreed with his statement. Clara adamantly opposed this evaluation. Either she had access to facts which I did not possess or she had already judged the man's heart. I always tried to avoid such judgments, having worked in the prisons of New York City with the so-called "dregs" of humanity. There I had met many "diamonds in the rough," whose true moral and spiritual value had been untapped. When someone cared about them and sincerely expressed it, they tended to blossom into beautiful human beings. Intuitively, I sensed that whatever David's background, there was a vibrant spiritual spark in his heart. Perhaps he was an honest seeker who had not fully found his way yet. All of these thoughts raced through my mind, but I recoiled from discussing them with Clara because she had made up her mind concerning David.

The next time David and I met we almost collided in the street outside the majestic old church building, where he sometimes held musical programs. We chitchatted while he ambled toward the entrance to set up for the evening's concert, which he was conducting. "You're not married, are you?" David inquired spontaneously. When I responded in the negative, he informed me that he had a very nice looking friend who was also still single, also a believer. "Would you like to meet him?"

My heart pounded. David appeared to be nobler than Clara had described him. "Why, yes," I answered cautiously, "It might be nice to meet him." A sense of ambivalence rose up inside. Years of living as a single were filled with some disappointments and wrong choices, and I was inclined to be skeptical about such a meeting. David then presented a proposal I had to ponder. He informed me he would bring his friend to the next concert in the area and I could meet him there.

I tried to appear as casual as possible, even though I was the first person at the church door for the next performance. When David finally arrived, I was disappointed. He was alone. He had forgotten.

The room had filled with Israelis as I found my way to a seat. I sighed as I listened to David perform on the violin. I loved classical music; it had the power to nourish my soul. I studied the man himself as I heard the tenderness of the strings being stroked. I saw a wild flicker of pain flash across his eyes like a wounded animal. David was obviously hurting about something. I assured myself I would not get involved. I slipped out of the crowd unnoticed at the end of the concert, but there was an aching feeling I carried along inside.

Long stormy months passed in both our lives. Like ships passing in the night our paths crisscrossed again and again. We addressed each other always in fleeting moments of different agendas. Our orbits collided only by circumstance, but we always exchanged superficial greetings. Like a scared snail I always recoiled into the shelter of my shell. I was determined never to fall prey to any man who was identified as a "womanizer" who would use and abuse a woman's affection. The brief times we met he never mentioned his friend again.

I looked forward to the regular concerts which took place in the magnificent old church. I loved the acoustical atmosphere there. The music magnified itself within the majestic walls and attending such an event was a welcomed diversion from the academic routine that consumed most of my time. Each performance was different in providing an exciting exercise of seeing modern day Israelis in ancient churches performing concerts of the masters and sometimes reciting contemporary poetry. Each time David was there I saw the cry of a wounded animal in his eyes. It was begging me for help every time his eyes met mine. During the week my thoughts turned to him often and I found myself frequently praying for him.

One evening when I was looking forward to finding refuge in the majestic music of Bach, I bumped into David at the doorway. In an abrupt Israeli manner, very unlike David typically, he murmured "I am divorced now, would you like to be my *friend*?" His question struck me like a bolt of lightening. I knew that the term "friend" in Hebrew in the way he used it, meant a steady relationship with one person. My defenses had already shut him out. His expressed interest in me did not penetrate. I simply did not take him seriously.

The next musical performance I attended was in a different church. The rich music of the visiting world renowned German organist transported me above all the pettiness and hassle of daily life in the pressure cooker. I felt as if I had just survived a long spiritual winter, and the music served to release a burst of new life within me like a fountain of spring forsythia. When I really reflected, I chuckled with amusement over the previous evening I had spent with the son of a well intentioned match-minded mother. The evening alone, with candlelight, warm free conversation and a tasty dinner with an Americanized Israeli had reminded me that I was a woman again. All of the fascinating feelings of the uniqueness of my gender were newly ignited. I cherished my femininity. The "date" was the first of its kind in months and months of standing in rigid guard over my affections. It left me more deeply aware of my need for a man's companionship.

After the program was over, everyone rushed to the cozy church lounge for coffee and lively conversation. When I entered the room, only one seat was available. It was between the German cultural attaché and David. Instantly both men motioned for me to come as if they had been reserving the spot. The German diplomat wasted no time in drawing out my history in his Land with obvious discomfort. I interspersed my German dialogue with interludes of Hebrew with David. By this time I had become more proficient.

Suddenly, as I turned toward David to elicit his opinion on the highlight of the performance, he looked straight into my eyes as if he had not heard a word I said and announced "*I love you*" in Hebrew!

His declaration precipitated one of those "E.F. Hutton moments." Everyone in the room became silent and all peered in our direction. For a moment I was breathless with shock and embarrassment. Then I realized that many occupants of the room did not know Hebrew, since German was the prevailing language that night. As I scanned their faces I felt that they understood in some uncanny way as they overheard David's overture to me.

Seizing control, I quickly retorted in a lighthearted way, "Oh David, you love *all* the women!" I mimicked Clara's commentary on his character.

"No" David insisted adamantly. "You don't *know* me."

"But I know your type!" I contradicted him, tilting my head back in laughter. I determined that the whole matter was a big joke and I was reading his "line"! I could not possibly accredit him with any seriousness there in that room of foreigners stepping out into the spotlight and declaring his love for me. Latins might do that in the Twentieth Century, but not Israeli sabras!

A dark cloud fell over David's face. "You don't *know* me!" he interjected with a pleading tone. His answer was more emphatic than before, shattering my glib guard against the charming gentle giant of a man. His response disarmed me so severely that I examined myself carefully. What did I really know about this man? I knew only what I had heard.

I had accepted Clara's integrity as being impeccable. However, I argued with myself that she, like most people, just might be guilty of judging another person she did not really know. Moreover, I saw Clara as a kind of prototype of many of the more traditional religious Christians living in Israel, and from the outside, David was the "typical" sabra. Sabras were often viewed as charming con-artists, connivers who had inherited their cunning skill from their ancestor Jacob.

On the other hand, although many Christians were living in Israel to serve the people, there sometimes appeared to be a spiritual "iron curtain" between them and the Israelis, who were "so near and yet so far." Neither group trusted the other. The cultural chasm was almost insurmountable for most foreigners. Something inside of me yearned to build a bridge in my relationship to the Land and people.

I peered deeply into David's eyes. I decided to give this man the benefit of the doubt. I looked at him again. His full black curly hair encompassed a handsome face, but unmistaken suffering shone through his warm brown eyes. For some seconds a stream of compassion surged in my spirit. I spoke hesitatingly. "I have wanted to talk to you...but from my heart."

"You just name the time and place," he said. A spark of hope flickered in his eyes.

"I'll tell you what," I answered. "I'm not sure whether I can make the next concert or not, but let's get together afterwards, if that is all right with you."

"That's fine with me." A new light danced in his eyes. He began to confide in me the poetry he had published, as well as the musical compositions he had written. I noticed how hungry he was for my acceptance and approval. In turn, I exchanged information with him about my own writing and the book I had published. This ignited his attentiveness even more and he expressed interest in reading it.

Our brief encounter seemed to have suspended all the activity in the room around us. It was as if everyone could feel the intensity of this encounter of two magnetic opposite poles colliding. As I walked out of the church complex, I stopped by my car and pulled out a copy of my book for him. He beamed in gratitude. As I drove away I began to wrestle with my decision. Instinctively I sensed much danger. I thrust the matter into the hands of the Almighty. I would simply make another meeting the matter of serious prayer.

As the week unwound and the Sabbath was approaching I had planned to attend a Sabbath evening concert. Little bubbles of anticipation burst into my thoughts. I determined that if a meeting with him was not appropriate I would not go. I submitted this matter to serious prayer. In view of any potential romantic explosion that might erupt from both of our needy lives, I determined not to go unless God overruled. I had secretly hoped He would.

Of all the weekends that Naomi had chosen to take a rest from life on the kibbutz, it happened to be the one that I would be meeting with David. She was planning on staying at the church hostel where there were rooms for visitors to stay. Naomi knew a number of people in the area and had a standing invitation of hospitality. She had also become friends with Clara and was planning on staying with her.

I had to meet Naomi at the church hostel in the afternoon in the same location where the concerts were held. As I climbed out of the car in the parking lot, the first person who stepped into my path was David. He had arrived ahead of his regular time in order to practice with the musicians.

"Shalom!" his eyes sparkled enthusiastically. "Are we going to see each other tonight?"

"Yes,"

"When would you like?" He asked.

"I guess right after the concert is the best time. We can sit in the lounge and have a cup of coffee there." I suggested.

"All right," he agreed and disappeared into the building. The wild wounded look was no longer in his eyes. David played one of his better performances in Brahms. After the concert I could tell that we were both enduring all of the customary niceties with the crowd and coffee klatch. Both of us seemed distracted. Our thoughts were already engaged in the upcoming encounter.

In spite of all the dangers, warnings, and taboos that any kind of emotional intimacy between the two of us might generate, I felt very secure that it was God who was directing our steps, since I had truly committed my path to Him.

As the last musical fan faded through the doorway, David pulled me aside to a corner. "Listen, I would feel better if we did not meet here in this building...you know, I don't really feel comfortable talking in this atmosphere."

"Why?" I asked.

"Because in Israel everybody listens in on others' business! When I sneeze in the north, they know it immediately in the south."

"All right, then, we'll go to some café," I suggested. I felt butterflies soar in my stomach. I wondered whether he was "up to something."

David courteously dismissed all the guests, handled business matters with the pastor and discussed future details of the next concert with Clara. I anxiously mulled over a hurdle that needed to be addressed. I was scheduled to stay overnight with Naomi at Clara's place. It would not appear appropriate to the others for me to slip away at that late hour with David. I certainly did not want Clara to see me with him. Wrestling with all the real and imagined opinions of those around me, I came upon an ingenious strategy.

I had confided in Naomi that David and I were desirous of some time together. Naomi had already exulted in adopting her role with me as my "Yiddish mama", and nothing delighted her more than standing watchdog over the door when I returned from my rendezvous with David. I felt this was very important because Clara ruled over the affairs of the hostel and had her own rooms adjacent to the entrance. Although there was nothing illicit in our secret appointment, Clara's outspoken judgment of David stood as a wall before us. I formulated the plot.

My precious friend, Efes, always accompanied me on any overnight visit. Instead of walking away with David, I decided to take my furry pal for a late night stroll before going to bed. That suited her just fine. Efes and I would meet David just around the corner, and together we would all go out. In turn, Naomi would unlock the door upon my return and Clara would never have to fill her mind with negative thoughts. Besides, if there was any truth to her allegations, Efes would be sure to protect me. She had intervened on another occasion when Boris's impassioned advances did not meet with her pleasure. She had whined and whimpered and placed herself between us, informing Boris that he was not to touch me.

Efes usually jumped in ecstasy when I grabbed her leash, and this night was no exception. She strutted proudly, pulling me along behind her as we walked the lonely alley beside the church. David was waiting in his little Renault with its engine purring patiently when we rounded the bend.

The January night in Jerusalem was especially crisp, but a blanket of warm breeze permeated the car as Efes and I climbed inside. She situated herself splendidly like a queen in the center of my lap. She appeared ready to enjoy whatever adventure awaited her.

Finding a place open at that hour of the night was no obstacle, but finding a quiet place to talk was. We finally drove up to a simple short order house on the outskirts of town. What it lacked in atmosphere, it made up for in privacy, since we were stationed in a back dim corner. The owner greeted David with a knowing nod.

David wasted no time in reaching across the table for my hand. I stiffened. Perhaps Clara had been right. Or? Perhaps he needed reassurance. He had taken my hand in a friendly non-seductive grip. Still, my caution bristled.

I knew that David must find out just where I stood before we proceeded any further. I did not know how to be any other way than candid. Quickly, I took the reigns of the conversation. "You know I have really been wanting to talk to you....because I can see that you are going through a lot of pain in your life...." The counselor in me had risen up.

"Yes," David interrupted. "I have just gone through the nightmare of a divorce," he quickly retorted. He related that he had suffered through a horrible marriage for many years, but it still came as a shock when he found divorce papers in his mail box. He had not only the agony of his own personal failure to face but also the stigma of a divorce in the small land of Israel. He felt everyone knew his business since his work was fairly high profile. There was also the trauma of his two beautiful children to worry about. David was still grieving the loss.

I attempted to untie any knots while he unraveled his story. Inside I was questioning whether he was a con artist, spinning the favorite yarn for the unsuspecting foreigner, or was he a hurting, vulnerable man longing for emotional support in his current pain. His body language evoked the honesty of his feelings as I studied him carefully. The same wounded look flashed across his face from time to time, but the presence of my hand seemed to subdue it. When he stopped, I began.

"David, I am sure that all of this is happening for a purpose." I sought to encourage him. "I know that God has a beautiful plan for your life. Even this heartache has a role to play in bringing you closer to Him....you see, my being imprisoned by the Communists turned out to be one of the biggest blessings of my life in the end.... I am sure you know the story of Joseph in the Bible, and how his own brothers betrayed him and sold him as a slave to the Egyptians. The prison was only a preparation for something far greater that Joseph had to do in life. In fact, he left prison with the attitude that his brothers "meant it for evil, but God meant it for good."

David drank the words that I poured out. I had not even noticed that I was unraveling my own life story in Hebrew, until I hit upon a point where a word was missing. I had never felt such a flow of Hebrew before.

"You see," I continued, "I had been searching all my life—through education, travel, romance, anything to fill a void I felt inside. In fact, I was always looking for 'the right man' to make me complete...." I noticed that David took special note of these words..."I looked in the wrong places and found the wrong relationships....until I discovered that what I was looking for was not to be found in any human, but only in God! It also became clear to me that I could not be happy with just any man—any human man—who did not want God to be the first priority in his life. I know that relationships are twisted when people try to make idols of each other or play god in one another's life!"

David sat frozen to his chair, eager to digest every word that flowed, however awkwardly, from my lips in his native language. "The real turning point came when I got out of prison," I explained. "God had allowed me to experience genuine love for my enemies and to forgive them before I returned and faced a spiritual wasteland in America. It was too much to bear.

My family let me down...although they could not help. They were not believers themselves. They had suffered perhaps more from my imprisonment than I had. Then I tried turning to a church for comfort. Quickly I learned that the pastor was his own god and did not really believe in the Bible. I refused to subject myself to the emptiness of someone's man made religion.

I was trembling inside. David was glued to every utterance that left my lips. "Then something kept telling me to 'give up'....that it was not worth fighting....to stop trying. And so I did. Into the vacuum of my despair walked a man. The wrong man! He was evil but I did not know it." I heaved a sigh of sudden memory. "I was so hungry for genuine love and comfort that I 'stopped fighting'! He did not tell me he was married! I was deceived and defeated at the same time!" David tightened his hand upon mine.

David continually nodded in affirmation while I poured out my story. He never looked away while I shared.

"I didn't realize that all this had been brought to me from the Evil One. I had not previously believed in a personal devil. However, I quickly discovered that he is alive and well on planet earth! He was the one who sent that man into my life and began to drag me down."

I dropped my eyes. David was hanging on my every word, warm and empathetic as I spoke. "I was pulled into a very destructive relationship with a genuine womanizer! The good news is that my spiritual detour was short lived. The bad news was that the relationship was destructive both emotionally and spiritually!"

"You know, David, it was then that I found myself in a worse prison than I had been behind bars! When you are locked up, you know that one day they must let you out. However, when you are captive to an inner prison, there is no way to get out alone...." I paused and looked him squarely in the eye. "Only God can unlock the door of the inner prison!"

David nodded in agreement. I waited for him to speak, but he encouraged me to continue.

"I was so desperate I could not sleep for three months. I took alcohol and tranquilizers together trying to sleep, but I had maybe one or two hours a night! Finally, I felt I was truly at the end of my rope. I had to give God one last attempt. If He failed to come through, I decided I was going to take my own life. I cried out, '*God, if you are real, you've got to help me!"*

"Oh David, it was so remarkable. A couple of nights later I was lying in bed in another sleepless stupor when suddenly a voice spoke to me.... it was not audible....but a voice from deep within my spirit....not my mind, either. I could tell the difference. The voice asked, '*Why do you reject me?* Why do you reject me? Why do you reject me?' Three times. It was the most tender pleading voice I had ever known." I hesitated carefully to choose my words. "David, instantly, I knew that it was the voice of *Yeshua!* He was asking, 'Why don't you give me your burdens....your guilt, loneliness, heartache and despair? Why are you carrying them yourself? You are carrying the whole world on your shoulders! Why don't you give it all to me?'"

I watched David's expression very closely. He did not flinch with the slightest disapproval. He nodded knowingly, beaming with the most loving expression I had ever seen.

"You know something, David. I did not know how to give my burdens to Yeshua. Moreover, I did not even know that he was speaking to people in the Twentieth Century! I knew that he was a Jew who had lived in this country two thousand years ago, who had come to save the world from their sins, and I believed that he would return to earth as the awaited Messiah. But I did not know that he was actually relating to people on earth now. Yet, I knew he was asking to lift the tremendous emotional and spiritual load from my life."

David continued to nod. His face was filled with a tender compassion and he nodded affirmatively, as if he deeply understood everything I was saying.

"I could sleep peacefully for the first time in months. A few days later miracles began to happen in my life!" I told him. I sighed in deep relief. Hebrew words that had not heretofore existed in my daily vocabulary were coming to me, even though my expression was very simple and direct. I wondered if David could really understand all I was saying. He seemed to. Before I continued, he spoke.

"Not too long ago, I split my head open in a parachute jump into the enemy territory on the Golan Heights during the war. I came very close to death." He motioned with two fingers spread apart on his forehead. "I *know* how real God is! He showed me at that time."

David pushed back his wavy hair and displayed a long scar on his forehead. I knew he understood at that moment.

I continued. "The turning point in my life came after God sent a total stranger to travel over 1000 miles to come and get me and take me to a group of people where I could learn about His ways. It was there I met a man who had also had a real revelation of Yeshua and the power of God's Spirit..."

David again nodded empathetically, holding my hand tightly.

"Well, when I learned that it is really possible to live the way the people of the Bible did...you know...with a real relationship with God....the miracles of Elijah, Moses...Yeshua healing the sick... raising the dead...then I knew that this was what I had been looking for all my life! This kind of relationship with God! I asked how I could receive such a relationship. He then asked me whether I had really received *the forgiveness of my sins through the atonement of Yeshua on the cross*. I had to admit that I had not completely turned my life over to God in repentance until such time. However, that day I did receive genuine forgiveness and acceptance of Yeshua's atonement—his willing sacrificial death on the cross to forgive my sins. Later, God's Spirit came upon my life with such a presence I can only describe as "liquid love" and power to live my life on the basis of His word and Spirit! Then, I received the wonderful revelation of Israel, God's incredible love for that nation, and His desire for me to come here and be a servant to His people."

David gazed at me with loving eyes. He responded with a flow of words in Hebrew, many of which were unfamiliar. "When I was a boy of fifteen, I began to talk to God," he explained. "I know how real He is..."

The more David spoke from his heart, the more magnificent he became in my eyes. His voice rang with sincerity, but I sensed that some dark shadow had also overtaken him as well, perhaps in the circle of some of his friends. The light of God's presence was truly in his heart, but it had been buried under some rubble and darkness. He intimated that there had been compromise in his life as he shared some of the pain and disappointment in his misguided marriage which was in the process of being dissolved in the divorce courts. Suddenly, I glanced at my watch. "Why it is after midnight!" I exclaimed.

"And poor little Efes is out in that cold car alone," he added. "I love dogs as much as you do!" Efes had already tuned in on this trait in David. They had mutual admiration for each other. David was also the first man that had come into my life that Efes had received with complete acceptance!

"I must get back!" I urged. I thought of Clara and all the scandal I could arouse getting caught slipping into her apartment after midnight after being out with such a "rascal" as David.

"Wait!" David tightened his grip on my hand as I attempted to rise. "When are we going to see each other again?"

I paused for an extended time. "Why I don't intend to see you anymore…that is, unless I know that God really wants me to! Let's just leave it at that. You know how to reach me, but please *don't* unless you are sure that God wants it."

"I know He wants it!" David said with confidence.

I thought about the longing in David's expression as he let me out of the car. I ran to the house and tapped on the window. Naomi tiptoed to the door to let me in. I quickly hugged her in gratitude. I was back again where I felt safe and secure. Clara did not awaken, and no one had missed me.

I gave Naomi a brief account of our evening and fell into bed exhausted. My heart was still racing as I lay reviewing the details of the night. I felt very drawn to David, but I was also very scared. I did not want to get pulled into any more turmoil than I had experienced. I knew very little about the circumstances of his divorce. "Oh God," I groaned. "Please don't let him contact me unless you want us together!" I prayed as I drifted off to sleep.

My conflict concerning my feelings was great. I felt as if I had just crossed the threshold into another world. I sensed it was permeated with murky darkness I could not understand. Yet, underneath the cloud that covered David's life, I thought I saw a wounded man, hungry for love and searching for truth. Something drew me toward him and compelled me to share the light and love I had discovered in my own life. At the same time, I was powerfully repelled by fear. There were many questions that were unanswered. Truly, I wanted to make the right choice in this relationship, and I knew I needed God's guidance to do so. I dared not do anything except what God was initiating. In the same way God had used my friendship with Naomi, I felt drawn to David.

A MAN AND A WOMAN

"There are three things which are too wonderful for me, four which I do not understand: The way of an eagle in the sky, the way of a serpent on a rock the way of a ship in the middle of the sea, and the way of a man with a maid." (Proverbs 30:18, 19)

Undeniably, I had been born with a characteristic that was often attributed to Jews—an insatiable appetite for learning. I dove into my studies at the Hebrew University with the anticipation of meeting another new discovery just over each intellectual mountain. I especially loved my studies in Zionism, and greatly identified with those earthly pioneers of the land, *Eretz Israel*. I felt that Messianic believers were the spiritual pioneers of Israel's future frontier, the New Jerusalem that the prophets wrote so passionately about and longed for. They would inaugurate a time when the lion and lamb would lie down together and there would be true *shalom* in both heaven and earth. From my faith I believed that this peace was only attainable when people truly had a change of heart, genuine *tschuva* (repentance) before God and man. I believed that Messiah was ready to transplant those hard hearts which turned to him. That was the promise I held in my heart for the future of the Promised Land. With each piece of new knowledge, the puzzle of her tomorrow took shape before my eyes.

At the Hebrew University my classes in Israeli Studies on the political structure of Israel were very enlightening and intriguing. I began to understand that my painful rejection by the Chief Rabbi was even more political than religious. In some classes, I was greatly disappointed to see the professors sweep the national rubbish of injustice under the carpets of self justification. One professor who was prone to whitewash the clash between religion and state appalled me when he recommended that "*one is justified in lying to the religious authorities to enable marriage between a Jew and a non Jew.*"

After I posed the question, the instructor confided that he personally knew of many cases where religious law was outmaneuvered. *Simply send down two witnesses to the Rabbinate to swear that both parties are legitimate Jews and that would alleviate the problem!*

I could not bring myself to succumb to such tactics. However, many Jews I met said that I was "more Jewish than they were." I assumed that they referred to my love for their God, their Land, and their people. Whether they called me a Christian Zionist or a spiritual Jew (not rabbinical), it did not really matter. I just wanted to be at their side as they rebuilt their nation and join with them in the restoration of their Land.

One day Efes and I were returning from an afternoon promenade in the Arab quarter when the upstairs neighbor caught me unlocking the door. "While you were out, you received a call. It was some gentleman. Here is the number." Mrs. Mizrachi handed me a paper.

"I am sorry for the intrusion, but I am hoping to get a telephone soon," I answered. "Thanks a lot." I rushed inside; my chest was pounding. I removed the leash from Efes and dashed up the stairs to borrow the neighbor's phone. It rang and rang without responding. As I climbed down the stairs my heart climbed down with me in disappointment. I returned to my room in the "International Boarding House of Jerusalem", which we called our little apartment. Another resident had been recently added when Maureen from Scotland moved in with the landlady, Molly, Efes and me.

I decided to annoy the Mizrachis once more for their telephone. I determined that if I had no success in getting through, I would turn to the impossible Israeli pay phone system. Special tokens were required to use public phones, and I had already discovered that I could drive from Jerusalem to Tel Aviv more quickly than I could place a call.

I dialed the number. One ring, two rings, three rings, four rings.... Suddenly, "Hello".

"David?"

"Yael!" A long pause followed. "How are you Yael?"

"Oh, I'm fine, David....but what about you?"

"I want to see you, Yael."

"When?"

"I'm traveling around the country this week with various engagements, but I'll be back by the weekend. Can I come by on Thursday?"

"That's the 3rd, isn't it? That's my anniversary...my liberation day from prison! That's a perfect time to come.....Something special always happens on that day!"

"I'll be there, Yael."

"Shalom, David. Until then."

I raced straight to my room, closed the door and fell across the bed. Waves of pure joy pulsed through my body. I had consistently prayed to remove this man from my life unless God had a purpose in our being together. It was a moment of promise when I heard his voice on the other end.

From the moment I had said "goodbye" to David, the time seemed to stand still. It appeared that February 3, was longer arriving than normal, just like the day of my release from prison. I had waited from early morning until midnight before I was released. I marveled that God seemed to be telling me "it's all right to love this man who needs your love so much! It's all right to walk into his dark world and extend your hand to him!"

Unlike the rest of my family, classical music had always been an inseparable part of my life. Through college and the subsequent years, my stereo had been my constant companion, and it played continually in the background of my life. In Israel I had no stereo, but now David was bringing a new concerto into my life!

Freedom day dawned with a brilliant Jerusalem sky. The clouds stood starch stiff against the crisp morning air. I decided to cut class on Scopus, just in case I might be late for his arrival. He was not arriving until late afternoon or evening, but the apartment needed much tidying with three women scurrying about the premises, all mostly on the run. My hair, my nails, the kitchen sink, the towels in the bathroom, and the dust on the end tables in the living room provided the long list of chores that needed immediate attention.

Twilight finally faded into the hills of Jerusalem, silhouetting a mysterious mixture of minarets, domes, and square roofed block-houses. Still no sign of David had appeared on the scene. By 10:00 p.m., I decided to turn out the light and call it a night. It was painful to consider that David was not a man of his word. I wanted to believe in him, no matter what all the Claras in the world had said against him. Naomi had also questioned my judgment when I told her about David's visit. "Wait and see," was Naomi's protective response.

I hashed and rehashed every word and every contact of our encounter as I lay across the bed. Suddenly, I felt a strong awareness that David was reaching out to me from somewhere and hindered from coming.. I dozed off in a wonderful peace and did not awaken until the first golden streaks of daylight streamed through the drapes. Why I had dreamed that David and I were on the way to see each other. Somewhere in between we had bumped into each other!

After the dashed hopes and then the unusual experience of the preceding night I did not feel I could concentrate on academics. While I was still dissecting these events, a loud knock sounded at the door. Mrs. Mizrachi yelled to tell me that a call was waiting for me upstairs. I grabbed my robe and bounded up the stairs and took the phone.

"Hello."

"Yael!"

"David!"

"Yael....I am so sorry....I wanted so much to come and see you, but I had a high fever and I was unable to move! I want you to know that *I thought about you the whole time.*

"I know," I answered. "Because I was thinking about you, as well! It was almost as if you were there with me!"

"In a way, I was. I was thinking about you!"

"I will see you as soon as I can arrange it...when I get back on my feet again."

"David, please take care of yourself. When we can, we'll get together."

"Thank you, Yael.....I love you!"

"Shalom, David." I love you, too!"

I put the telephone down and slowly walked down the stairs. I felt dazed. I could not explain what had happened but it was very real. Never in my life had anything like that happened, but it was very real and pure. There was a magnetic power that drew us together in pure unselfish love. The recognition that David had not let me down lifted me up to another plane. The knowledge that he was loving and unselfish melted away some of my fears about him. Unbeknown to him, while I had felt him reaching out to me for love and comfort, I was also reaching up to God on his behalf, asking Him to bless him.

David's recovery and subsequent call appeared to take forever before they reached me. In the interim of waiting, an old inner tape warned me that he would let me down. He was not to be trusted. David again proved himself loyal. He called. This time we were going to meet in Jerusalem at the huge YMCA, across from the elegant King David Hotel. David was en route to a concert and had arranged to take off the afternoon to spend with me.

I began to feel a longing to proceed across the bridge to David's world with utmost caution, but both of us had volcanic emotions and I knew it would not be easy. My defenses dissolved before the eyes and ears of the world as he strolled into the YMCA in Jerusalem to meet me. He spotted me instantly in a lounge chair and bounded right to me, lifting me up into his arms and giving me a generous kiss right there in the lobby.

The glorious interlude of our afternoon was interrupted when David had to depart for the Galilee, where he was presenting a series of performances. His bold avowal of love right there on the stage of the golden City both frightened and exhilarated me. He did not yet know my history in his Land; nor did I know his. We both felt secure that the Heavenly Father was saying "yes" to our love. We began to see one another whenever the opportunity would avail itself, but it was not without warfare. So far, I saw none of the rogue reputation that Clara had labeled him with. I saw a tender warrior who was deeply affectionate and who was finding his way out of the miry clay of his past. Later, when he knew he had gained my trust and I had gained his love, he confided the horror of being bound to a woman who was mentally ill and bent on his destruction. There had been nothing satisfying in such a relationship. He greatly desired a loving intimate relationship with a woman in marriage.

I trusted him thus far, but we needed time to really discover each other.

There was urgency about Israel that gave a special passion to all of life. Daily there was the pressure to live life to the fullest, because one never knew about tomorrow. The history of the reborn nation was one of ceaseless wars screaming for her destruction. Israelis stood undaunted in the face of death daily and lived every moment with the intensity of life—L'chaim!

I already felt a passionate attachment to the nation. I could not partake enough of her culture. I was always longing to know her more deeply and intimately. My university courses were mere appetizers of a wealth of experience, history and life. This power of her heritage was magnified and intensified in her native son, David, the musician and poet. The heartbeat of his history was inseparable from the man. Indeed, he did remind me of his namesake, David, the beloved King of Israel.

I wondered how David would feel if he knew that I was not Jewish—at least in the sense of being "kosher" according to the rabbinate. I had not even thought about that, but I sensed no racism or prejudice in his heart. Nevertheless, I knew at some point we would have to talk about it. There was always too little time for us to say all the things we wanted to when we came together. I also felt I needed to learn more from him about his divorce. I knew that there were "two sides" to every divorce, but I wanted to make sure I was not stepping into the middle of unfinished business in their lives.

At this very point I discovered Maureen at my doorstep. Actually she became a resident along with me at Molly's house. Her life story began to erase many of my preconceptions and legalisms about marriage and divorce. This little effervescent Christian lady in her fifties had served as a missionary in other countries for many years. Yet, after twelve years of ministry and marriage as a team with her spouse, her husband served her divorce papers. He had walked off to live with another woman.

This presented a deep enigma to me. My firm and unquestionable belief was that two married persons, who had a genuine relationship with God did not need to get a divorce. God was able to grant power to overcome their obstacles. Dear little Maureen had prayed, pleaded, and petitioned God to restore her home, but when two years passed with a greater gulf of alienation between her and her spouse, she sought direction from God. She felt He had given her a word, *"I will comfort you in Jerusalem."* She had decided to grant the divorce her husband was seeking and move to Jerusalem.

All of this threw me into a tail spin of questioning and uncertainty about the issue of marriage and divorce. Every time I sought spiritual answers about how this applied to my current situation, the answer I always got was *"I WILL HAVE MERCY ON WHOM I WILL HAVE MERCY!"*

"Oh God, teach me more about your mercy." I cried. "I don't really know what mercy means." I did know, though, that God had commanded the Gentile Christians to show mercy to Israel!

Maureen explained to me that her husband, a minister with a powerful and influential ministry, had never learned *to love.* He could experience the "signs and wonders the Bible spoke about, but he could not love. God had continually tried to win his heart to the breaking point, but he became increasingly recalcitrant. This man did not really know God—the true God who is love, but he knew religion.

For the first time, I began to understand the words of Jesus:

"Not everyone who says to me "Lord, Lord," will enter the kingdom of heaven, but *only he who does the will of my Father,* who is in heaven."

I concluded that Maureen's husband had chosen not to belong to the Lord. It appeared that God in His mercy was freeing her from the bondage to him.

Of course in David's case I knew none of the details of his marriage and divorce, but I owed it to myself to find out before he had irretrievably captured my heart. Every marriage and divorce in

Israel had to go through the rabbinical courts and the outcome could be very subjective according to whoever was handling the case.

As I sprayed a cloud of my best French perfume behind my ears, chose my favorite skirt and put the finishing touches on my face, my emotions were tingling with anticipation. David had invited me to a concert where he was performing in one of the outlying towns of the area. We agreed that the best arrangement for time would be for me to drive to his place and we would go together in his car.

David's eyes danced with delight when we met in his doorway. With one huge swoop he swept me from the hallway into his arms with a spontaneous kiss, leaving the door ajar. I quickly looked over my shoulder to determine whether anyone saw us. "Please, no," I begged. "I have no intention for us to start off like this."

"I hadn't planned it either, but I couldn't resist!" David reassured me.

Clara's words rose up like a specter over me. My suspicions mounted again. Molten steel began to flow up my spine. Distrust overshadowed our drive the rest of the way. I was tense and also haunted by the prospect of appearing in public with this well known Israeli man. What if those secret conspirators who had set me up before were still keeping tabs on me? I was certain that they would never approve of any romance with one of their native sons. Pure and innocent as I felt it was, I feared Israel would not be ready for such a liaison. David was too well known.

We inaugurated the Sabbath in the home a warm Sephardic family who were close friends of David. I sat stiffly at their long table like an alien immigrant, hiding behind a friendly mask. Afterwards, we drove together to the hall that hosted the event. The community center was packed. I was deeply touched by the tearful dirge from Mozart's "Requiem". Afterwards, David wanted my review of the performance. I desired to please him, but the adrenalin in my body was still working overtime with my fears. I assured him of all the appropriate niceties, and declared that I was so sick that I would immediately have to return home. David appeared dejected when I told him, because we both had been invited to a celebration of the performers in a private home. "Would it be possible to stay for a little while and then return?" he wondered out loud.

"Oh no! I simply do not feel able." I responded. I would have had to exert my last ounce of strength to comply, but I could not muster it. Numb with emotions my body could not handle, I suggested an alternate plan to his having to drive so far to take me home. "Why don't you just drop me off at the car, or let me get a taxi. I want you to go ahead to the party."

With all the chivalry that was uncommon to Israelis, David insisted that he take me home. David was always gracious with me. Still I demanded that he stay because I knew how important it was to him. David protested and led me to his Renault, mumbling an announcement to his friend which I could not understand.

There was a strange look in his eyes as he turned the key. The engine refused to budge. It clicked several times without the engine turning over. I moaned my disapproval at his driving me back. "Please, you stay with your friends and let me get a taxi."

"Are you sure that's all right? He asked. He was very reluctant to submit to this plan.

When I insisted, he hailed a cab, briefly discoursed with the driver, handed him some money, pecked me on the cheek and helped me climb in. I began to breathe again. I was suspicious that the engine trouble with his car was contrived. While the cab sped the twenty-five kilometers back to the security of the City, I determined that I could not handle this relationship with this man that I was afraid to trust. I thought I probably should have heeded Clara's warning from the beginning.

"No," I assured David when he called me on the eve of his next musical program. "I believe that it is better not to see you anymore." He had no time to engage in debate but informed me that he would contest my decision later.

Despite my resolve, I was inexplicably compelled back to the magnificent old church where David was involved with his next concert. I hid away in a corner of the balcony. When David finally spotted me, he met my cool stare with hurt and disapproval. Suddenly in the midst of the program, he appeared to have difficulty with his instrument. Pangs of guilt and remorse shot through my heart, because I could see he was under great stress. During the intermission he marched directly up to the balcony and addressed me in front of everyone. "I've just received news that my father has been rushed to the hospital!" The wounded animal look appeared once again in his eyes, accompanied with great fear.

When we were finally able to talk by phone, David reassured me that he had frequent problems with his car. I was still frightened that he might be lying, for which I had zero tolerance. His voice rang with sincerity. I felt repentant. My own exaggerated fear had caused me to misjudge him.

In the meantime, Maureen had become my confidante and prayer partner. She had met a Moslem whom she felt especially drawn to in the Old City. "Maureen! How could you possibly be so reckless?" I had misgiving when I heard the news.

"Maureen, there is absolutely no question about it, you are deceived!" I declared. I offered motherly advice to the woman who was several years my senior. "Many Western women fall into the same trap here in the Middle East. The men tend to be very manipulative and deceitful."

"But we talked about his relationship with God, and he was so open and responsive..." she contradicted me. "He even asked me to pray with him for a wife!"

I learned that the Arab man she had met was several years her junior, and it was common knowledge that the Anglo Saxon women in particular fell prey to the hot-blooded natives of the Middle East. There were elements in the opposing chemistry of their respective cultures that very easily ignited. Maureen argued adamantly with me that she "knew well the voice of God," and that she was not a romantic like me. She was certain that God wanted her to reach this man. I said no more but urged her to truly seek God's will continually in her relationship, take her own hands off, and leave the outcome to Him. She heartily agreed with me. She cut off relations with him, released him back to God and asked God to remove him from her life, unless He had some purpose for their relationship.

The following day, there was knock on the door. When I opened it, there stood a nice young Arab Moslem man at our front door! It was the only time he ever came to the house to see her!

I concluded that maybe I was wrong. Who was I to tell God how to run His program in the Middle East? I decided, though, that I must urgently consult and pray with some of my Christian friends in the country concerning my relationship with David. I had to be sure. Too much was at stake.

I conferred with one of my Messianic believing friends in Jerusalem. His advice was for me to proceed with caution in the relationship, as long as I kept my own self will completely yielded to the Lord. Only then could I be sure that God would guide me safely through all the obstacles. I concluded as well that I must be vigilant and prayerful to be protected from deception. I also decided to spend a weekend with my Jewish friend, Lana, who had moved out into the country to a *moshav* in central Israel. Naomi decided to meet with us there together.

It was not just the unknown about David's former marriage that troubled me, nor his integrity, but the depth of commitment to God. I was conscious of having some special purpose for my life that I wanted to fulfill. I did not want to be diverted.

Naomi, Lana and I sat in a simple square room out in the wilderness. Efes lay snoring on one of the beds. She had spent a long afternoon chasing strange creatures out in the pasture. After all of us had finished discharging the latest news of our lives, we decided to have a prayer time together.

Lana was still young in her faith, but she had been growing spiritually in leaps and bounds in the last months. She was an American Jewish immigrant to Israel, who had lived there many years. Her expressions, actions, and gestures were Israeli, but her self identity was not with her own people. I had spent much time in helping her appreciate, affirm, and even adopt her own Jewish roots in a greater depth of soil. Lana's life had been literally rescued from deep moral degradation before she met Messiah.

Lana dozed off while Naomi and I were praying out loud. As soon as the two of us had uttered "amen," Lana jerked her head up straight. "I have just had the weirdest dream about a relationship with a man that I loved more than God and with whom I encountered many difficulties! The purpose of it all was for "religious discipline!"

Fear gripped me. I immediately thought about my relationship with David. I instantly decided to stop seeing David, at least for a while, until I knew what was happening in his life. I decided to write him a note and tell him that it was better not to see him at this time.

Dear David.

I want to thank you for sharing so much of yourself with me. I appreciate the things I have learned from you. I have really prayed much for direction in my life. I am so afraid that I might be misguided in our relationship. I believe that it is probably best that we do not see each other anymore. Please do not call.

I dropped the letter into the mailbox the following day. As far as I was concerned, the story of David and Yael was a closed book. I did not want anything to come between me and God!

ENTREAT ME NOT TO LEAVE

"Don't urge me to leave you or to turn back from you. Where you go, I will go, and where you stay, I will stay. Your people will be my people, and your God, my God. Where you die, I will die, and there I will be buried. May the Lord deal with me, be it ever so severely if anything but death separates you and me."
(Ruth 1:16-18)

Rinnnnnnng! Rinnnnnnnnng!" The telephone screamed. It had been installed only a couple of days and was already demanding my attention. I had just glided into the apartment on a new cloud of knowledge from my Israeli studies. Learning about the Land of Promise was always exciting because of my love affair with Israel. I plunged forward to grab the receiver of the insistent black box, which I really welcomed.

"Hello."

"Yael!"

"David!" There were no violins this time. Only fear. "I thought I told you not to call."

"You're wrong, Yael! I just returned from a tour. I got your note. Now I know why I've been under a depression all week. It is because you cut me off. You're too impulsive. You've jumped to conclusions again."

I remained silent. I slowly digested his words. They sounded logical. The moment he pronounced them, they brought life to my spirit. Maybe he was right. "David, maybe you are right, but I don't understand. I'm scared!"

"Please don't cut me off! We should be together. I need you."

"I don't understand, but my heart tells me that you are right!" I answered.

"My next concert is scheduled this Sunday afternoon at the art museum. Why don't we see each other then?"

"All right, David, I'll see you then."

I hung up the receiver and signaled a desperate SOS heavenward. "Help! What is going on here?"

I was reminded that indeed I was sometimes very impulsive, but I was also *afraid.* I reviewed all of the events of the past days and realized I had jumped to conclusions based on Lana's own struggles reflected in her dream and our conversation. I was still plagued by the poisonous darts that Clara and one of the deacons of her church had spoken about David. They had slandered him. But how could I be sure that it was not true? I needed him as much as he needed me.

As I wandered through the paintings of Renoir and Cezanne in the spacious art museum, I was thinking about Naomi's faithful and undying love for me as a person. It was unconditional and God had put it in her heart for the lonely foreigner who had chosen her Land. The Almighty had knit our hearts together, like Naomi and Ruth in the Bible. She was my "Jewish mother" and I was her spiritual sister. Naomi believed in my love for David.

This time David had been asked to conduct a chamber orchestra in Tel Aviv. As I watched him waving his wand before the orchestra, I noted that he truly had the characteristic flair of an artistic temperament. David totally thrust himself into his music and was oblivious to the world outside when he was performing. He displayed an intensity and utter abandonment to the object of his heart. That very trait was the reason the Jewish people had excelled in the realm of music. I loved it.

Watching David perform reminded me of the concert following our very first encounter after I had shared the reality of his Messiah in my own life. Soon thereafter he had conducted Handel's "Messiah" before the Prime Minister and a group of Israeli leaders. At that time, the Prime Minister had told him that there was something very "special" about his music. Another elderly gentleman had said the same. David then confided, "It is because I am talking to Him, while I am conducting." He had motioned upward to heaven. It was evident that God was bestowing His blessing upon David's music, because he was drawing on divine inspiration.

While I listened to the concert, I was reviewing our history together. Had David really ever let me down yet? Well, no, I could not find a time when that was true. I could see some glaring weaknesses in his life, but that was true of me as well. I thought about my relationship with Naomi—how she needed my support and even "adored" me in the beginning, until she could stand alone with her God. It was amusing that I adopted her as my Yiddish mother and she adopted me as her "spiritual" mother. I felt I had only been a spiritual bridge that she could walk over to the other side. Now, David needed a bridge and I loved him, just as I loved Naomi.

It has been said by the sages that "man proposes, but God disposes." This was no less true in the biblical story of Boaz and Ruth. Her intentions were earnest to keep her footsteps firmly planted in the way of the God of Israel and stand at her mother-in-law's side. Boaz was a loyal son of his people. Surely this great man must have stopped to count the cost, when he considered that the lovely woman's origin was Moabite and not Jewish. The Moabites were the despised enemies of Israel.

For a moment I imagined the scene in heaven. God must have leaned back on His majestic armchair, given a great chuckle, and dispatched a host of angels to chase down all the foes of this beautiful couple. They were in need of help. After all, no one enjoyed an intriguing romance any more than the Creator of man and woman. He was the playwright who wrote the drama in the first place. It seemed like the right time for a good Yiddish mama to come onstage. Ruth needed an extra boost of boldness, since she was still the outsider and not yet a Jew.

I ran to the arms of my Jewish mother, Naomi. Dear Naomi always managed to be at my side when I needed her, even though there were wars to fight on her own home front. Her husband had to live in a wheel chair after a major stroke. She had to shuffle from one hospital to another for months. More recently, her misfortune became my good fortune. Her husband had been moved to a location close to David's neighborhood. In her spare time, she would be able to visit David, a desire which burned in my heart of late.

One afternoon all three of us were able to juggle our schedules to coincide at David's apartment. David adamantly insisted on serving us, instead of being served. I wanted Naomi's counsel on our relationship, since she knew her own people better than I. While Efes and I were organizing the cleanup of the kitchen, David and Naomi engaged in lively palaver in Hebrew. I was unable to catch all the words at the pace they were chatting, so I tuned out and tidied the kitchen. The evening unfolded in wonderful fun and fellowship for the three of us. Later, while I was driving Naomi to her residence nearby, she dropped a "bomb" on me. "You know, I was surprised that David *did not even realize that you are not Jewish!"* she laughed, half serious.

"Oh no!" I groaned. "How did you two get onto that subject?" The question was really rhetorical, because it appeared to be central to Jewish identity. "Naomi, I thought David already knew! At least, that I am not a "certified" Jew! I feel more Jewish than many who have a pure bloodline to back them up. Many of my Jewish friends have already informed me in no uncertain terms that I am "more Jewish" than they are! The real problem is that there is no consensus on "who is a Jew!"

"He was just asking me about your family," Naomi sputtered defensively. She was taken aback by the vigor of my response. "It did seem to shock him, though, to learn that you are not."

Rumblings of rage and fear welled up inside. "Why does it have to matter so much? Can we not transcend those categories that separate the human race more than uniting it? I have already proven myself to be more than willing to take on the Jewish culture with greater zeal and fervor than most Jews! I am amazed that David, a native son of Israel, deeply rooted in a passionate love for his people and culture, did not even know that I was not Jewish!—of course, that is according to rabbinical definition! That merely proves that in my spirit I am Jewish! I am quite certain that the Moabite, Ruth, did not have the stamp of approval from any rabbi when she joined her life to Boaz and the nation of Israel!"

It was unfair for me to dump my indignation on poor Naomi, who had greatly rushed to my defense and David's reassurance when the news had touched off a spark of fear in him. She had given me a higher recommendation than she would have her own kinsmen. It seemed as if some of David's fervor had cooled at my departure at the doorstep. It appeared that a can of worms was being opened up in both of our lives.

At this juncture, Naomi and I both agreed to pray for understanding. The powerful national spirit that had reared its divisive head like a black shadow threatened to throw a wall between us as well. I had first discovered that a spiritual wall truly exists between Jews and Gentiles while I was trying to learn Hebrew. I did not have to discover it in person. The Bible speaks of a "wall of partition between Jews and Gentiles." Through Messiah, this wall is removed, because those Gentiles, who believe in the Jewish Messiah and live in faith in the God of Israel, are brought into the same covenant of Abraham. The promises given to Abraham and his descendants are depicted in the *Torah, Tanach*, and the New Testament. The promise of the land is given to the Jew. However, the prophets stated that Gentiles would join with them, as well.

I committed myself to fasting and prayer for David. I had seen great power and miraculous solutions released when God's Spirit prevailed through fasting and prayer. Fasting is a form of self denial that can bring a greater presence of God's spiritual reality and purpose into being through the frailty of human beings.

I reminded Naomi that God's love story with Israel is mirrored in the life of every believer. When Israel left the oppression of Egypt, God carried her across the sea by a great miracle. Out in the howling wilderness the testing began. God wanted to determine whether she really loved the Lord, her God, with all her heart, soul, and mind as she had been commanded to do. Although Israel rebelled, God remained merciful to her, feeding her with supernatural manna from heaven, preserving her clothes, even the shoes on her feet, and leading her divinely with both cloud and fire. Still, most of the people of that generation refused to trust and obey. Therefore, only a few could enter the Promised Land.

It had been a simple matter for God to remove Israel from Egypt—just one miracle away, although many were performed to glorify Israel's God and bring judgment upon the Egyptians. But to "remove Egypt" out of Israel's heart proved to be more difficult. That was because Israel's self will was involved! When she was not lusting after the leeks and garlic of Egypt, she was longing for the false security of slavery, where someone else had to make the decisions for her! Forty years of testing were needed to work out the false values and idols from her heart before she could receive what God had prepared for her. My own spiritual history had been no different than Israel's. Nor was it other than the way of every true believer who genuinely enters into an intimate relationship of faith with God.

Within a few days, Naomi joyously reported back the results of her intense prayer. After hours of agonizing prayer, Naomi felt she had touched God. She felt *we would be married.* It had to be a work of God's Spirit, though, and not our own. There were too many obstacles to be overcome. I believed in God's power to overcome them all. In Jewish law at least two witnesses were required to establish a matter. I was challenged to hear from God myself in this matter. I decided to embark on an eight day fast. Eight was the number of "new beginnings." God's covenant with His people was instituted through circumcision on the eighth day. The circumcision, not of the body alone, but of the heart, was the token of the true Jew, according to Jeremiah the Prophet.

The fast became one of the most difficult in my life. More than fighting hunger pangs, I fought weakness. I felt as if I stood with the Red Sea before me and the armies of Egypt behind me. The God of Israel simply had to act on my behalf.

The last fast day fell on a concert night, when David was playing in our favorite old church in Jerusalem. Of course I would be there, and I invited Naomi to accompany me, if she was able to leave her sick husband.

On the eve of the performance at the old church, the weather was moody. Like a symphonic poem of contrasts, it interwove dark clouds with light ones, threatening at any moment to burst into a crescendo of rain. I planned to stop by David's place for a brief interlude on my on my way to pick up Naomi at the hospital. It was the last day of my fast, and I was anticipating an answer from the Lord.

David welcomed me warmly and we tossed around the latest chitchat. He suddenly pulled me out of the armchair onto the couch, close to his side. He hated distance. David was the kind of person to move right up to my nose or nestle close to my side, or bury my palm in his large hand. Touch was vital to him.

With my head tucked in the curve of his arm, David suddenly turned to me and with great tenderness looked into my eyes and asked "Yael, *do you love Israel?*" I could not speak from choking back the tears. My words to the Israeli Intelligence flashed back to my mind. I had told them that I had not yet married because I had not found a man who loved Israel and God at the same time. David was testing me.

"David, I love Israel so much that I would die for her!" I exclaimed. I had already died many deaths on her spiritual battlefield. My unspoken question to David was "Do you love God, your God, the God of Israel?" I decided not to ask it just yet.

Our brief moments together were the most tender we had ever known, and I poured out my struggles with the Chief Rabbi and becoming Jewish. "In fact, David, just like Israel herself, my life has been one constant fight to survive!"

David looked into my eyes, tilted my chin backward and declared, "*I will fight for you!*" His spirit had transcended his culture! He was not greatly bothered that the Chief Rabbi and I did not see things eye to eye. Those were the most hope-filled words I had heard since I had been in Israel.

When the hour of departure struck, David hopped into his Renault and I into my little VW. I felt safer not making any public appearance with him just yet. Israel was a tiny nation, where everyone knew everyone else's business. David had said, "When I sneeze in the north, they know it in the south!" I knew I was protecting our future together until the time was right. As I followed him around a curve in the winding road, suddenly he was stuck on the roadside. His car refused to budge.

I had to laugh as I thought about my accusation of him deceiving me on the very first breakdown. Fortunately, I was behind him. It now meant I had to drive him to the auditorium where the concert was held. He appeared nervous when I told him I first needed to stop at the hospital and pick up Naomi. He glanced at his watch. He felt there was too little time, but he reluctantly complied.

I eagerly hoped that Naomi would be able to get away for this special night. She had been fasting, too. Heavy wet clouds began to whip into the area from the coastal region, and would probably discourage musical fans from going out on such a night. As I pulled around the circular drive at the hospital entrance, there stood Naomi, already waiting for me outside. For some inexplicable reason, she had known I would be coming to get her, even though she had not called.

With the three of us gathered in my little VW, the vehicle filled with a beautiful presence I recognized as the Spirit of God. A cloud of love descended upon us. David and Naomi responded with a great outburst of lively conversation. They traded tidbits about the preceding week's concert. Naomi recalled one of the Brahms' *Lieder* that David had performed. One of these love songs had been titled, *"Don't Believe It If Someone Speaks Evil About Your Friend!"* The title hit me with a moment of truth. That was exactly what I had done. I had believed evil about David and mistrusted him. Clara's report had poisoned my mind about him. I resolved to trust him from that moment forward.

I could see that David was very happy. He began to share with us about beautiful Christian friends he had discovered in Switzerland. As he told the story, I could sense that God had been drawing him closer to Himself through these people in a significant way.

When we arrived at the church, I dropped David off at the front of the church and then drove into an alley where Naomi and I could pray. When I switched off the ignition, Naomi looked into my eyes with deep love. "What do you think?" she probed hesitantly.

"I....think....David is the one that God intends for me!" I was overwhelmed with a feeling of gratitude.

"Oh, how could you ever doubt you intuition?" she asked.

"Only because I have been deceived before by my own emotions...." I have learned caution from real life experience, not "doubting". "Doubting is healthy where deception occurs." I sat silently, awestruck. I was unable to utter a word. Reverence and joy surged upward in my emotions like a Bach fugue.

Finally, I broke the still. "Let's pray...."

Naomi and I bowed before the Father in a hidden corner of His Land. We thanked Him for His incredible love and mercy. We praised Him in gratitude. When we finished, I realized that I had been able to pray in Hebrew for the first time in my life! Some spiritual barrier had been broken through!

The concert was a dramatic overture on a stormy night; only a few courageous music lovers had braved the storm. Wind and rain viciously buffeted the church tower, sharing in the sweetest music I had ever heard. It sounded as if a heavenly orchestra was joining the performers, and the musical nectar which was being served had been kept hidden for those who sought only the best.

Melodic strains of Schubert began filling the naves and arches of the church. The atmosphere was a psalm of praise to the Most High. My own spirit was soaring with the music, when suddenly I saw a picture in my mind. I was standing before the Throne of God. Yeshua was standing there before the majesty of the Almighty, holding my hand on his right and David's hand on his left. He was addressing the Father. "Father, see what I have accomplished for Your glory!" He was presenting us both to the Father.

All around the Throne there was great rejoicing in heaven, not only because two stormy souls had found their way into God's plan, in spite of a long and treacherous way, but Jew and Gentile were blended into a union of love that crossed all borders of culture, race, and religion! Yeshua turned to address me, saying "It is all right to love David that much—the intensity and passion you feel." In the moment that he gave me permission, and my heart's desire was fulfilled, I knew I could release David back into God's keeping. Then, I turned and looked at Yeshua, and I knew I loved him even more!

This realization was absolutely vital for my inner wholeness. I had been afraid that I would love a human man more than I loved God. God had brought me to a man I could love with the totality of my being in David, and yet in the instant and release of that freedom to love, I discovered an even greater love for my Lord. The experience was sublime. In losing myself in love for David, I was able to find God's greater reckless love for all the lost, sinful, rejects of the world at the same time. The depths to which God would stoop to tell them He loved them were immeasurable!

Then, with a swift stroke of the wand, the symphonic sound changed to Shostakovich. The music presented the dark tragic overtones of a memorial to the Holocaust to my mind. Death camps and darkness filled the church with agony and pain. Generations of Jewish suffering swelled before my eyes. Suddenly, through the gloom, I saw a cross. Yeshua, by an act of his own will had chosen to suffer the same agony, pain and rejection that his own people would undergo. He had willingly chosen to accept it, despising its shame, as atonement for his own people and the entire world! How intertwined was his personal history with the national history of Israel. Perfect Love had chosen to suffer on behalf of the beloved. Yes, David, I am willing to suffer for you to know your God. Yes, Israel, I will suffer for your resurrection. The world is waiting to see God's glory through you!

Two witnesses had spoken. What further confirmation did I need for our two lives? Upon arriving home that night, I decided to write him a letter.

Dearest David,

"Delight yourself in the Lord, and He will give you the desires of your heart."

Saturday evening, God made it plain to me that you are the desire of my heart! I know how important your career is. I know that if you pursue it for God's glory, He will bless you without limitation! I want to be at your side, loving you, supporting you, and above all, praying for you—if you want me. Just as Ruth went and offered herself to Boaz, I offer my love to you with her words:

> "Entreat me not to leave you, for where you go I will go; and where you lodge, I will lodge; your people shall be my people, and your God, my God; Where you die, I will die, and there will I be buried. The Lord do so to me and more also, if anything but death parts me from you."(Ruth 1:16-17, KJV)

> "Seal me in your heart with permanent betrothal, for love is strong as death. Many waters cannot quench the flame of love; neither can the floods drown it. If a man tried to buy it with everything he owned he could not do it."(Song of Songs 8:6-7, TLB)

I mailed it to him with much trepidation. The woman who was not one of his people had literally placed herself at his feet. There would be a price to pay for the acceptance of this love. The thought of his rejection no longer mattered to me. How could anyone possibly turn away from the love which flowed from God through my heart to this man? I felt I would have died out of sheer love if I had not expressed it somehow. I deposited it into the mailbox because I knew he would be traveling.

A THREE STRAND CORD

"Two are better than one, because they have a good return for their work; if one falls down, his friend can help him up. But pity the man who falls and has no one to help him up! Also, if two lie down together, they will keep warm. But how can one keep warm alone? Though one may be overpowered, two can defend themselves. A cord of three strands is not quickly broken." (Ecclesiastes 4:9-12)

As far as I was concerned, real faith is "the assurance of things hoped for, the evidence of things not seen," as the writer of the book of Hebrews confidently declared in the New Testament. Translated into everyday language, this meant to me that my marriage to David had already been promised and performed in heaven! All that remained for us to do was remove the rubble that was lying in the path of His purposes and fulfill on earth what was intended by God. No matter what any circumstances looked like on the outside, when God had spoken, the eyes of faith could see beyond all outward evidence to the contrary.

My ardent and forthright declaration to David had struck the deepest chords of his heart. In a tender moment he confided that he carried my letter in his wallet. At the same time, it stirred up a nest of fears that swarmed at him like hornets. My non Jewish identity, another commitment in marriage after one fiasco, the meaning of total surrender to God—which was the unspoken price on my head, and crossing conflicting cultures with two scarred children all buzzed around him in confusion. Each time I could see the dilemma swimming across his eyes, I reminded him and myself that GOD'S LOVE CONQUERS ALL. That was the doctrine of any true believer, which I was committed to follow. More than that, though, it was the statement of faith in the God Who is Love.

I had collected very few details about David's family life because it was a matter still filled with pain. I had never heard him say anything unkind about his ex-wife, which both stirred my admiration and alarm. I was biding my time until I could meet his parents, who lived—of all places—on the same kibbutz as one of Naomi's children. I had remarked that God was truly joining our two "families", since Naomi was my real family in Israel.

When I dared think about his two daughters, I already loved them through his heart. I felt that my social work training and my experience in working with foster and adopted children would help me relate to them. Most of the time, however, I pushed them to the back of my mind. There was the danger that they would not want to accept me, the language barrier with my floundering Hebrew, and the poison of the hatred of some people in Israel. Like Scarlet O'Hara in "Gone with the Wind", I decided to "think about that tomorrow." Tomorrow came much sooner than expected and took me by surprise.

Since I felt a certainty in my own mind and heart that David was to be my husband, I entered into a new freedom in my relationship with him. All the fears of his taking advantage of me had been dissolved in a sweet pool of trust. One of the weekends he was not tied up with his work, I decided to shuttle over to his apartment where we could spend a quiet evening together, which was very rare.

The first time I had crossed the threshold of his doorway had been a delightful revelation. I literally met his humanity almost in the raw. I not only caught him in his underwear but discovered just how human this larger than life man really was. He needed a woman. If for no other reason than to tidy, clean, and order the place—although I knew the feminists would devour that one! The realization of catching him without any defenses let me know just how much I really loved him. Normally, I had a tendency to be exacting with a man, but in his case I felt nothing but an endearing inner urge to step in and fill whatever was lacking in his life.

On this visit, when I tried to cook our supper, David interfered, insisting that he really wanted to do something for me. After a generous portion of fried eggs, cucumbers, tomatoes, and potatoes—*a la Israeli*, I was collecting the leftovers when David blocked me. With two giant steps across the living room, David strode over to the dining table and captured me in a bear lock. He shuffled us both over to the sofa and plopped me in a corner.

Efes, who had been an invited guest, had been carried away with the leftovers until this moment. She quickly ran and hopped into the armchair adjoining the couch and nervously observed David's affectionate overtures. I was faintly beginning to feel my boundaries melting when Efes jumped into the middle of my lap and began whimpering. I concluded that my furry friend must be jealous, although she usually allowed any expression of affection between David and me. Fear filled her canine eyes. Efes was warning me of some danger. David and I were becoming too emotionally intoxicated to pay Efes too much attention.

Suddenly loud banging sounded on the door startling me to sobriety. It was followed by urgent ringing of the doorbell. David lunged toward the door, while my heart raced wildly.

A striking young girl of eleven with soft brown eyes and long chestnut hair barged into the room. "*Abba!*" She cried. "Why did it take you so long to answer the door?" She darted her eyes in my direction. My body felt like wax and I desperately desired to dissolve into the floor.

David immediately introduced me to his lovely daughter, Miri, and her attention quickly shifted to Efes, who was stationed in her father's armchair. She instantly made friends with my fluffy pal and beckoned her Abba to help her carry in a big trunk from the street. David excused himself momentarily to assist his daughter and promised to return at once.

I grabbed Efes for my protection, not hers. David was the only man in my life in Israel that she had completely accepted: however, when she thought we might be losing ourselves on the sofa, she whined a warning. She had been trying to tell me something which

I could not analyze. I felt as if I had been caught with my paw in the cookie jar when Miri rushed into the room. That was not the way I wanted to meet her at the beginning. I had hoped to meet his children under different circumstances.

David returned breathless and scrutinized my stunned expression. "I've been meaning to tell you," he announced half assertively and half apologetically, "that you are going to have to get used to having my daughters drop in like this. They live down the street with their mother and spend half the time with me and half the time with her."

He instantly took me into his arms and held me to comfort me from the fear that had frozen my body. Knowing that he had a family, and facing it in reality were two entirely different frames of reference for me. It gave a new status to our relationship which I would have to define for myself. My stomach was churning in distress. The fact that his ex-wife lived just down the street gave me anything but consolation. I had never faced such a situation before and felt a longing to hop into my track shoes and run in the other direction.

David had an uncanny ability to tune into every vibration of anxiety and fear that flowed through my body. The thought of losing me to my fears created a momentary desperation in him. He tightened his hold on me and wanted to smother me with encouragement.

Efes had a conniption and plunged herself upon both of us. Frantic "ding-dongs" began screaming at the doorway again. Instinctively, this time I ran for cover in the bathroom. I had no idea what awaited us. I felt unprepared for further appearances. Nor was it the time or the place for any unexpected introductions. I needed physical and emotional preparation before I met new people. After running a comb through my hair and spending a few seconds shivering on the edge of the bathtub, I heard a loud female voice arguing with David in Hebrew. At once, he appeared at the door of my "hiding place" and told me to come out and present myself to—of all people—his ex-wife!

White as a sheet, I marched out of the bathroom to the tune of "Pomp and Ceremony", holding my head high, but feeling like "the other woman" inside. I had never faced anything like this and I was feeling guilty for what I did not know. An attractive woman with blond hair was standing in the room. "It is so nice to meet you!" she said in a sweet syrupy voice. "I recognize your face from your picture on the back of your book! You *two* will have to come over and visit me sometime! My name is Shula."

The gracious acceptance which the lovely lady proffered me in English demolished my defenses. Her tone of voice sounded anything but genuine. Just as readily as she had so sweetly received me, she spun on her heels and began to attack David in English! If he had the "right" to have women in his place before all the final divorce details were settled, then she would have her "friend"in, too. She announced that what he was doing was totally unfair to her!

David weakly defended himself in English also. Then she became hysterical and with a strong sense of artistic snobbery began to attack his ability as a musician. The two entered into a *Kulturkampf* right there before my very eyes. She was on the offense and he was on the defense. He finally interrupted her tirade with an accusation of some affair she had had with an old man. I watched the ping pong match of words all in my native language with the feeling that the performance was for me. It would have made a wonderful comedy if I had not seen their other precious daughter, a fair haired angelic looking child, standing by herself with big sad eyes. Her blond hair was pulled back with pony tails on both sides of her head. She rushed to her Abba and clung to him tightly at the edge of the firing line.

After they had performed for me a while, I bravely interrupted the shouting match. I asked Shula why she desired this divorce so much. Now it was my turn to disarm her. She hemmed, hawed, stuttered, sputtered and then said that there were "reasons" she had "rather not talk about at this time." Obviously, she had set out to destroy him in my eyes. She missed her golden opportunity by not answering my question. I was genuinely interested in her answer because my little mental computer had already sought help for finding an explanation.

Huffing with indignation, she stormed out of the apartment, demanding David to take care of certain undefined things I could not figure out. The two girls held fast to her coattail. David closed the door behind her and turned to me. My emotions were in shambles. Fragments of my trust lay splintered around his apartment.

David dropped his shoulders in defeat. He slumped down on the sofa. He had already previously apologized for his décor because his ex had made off with most of the furniture. She had even gone so far as to "steal" his piano when he was not home.

I broke the gloom with a question. "I thought that your divorce settlement was already completed?"

"Well, it really is, but there are still several matters relating to property and the children that have to be worked out," He replied with resignation.

"Oh David, I cannot get involved in this kind of relationship with you!" I felt intense sorrow and guilt for being in what had been their home together. My dejection was mingled with love for him and compassion for her in her hurt.

Now it was David's turn to be afraid. This was a moment when he most needed my support, and I had slugged him hard with the threat of rejection. As if it were a variation on a theme in our relationship, David rose up when I was knocked down. *"I can wait!"* He answered absolutely. There was such faith and confidence in his voice that my defenses crumbled again. The loving assurance that David was willing to pay a price for me dispelled my fear and confusion. I reevaluated my impulsive outburst.

"I don't understand," I lamented. "In some ways your 'ex-wife' seemed to be so nice." Her behavior had crushed the foundation of my confidence.

"She's pretty on the outside, but very ugly on the inside," he announced absolutely. You have no idea of all the things she has done to me....lied, stolen...." He stopped himself. He had been married to this woman and no matter how bad she was, she was still the mother of his children. I listened carefully, but I heard no shred of vindictiveness in his voice. His protest was self defense. "She's very sly and deceitful," he concluded.

I left crestfallen that night. A whirlwind of doubt and confusion assailed me. I intensely loved this man and knew he needed me. I was willing to let go of him if God so willed. I feared falling into a snare. I hurt for his beautiful children.

I thrust myself upon the Lord. No, I did not understand. On Sunday, I fled to the refuge of the big church, where a pastor from Europe was presiding. He read the text from Jeremiah 33.

> And I will cleanse away their sins against me and pardon them....The Lord declares that the happy voices of bridegrooms and of brides, and the joyous songs of those bringing thanksgiving offerings to the Lord will be heard again in this doomed land. The people will sing: Praise the Lord! For He is good and His mercy endures forever....If you can break my covenant with the day and with the night so that day and night don't come on their usual schedule, only then will my covenant with David my servant be broken.

The sermon turned out to be based on the verse that had been impressed upon me every time I cried out to God about marriage: "Blessed is she who has believed that there would be a fulfillment of those things spoken to her by the Lord!" This was Elizabeth's exultation to Mary, who believed the Word of the Lord to her heart concerning Yeshua.

The minister then talked at length about Mary's faith. Was it a coincidence that my real first name was Mary, and God was speaking with me? He elaborated on the fact that some people are called to a special task, and those words leapt out at me. Everyone had a task and it was our responsibility to find out our task and move into it.

I felt encouraged as I walked out of the massive structure. The message had sunk straight into my heart. However, I had learned two new things. First, fierce testing follows any real revelation from God to man. Secondly, God's ways are not man's ways, especially with the nation of Israel!

I still walked around with an inner turmoil as I reviewed David's situation. How could it possibly be God's will to plunge me into the middle of this enigmatic maze of circumstances? Some answers began to fall into place. God chooses whom He will! He announced, "Jacob I have loved and Esau I have hated!" It appeared unjust that God had chosen Jacob before his birth and even though he was a conniver. Then, the Lord impressed me again with "*I will have mercy on whom I will have mercy!* King David's relationship with Bathsheba began in adultery, but Solomon was the offspring of their relationship and later king of Israel. From the beginning to the end of the Book, I could see that God's ways are not man's ways. I resolved myself to the fact that I could *trust* God but not always understand.

As I thought about David I saw him as a prototype of his beloved land and people. He was abundantly gifted with talent. There was the sweet psalmist of his ancestor, David, hidden away in his heart. Most of all I deeply admired the scope of his compassion. I remembered the night we had talked about Israel's relationship with the rest of the world. Tears were in his eyes as he spoke about the suffering of the Vietnamese people. He was not selfish or myopic in his focus but cared for the rest of the world as much as he did for his own nation. The prophets of Israel continually called the nation "God's wife". She had been estranged from Him by going her own way. I recognized in David what the Jewish apostle Paul spoke about in his letter to the Romans. When Israel truly returned to her God, to "love Him with all her heart and soul and strength," it would be like the "*resurrection of the dead for the whole world.*" Israel had a glorious destiny awaiting her. David was one of her true sons.

I also thought about Israel's prophets whose life and words were recorded in the *Tanach*. The prophets always had to go outside the camp, away from public opinion, in order to stand alone as God's spokesmen. They had to learn how to "stand against the people" in order to "stand with God". David's failed marriage, for whatever reason, had ejected him from the security of social acceptability in some circles already. His acceptance of me as a believer in Yeshua as the Messiah of Israel, as well as his willingness to take an open stand for his Messiah would cost him everything! Would he be willing to pay the price? For an Israeli Jew to believe, it might cost him great rejection of family and friends.

Later, when we were together at the house, Maureen and I traded our stories with each other. Inside I was continually questioning her relationship with her Moslem friend. At this point I did not know whether to challenge her or not. I was in a school of learning more about the sovereignty of God myself. At times it seemed that Maureen's and my lives were running on parallel courses. Every fluctuation that occurred with her Ishmael rippled a similar response with David and me. It was uncanny. It was natural when she decided to move out of the little Jerusalem flat into another neighborhood to be closer to her beloved. I wondered whether I would follow in her steps. David was in the process of moving to Tel Aviv.

Meanwhile, I kept Lana posted on the latest events in the story. I detected a strong judgmental attitude toward me in my current conflict. When I explained the unusual circumstances surrounding David's divorce settlement, she turned to me and fiercely declared "you definitely should stop seeing him until all this is settled!"

None of my explanations about the long weary entanglements his ex-wife engineered at the Rabbinate sufficed to calm her. I was hurt that of all people she, who had gone through divorce herself, was relating to me in a hardened, legalistic way. I felt a growing alienation from her which was very painful because I had given so much of myself to her in our friendship. There was no such thing as secular divorce in Israel. Every Jew had to be married or divorced through the rabbinical authorities whether they wanted to or not.

In addition to the condemnation I was receiving from Lana, I was fighting growing apprehension about the settlement that would take place concerning David's children. After the severe slander that had taken place against me from the Chief Rabbi, I was convinced it would be used against David at this vulnerable time in his life if he were known to be associated with me in any way. I knew that he was trying very hard to protect his children from some of the bizarre shenanigans of his estranged wife.

Storm clouds were gathering around our two lives at the same time they were reflected in the political arena of Israel's destiny. Kissinger had just failed in his mission to the Middle East. We were approaching the season of Passover, the time of redemption, hope and resurrection. Surely, there would be a breakthrough in the unending warfare that was the distinct hallmark of life in Israel.

David had invited me to celebrate Passover with him and his family on the kibbutz. Naomi would be there, too, with her daughter and grandchildren. It sounded like a wonderful opportunity for a family gathering of rejoicing in the midst of the storm. I deeply desired to be with him; however, the more I contemplated the event, the less comfortable I felt about going. I was longing to meet David's Mother. I had already determined that she would love me if she was the kind of woman he had described her to be. I was convinced, though, that public exposure of David with someone who had been slandered as severely as I had would jeopardize his settlement with his children. With great reluctance I chose to be unselfish and refuse the invitation for the sake of the children.

I had also wanted very much to be with Naomi. I took her aside and carefully instructed her to take David under her "Yiddish" wing in my absence of being able to celebrate their great festival of redemption with them. Later, someone I barely knew invited me to a Messianic Seder upon the Mount of Olives in Jerusalem.

My heart was with Naomi and David on the night of the Passover Seder. My future relationship with David's precious daughters was weighing heavily on me as I drove up the steep road to the top of the Mount of Olives. It was one of the loveliest spots in all Jerusalem. Outside in the garden behind the building where we met I had a glorious view of the City. Ribbons of golden light from the setting sun enveloped the City in a glistening hue of gold. I immediately strolled over in the direction of a huge slab of rock that sat on the side of the mountain. I chose it as my bench to meditate alone.

Suddenly I heard a cry. "Yael! "Yael!" I twisted my body around and looked squarely into the face of the gorgeous eleven year old daughter of Moshe, the owner of the property where I sat. The little girl ran up and hugged me, as if she had missed me for years. I was very surprised that she remembered who I was because she had met me only once before. I was even more amazed that I had made such a deep impression on her. While we were chatting in my childlike Hebrew, again I heard a shout. "Yael! Yael!"

This time a young blond seven year old beauty with beaming eyes raced toward me. She was the daughter of another Messianic Jewish family I had met months before. I barely knew this child, and she was bubbling with delight in discovering me once again. What was happening?

I wrapped one of the little girls in the bend of my right arm and the other in the left and pulled them over to the stone slab. The three of us sat watching golden ribbons of light wrap the eternal City with streamers. We sang my entire repertoire of Hebrew songs together for some time until Passover had descended upon the Land.

Our heavenly Father was speaking to my heart. "*This is my Passover love gift to you. You see these two little girls, a blond one and a darker haired one, just like David's daughters. You can trust me to help you care for them!*"

Joy overflowed at the long Seder table with my Jewish brothers and sisters while they read the story of Israel's redemption from bondage and slavery. One part of the ceremony touched me in a special way. It was the tipping of the wine glass and spilling some of the wine before drinking it. This was a reminder that others had also suffered for Israel's redemption. The Egyptians had to suffer greatly when Israel was delivered from her captivity; therefore, Israel's joy was not allowed to be complete since others suffered at her expense. This represented the *spirit of the true Jew* to me. *Compassion!*

The Messianic Jewish believers I celebrated with reflected Israel's spiritual redemption through the Passover Lamb of God, Yeshua, who willingly chose to be sacrificed for the sins of his nation and the entire world. His sacrificial death freed both Jew and Gentile from bondage to sin and self. The presence of God's Spirit was so real that I was expecting another Passover miracle to take place! And so it did! The miracle that occurred was such a splendid sign from God that I knew there never would be room for doubt again about my beloved David and me.

I sat on one of the most venerated spots in all the Holy Land, the Mount of Olives, where Messiah would touch his feet upon return to the earth according to the Jewish prophet Zechariah. At the same time, David and Naomi received the beautiful evidence of "*my presence with them.*" Naomi had taken my motherly instructions to comfort David profoundly to heart. However, when she arrived at her daughter's kibbutz, she was seized with a sick feeling. Exhausted and weak from months of zigzagging from house to hospital and back, she no longer found strength to participate in the celebration. She lovingly shoved her daughter and grandchildren out to the dining hall and decided to stay in bed. As she stretched out on a cot in her daughter's room, slowly she began to be infused with strength. Remembering her promise to me to comfort David, she jumped up and headed for the kibbutz dining room.

When she arrived at the big hall, it looked like an anthill with hundreds of people scurrying around. There were long lines of kibbutzniks, relatives from within and outside the land, children, and the elderly standing and waiting for the number of their table assignment. Naomi was intent on finding her own family as she wove her way through the crowd. After bumping shoulders, scooting chairs, and shuffling her path through the human maze, she finally spotted her family table. Recalling her promise to me once again, she scanned the huge room to determine whether it was possible to detect a sign of David in the midst of the horde of eight hundred people. "How absurd," she reasoned, "to think that I could ever find him in this multitude!"

As Naomi sat down at the table, she turned to the right. There sat David right next to her, with one empty seat between! When I heard, I knew that it was my seat. Only a great "romantic" like God, could have ever arranged the seating out of all the mathematical possibilities of placing these two together with my empty seat between! God had given us all a *sign!*

David and Naomi saw each other at the same time. He had been wrestling with his own doubts and fears and was weighed down at the same time as she was. When he realized the miraculous event that had transpired before his own eyes, he turned to Naomi and said *"I guess God really does want it, doesn't He!"* He, too had been battling uncertainties about his relationship with me, and God had sent us all a sign as a Passover gift! The following day David went to visit Naomi's husband in the hospital in order to bring him comfort! Their hearts had been linked together in a deeper bond, as well. After Passover, my joy was so full that I forgot to spill a little of it out of the cup. In a world so filled with evil, the suffering was bound to arrive automatically on the footsteps of any great blessing in order to steal some of the joy away. And, so it did.

Lana appeared unable to endure my report of victorious divine comfort and confirmation about my relationship with David. It did not fit into her religious formulas. The real reason for her cool behavior was hidden by an insidious disguise. It was the green eyed monster of jealousy. Why should God allow me the joy of fulfillment with the right man, while it was yet denied her? As I shared my exuberance with her in her modest room on the *moshav,* she abruptly twirled around and addressed me with a glare. "I want that scarf you are wearing. I need it!"

I was stunned. I paused some moments. "Don't you remember? You gave it to me as a gift."

"No, I didn't. I want it back."

"All right," I meekly replied, "here take it." I untied the tiny knot at the base of my neck and handed her the worn, worthless scarf. An icy glaze covered her face, and she coldly took it from me. I mumbled something about having to hurry back to the city and fled to the refuge of my little car. After a couple of days, I learned that Lana had written a letter to two of my best friends and confidantes in Jerusalem who were leaders in the Christian community. She had instructed them to "discipline" me in my relationship with David, which she felt was against God's will. They approached me with admonishment and finally cool withdrawal. She had succeeded in completely damaging any lifeline I may have had to the Christian community.

I felt battered and crushed. I remembered what Maureen had been sharing with me of late about having to "go outside the camp". Now, I had to deal with rejection from both the Jewish and Christian camps. I knew that it was all a part of the "fellowship of his sufferings," which Yeshua endured on earth. I recalled the words of the prophetic psalm:

"Even my close friend, whom I trusted 'she' who shared my bread, has lifted up 'her' heel against me." There was no deeper wound and grueling pain than the rejection of those who were closest. It was also clear that the hatred directed against Yeshua from the religious leaders was rooted in jealousy itself. Many of the proud and self righteous religious leaders of his day were jealous of his favor with the people. They envied the miracles he performed. They despised the mercy and compassion he poured out in contrast to the heavy demands they placed on the people. Both religious legalism and jealousy were the forces motivating Lana to turn against me.

I was sitting in my room nursing my wounds after the latest attack, when a knock sounded on the door. I was in no mood to receive any visitor. Nevertheless, I opened the door and there stood a gray haired old patriarchal Arab at the threshold asking to see Molly, the landlady. I informed him she was not home. He did not budge. He obviously wanted an invitation inside. Not to ask him in would have been a flagrant violation of the Middle Eastern hospitality code, so I motioned the old man inside and offered him tea. He was a longstanding friend of Molly and worthy of our respect.

Maureen, who had been busy in her room, suddenly appeared and took over the customary amenities. I was grateful because I had every intention of fleeing back to the refuge of my self pity in the corner of my room. Nothing slipped past the keen eyes of this wise old elder. He immediately cornered me in conversation and commanded me to sit down and join the circle. My refusal was unacceptable.

When I reluctantly complied, the old man began to tug at me to disclose why I was so "low". As if he had instantly unzipped my heart, I began to spill out my latest setback. "My friend has just betrayed me!" I tearfully announced.

"That's nothing," the old man replied casually. "My own son has betrayed me. *That's the price of being a disciple of the Messiah!*"

His words removed the sting. This Arab patriarch was a true Christian who knew the cost of following his Lord. "God must have sent you to my doorstep," I said. For a few moments all the pain was gone. I knew I had lost the closeness and confidence of two good friends and strong leaders. This could not be repaired overnight. On the other hand, I had the privilege of entering into the fellowship of the suffering of my savior. "If they persecuted me, they will persecute you," he had said. Now Naomi and David were the only two living people in that land that loved me with a loyalty that was unyielding. Would the three of us be able to continue to stand in the face of opposition? Our three lives were inextricably intertwined in a divine plan which was the handiwork of God Almighty. Who was mere man to question His purposes?

After our Arab friend left, I turned to a favorite passage of the *Tanach,* from the book of Ecclesiastes. I had discovered it some years before while I was praying about a husband.

> Two are better than one, because they have a good return for their work.
> If one falls down, his friend can help him up.
> But pity the man who falls and has no one to help him up!
> Also, if two lie down together, they will keep warm.
> But how can one keep warm alone?
> Though one may be overpowered, two can defend themselves.
> A cord of three strands is not quickly broken.
> (Ecclesiastes 4:9-12)

WHITHER YOU GO I WILL GO

"Don't urge me to leave you or to turn back from you. Where you go, I will go, and where you stay, I will stay. Your people will be my people and your God my God. Where you die I will die, and there I will be buried. May the Lord deal with me, be it ever so severely, if anything but death separates you and me."
(Ruth 1:16-18)

I was awakened with a jerk and bounced upright in bed. Loud, long moans howled underneath my window. A shiver rattled my spine. I glanced around the room. All the objects were unfamiliar. "Where am I?" I strained to remember, but my memory was too tired to grant recall. A deep throated moaning was heard again. "Dear God, what is happening out there? Is someone dying?"

I tuned my ear attentively for some more minutes, pulled between paralysis and the desire to jump up and run for help. But, run where? I was in strange surroundings, and for the life of me could not focus myself in time and space. Like lightning came a realization. I fell back on the pillow and roared with laughter. I was in my new room in Tel Aviv, and those were the love calls of the local cats in mating season!

The passionate, aching screams rising from the alley shook me to the depths. They reminded me of just how I felt inside. I had to chuckle at the cats' caricature of us human beings. There was no question about it. The cats in Israel were much more passionate than those I had heard in America! I had never heard such longing in my life! Nor had I felt it before.

Overnight I had found myself situated in a transitional neighborhood which blended modern skyscrapers with crumbling old edifices a few blocks away from the red light district. My building was one of the older weather-beaten structures which would eventually opt to renovation or removal. There was nothing to impress anyone from the outside, except the scars of age and indentations from misfired weapons from the earlier wars. Inside, the building had a colorful history. It had been a place of early refuge from the British for some of the boat people making illegal entry into Palestine.

My spacious room also had its glory. From the back window I could watch a ballet of green, performed by the abundance of trees which enclosed a huge park. The visibility of so much verdure was a rare treat for anyone's dwelling in Tel Aviv. From my side door, which opened upon a wide outdoor balcony, I could immediately step out and be encompassed by the Mediterranean across the street. The thought of being surrounded by so much beauty brought bittersweet memories. Tears of recollection welled up in my eyes. My greatest difficulties had been born in the most beautiful surroundings.

As usual, it seemed supernatural how I had arrived there. Through the big church I often visited, an Israeli had wandered in looking for someone who would care for his ninety year old immigrant mother. She spoke no Hebrew, only German and was as stubborn as a Missouri mule. She had informed her family that she could manage quite well alone in her upper story apartment, thank you. No one was going to make her one of those senior citizens who folded up and died in senile dependence upon their children! This little lady had all the determination of the Jews and the Germans rolled up into stubborn independence which I immediately had to admire. She had both mental clarity and gracious dignity one seldom found in her age.

The disheartened Israeli son had combed the newspapers, scouted the streets, and even contacted all his friends to try and find a live-in companion for his mother. However, in all Israel, only a miracle could produce someone who spoke German well enough to converse with the lady and was willing to help with the chores and do it all freely without cash for a room and food. So where did this disheartened Jewish son go for a miracle, but to one of the Christian churches that happened to have German speakers in their midst. It was a last resort, mind you, but that was the place we bumped noses. Unfortunately, we had to engage in deception to smuggle me into the house. Our little lady had already managed many years alone since the death of her husband. Why should any intruder now alter her long established lifestyle? So, sonny boy cooked up a plan when he discovered I was scouting for a room in Tel Aviv. He invited me to Mama's for lunch, introducing me as a friend. I probably would have considered him to be if I had been allowed more time to get to know him. He let his mother know that I needed a place to stay. The clincher would be whether or not Mama was willing to offer me a place to live. Clever? Well, it was a situation where compassion overruled ethics.

At first sight, I fell in love with Frau Herz. She was truly all heart, encased in a rigid, Germanic, Jewish exterior. I was just the right granddaughter for her to grandmother. She needed a mission and a purpose to thrive, and I was ideal! Efes did not take to these extreme changes well. Weeks before the move, she sensed something in the air. She began to develop a neurosis. Strangely for no reason, she started limping. I examined and probed her paw time and time again, without any evidence of the slightest scratch. She became moody, depressed, and suffered from a loss of appetite. I had put her on forced fasts before when she stubbornly refused a change in her diet during the times I was short of cash and had only milk and bread to serve her. More than likely, this perceptive little creature was prematurely sensing that she would not be able to live in my new quarters. I was forced to find another place for her to live. The adjustment of a dynamic young companion was one thing for a ninety year old, but a curly canine? No, thank you! There was a limit one had to set, even at her age.

It was also no secret that there were two camps of thought concerning dogs in Israel. Many of the Eastern European Jews hated and scorned them out of fear. They had been the victims of the fury of Gentile dogs in their countries of origin. Some of the sabras and Western Jews had made their dogs a part of the family, depending on the cultures they came from. David and I both loved the little canine creatures. Efes resided with friends until I could find a new home for her.

Only a couple of weeks had passed since our Passover miracle. David and I were still riding on the crest of a euphoric wave. We were closer than ever before to each other in where we lived, as well as the tenderness we could express to each other. I brought him to my new "apartment" and introduced him to my dear little lady. He was also taken with her charm from the old country. David had recently relocated just outside Tel Aviv.

I lived in a large room at the back of the apartment. It had its own entrance, just inside the door to the main apartment, so I could come and go without disturbing Frau Herz. The living and sleeping room, as well as the kitchen were all on the other side of my wall, but I also had another door to that area. The rooms had European couches that were sat on in the day and folded out to make a bed at night.

I had invited David into my new apartment to have some tea. As David sat in an armchair in my room, sipping tea and sharing the current events in his life, I noticed that his eyes were brighter than before. There was a new light which I read as "hope" for the future. I was noticing that the more distance he gained from Shula, the less pain was visible in his face. He was squarely facing new truths about his own life and confident enough to share them with me.

He confided that Shula's behavior had become bizarre of late, and she had exhibited a complete breakdown into wild and unexpected actions. She had attempted to throw lawsuits at him, postpone dates at the Rabbinate again and again, which involved the settlement of the children's future. David was very hesitant as he turned to me and told me it might be better for me to be free, because it looked as if Shula was waging a war that was going to take a long time to resolve. His tender unselfishness touched me deeply. This time it was I who said, "I can wait!" I had decided that we belonged together, and I loved this man enough to wait as long as it took.

I could tell that David was moved by my affirmation. In the real niche of privacy that we had without any fear, he swept me up into his bear like arms. We made ourselves sick with longing. Both of us were filled with unexpressed emotion. However, out of our honoring the Lord we had set a limit on our affections.

David was scheduled for another taxing confrontation at the Rabbinate in a few days. The lines on his face revealed the great burden he was bearing as he told me about it. I told him that I would be fasting and praying for him. David then confided that he was seeing many things in his life more clearly, including the political pollution of the Rabbinate. On one of his earlier visits, one of the rabbis had offered him an "under-the-table arrangement" to settle all the disputes in the divorce proceedings. David was very startled when the offer was made, but he refused to compromise. God had been showing him the evils of wrong compromise, including in his own life. He said he felt like he was going into the lion's den every time he had to show up for one of the proceedings at the rabbinate.

The day preceding the court's scheduled decree, David dropped by for some added encouragement. I read a psalm to him:

> The Lord is righteous in all his ways and loving toward all
> he has made.
> The Lord is near to all who call on him, to all who call on
> him in truth.
> He fulfills the desires of those who fear him;
> He hears their cry and saves them.
> The Lord watches over all who love him, but all the wicked
> he will destroy.

The words brought comfort to his spirit, and for the first time I prayed aloud for him in his presence. Our relationship had never felt so whole. God's Spirit was overshadowing our love. I felt as if God had truly joined us together as one, even though it was not the time for genuine marital union. Unless I became Jewish there was no legal recourse in Israel for us to be married. Besides, until the mess with Shula and the Rabbinate was cleared up we could not be married. It was a dilemma, but we would have to wait and see what God was doing in our lives and when it was the time to make that life commitment to each other before God and the world. David began sharing some of his deepest questions concerning God's ways. As everyone, especially the Jews, he was greatly troubled about the problem of evil and suffering. He wanted us to talk about it some more. The more we shared our hearts openly, the more evident it became that the situation with his ex-wife was worse than I had ever imagined. I felt that because he had a limited understanding of evil, his spirit was passive toward it, accepting it from God.

I shared my own understanding. I did not believe as Moslems do that everything that happens in the world is the will of God. There is a devil, who is the spiritual being of evil, and who wants to destroy all that is good and godly. Anti-Semitism was the best example of evil I could think of. God has chosen Israel to be a blessing in the whole earth; and precisely for this reason Satan hates and wants to destroy the Jews. If he could succeed, he would defeat God's plan. Of course, he will never succeed, because God will not let him. However, God has given each of us free will to choose good or evil, and our own choices also shape and determine our destiny. When we choose to act harmoniously with God, we overcome evil with good.

We also talked about the difference between the wrath of God and the wrath of Satan. God is not out to destroy his own people but allows them to be disciplined, according to their own choices. Satan is always out to destroy and to thwart God's plans, and God's people. He works through the evil choices of men. Of course, God is ruler over all and even Satan is subject to Him.

Like most Jews, David was perplexed about the Holocaust. That was a very painful question that all Jews have had to wrestle with. I had no doubt that the depravity of it was the very wrath of Satan to attempt to annihilate the Jews before God could fulfill His promises to them. Could God have stopped it? If he had deprived man of free will he could have. In fact, He did stop it when he caused the allied forces to rise up and defeat the Nazis. Many other nationalities were killed along with the Jews. The good that God brought out of the ashes of the Holocaust was *the resurrection of the nation of Israel and the subsequent return of the Jews to their homeland.*

David was encouraged. His own faith mostly stood alone in his heart, outside the traditional circles of religious orthodoxy. At that time in Israel's history, Messianic congregations were few and far between. Most Jews did not feel free to appear in such a place because of rejection or persecution, so David and I had to share our hearts with one another about God, Israel, and our own lives. I was beginning to see that David and Yael where two little actors in a world drama that the Almighty was presenting. Under girding our own love story was the cosmic love story between God and Israel. David somehow represented the heart of Israel, deeply rooted with his culture, land, and his people. I represented Ruth whose heart had been drawn to the God of Israel and was reaching out to Boaz with His love. In some small way we reflected the Spirit of God wooing the spirit of Israel, and Israel's God wooing the Gentile church with her Jewish heritage, as a prophetic element in our relationship. We both felt God loving Israel, longing for complete union with His covenant people, seeking her total surrender and commitment to Himself.

Many of Israel's prophets had spoken of Israel's infidelity to her husband, the Lord. She courted the idols of other nations and chose Deceit as her spouse, instead of God's love, the pure love of her husband. The Almighty is described as a very jealous lover who could not tolerate her harlotry and unfaithfulness with her other lovers. In His fury, God sold her back into the slavery of her exile. The prophet Hosea most graphically depicts this relationship of God as the jealous husband, and Israel as the unfaithful wife. He also promises the day of her restoration.

> 'I will punish her for the days she burned incense to the Baals. She decked herself with rings and jewelry and went after her lovers, but me she forgot,' declares the Lord. 'Therefore, I am now going to allure her; I will lead her into the desert and speak tenderly to her. There I will give her back her vineyards, and will make the Valley of Troubles a Door of Hope. Then, she will sing as in the days of her youth, as in the day she came up out of Egypt. In that day,' declares the Lord, 'you will call me *my husband*; you will no longer call me my master.' (Hosea 2:13-16)

The day would come when Israel would long for intimacy with the Lord, her husband. How tenderly and passionately God desired to show His love to His beloved Israel. Yet, He had to discipline her by scattering her among the nations, exposing her shame, only in order to bring her into purity and fidelity with Himself. The nations raped, plundered and attempted to destroy her. The prophet Zechariah proclaimed that God never intended all the abuse the nations poured upon Israel. He promised to bring her to Himself once again and judge her enemies.

The prophet Hosea foretells one of the most beautiful promises of Israel's restoration to her God in the *Tanach*.

> I will betroth you to me forever; I will betroth you in righteousness and justice, and love and compassion. I will betroth you in faithfulness and you will acknowledge the LORD. (Hosea 2:19-20)

When David departed from his visit that day, both of our hearts were filled with hope for the future. I trusted that God was going to do something special at the Rabbinate. David's heart was sincerely searching to know His God in a much deeper way than ever before.

On the afternoon of the final settlement in the Rabbinical Court, I sat upon "pins and needles" of expectation. I glued myself next to the phone, because dear Frau Herz, who only spoke German and was partially deaf, had difficulty hearing and communicating with the callers. When she received any call in Hebrew, it stirred up frustration and anxiety in her. I had been praying for David the entire time he was scheduled for his hearing. Now I was awaiting the outcome any minute. One hour extended into two before the telephone rang.

I grabbed the receiver, only to discover to my disappointment that Frau Herz's son was calling. From my balcony I watched the twilight merge into the Mediterranean Sea, where evening shadows danced along swelling waves. At 8 p.m. I tried to reach him, but there was no answer. An eerie feeling of apprehension crept over me. Something must have gone wrong.

That night became the blackest I had known for some time. I was stiff with fear of the unknown. I lay in sleepless stupor. The beauty of a spiritual oneness we had felt after a time of sharing our lives so deeply with one another had been suddenly cut off.

The following morning I picked up the telephone to call as soon as I felt the time was reasonable. After numerous rings, a garbled sleepy voice on the other end answered. "Oh, it's you, Yael...Can you please call back later? I haven't had much sleep..."

"Why, yes...all right....later..." His words stung with a deep feeling of rejection. After an inner battle between anger and self pity, reason began to return to my thoughts. I realized that I was so busy thinking about myself that I could not hear how dejected he really was. The more I thought the more I realized that he sounded very discouraged. He probably had suffered a setback. "*Now it's my time to rise up again on his behalf.*

That same day the headlines of 'The Jerusalem Post' announced that war had been postponed. Israel's destiny and mine always seemed to run concurrently. I was deeply disappointed but not surprised when David called and told me his hearing for the settlement had been postponed until the end of May. David called in the afternoon to inform me of the details of the fiasco that had taken place at the Rabbinate. His "ex" had performed a star production with histrionics to perfection. According to him, the performance was filled with scandalous outrage, vicious accusation, lies and gross distortions! He had no desire to talk about it, and he had already admonished me against probing into any area he was not willing to discuss. If I touched upon a taboo subject he snapped his clam-like shell shut with an intensity that no amount of prying would budge. It appeared that the more David was emerging into the light of truth about himself and God, the more the forces of Satan's fury were unleashed upon him through his ex-wife.

David said it would be some time before he could see me.

In the midst of my deep disappointment, my old buddy, Barry, phoned from Bat Yam. He had experienced his own brand of thunderstorms of late. His third marriage had just exploded and sent Harriet skyrocketing back to the States in formal separation! If anyone was my Jewish big brother in Israel, it was Barry. I beckoned him over as soon as possible. He was driving nearby and agreed to stop by.

I felt very safe to unload my baggage upon Barry. I dumped his ears with piles of discouragement, so much so, that I felt I must have erased all the months of inspiration I had poured into his life in the past. "No," he reassured me, "there is a time for everyone to be weak, so that others might help." He said. His sweet Jewish wisdom was humbling but true.

In a most fatherly way Barry listened patiently to my fractured heart. He then made a sage-like suggestion. "Now, if I myself were really a *believer* …" he began, "I'd tell you that all of this is happening for a purpose. The light will come to you at the end of the tunnel…. I'm sure that's not too far away!" He sighed deeply and shifted in his chair. "You swim, don't you?" I nodded affirmatively, signaling him to continue. His words were feeding life into my spirit.

"Well….what you're going through now is like diving down into the depths of a pool. It feels as if you're never going to get air, and suddenly you break the surface of the water! Ahhhhh! There is that air! You can breathe again!

"Oh thank you, Barry. I know you are right. I've been knocked down and I am having difficulty getting up."

"Well….you know what I think….I believe that we are sometimes harder on ourselves than God is on us!"

"Yes, that's what David says to me, too." I answered.

"By the way," his tone and countenance took a new direction. "I've been meaning to talk to you. You know that Harriet and I have broken up ….She's back in the States…I really believe that she is not the right woman for me in the first place….It's really you that I have always loved! I believe that I am supposed to marry you!"

Shock jolted my system! The declaration fell like a concrete block on my chest. I waited until I could regain my composure. I ran a quick analysis of what could possibly be occurring in my friend Barry's heart. I had never viewed him in any other way than a father or big brother figure. Barry is desperately in search of *God's love*, I decided. This is the spark that attracted him to me.

"Barry, I am absolutely certain that I love David. I firmly believe that he is God's man for my life! There is no question about it….but I am deeply touched that you care….I believe that this is God's love that draws you to me. I know that I am not the one for you."

"Are you absolutely *sure?"* He asked emphatically.

"Yes, very much so," I replied.

"Well, if you know for certain....that's the main thing.....I just want your happiness! If David is who you really want, then that is what I desire for you!"

The realization that his feelings for me were totally unselfish gave me enormous gratitude. I felt safe and protected as his friend. "Oh, Barry, I am so moved by the selflessness of the love you have expressed. I know it comes from God. I simply must ask Him to bless you. Do you mind if I pray aloud?"

"No, of course, not!"

Many times Barry, Harriet and I had weathered emotional storms looking for God's help together. Barry felt lonely now that she was gone. I thanked God for Barry's unselfish heart and asked him to bless Barry and give him the guidance he needed. I also pleaded for David in his current dilemma. I begged God for my strength to carry on. There was a pause when I finished.

At once Barry spoke *"P.S. God, if Yael is not the woman for my life, please give her the happiness she so desires, and please bring Harriet back to me! I'm sorry for the way I have treated her, and I'll do better if you send her back."*

I chuckled as I realized that this request was what he really wanted, but he had reached out to a warm, loving female to relate to him in Harriet's absence! I sprang up from the armchair, and bounced off toward the kitchen to bring out some coffee and cookies.

When I returned, Barry was glowing. "You'll never believe what just happened to me!" he exclaimed.

"What?" I inquired.

"While you were in the kitchen, I burst out with the *Shema Yisrael* in Hebrew. I have not prayed that Jewish prayer since my Bar Mitzvah as a boy!"

I looked at the man in his mid-fifties with his shining silver hair. *"God's Spirit has just touched you,"* I declared! "God is *Love!* Your love for me is God's kind of love. It is unselfish. You sacrificed yourself for me. God has shown you He is pleased. Harriet will return!"

Both of us became high on the joy of the occasion. We rehashed old times, especially the time I made a surprise visit to him and

Harriet and ended up having to help get him out of an Israeli jail! It remained a blow to his dignity, which he was not yet fully able to laugh about. He was not the criminal type. After he had first arrived in Israel alone, a merry old widow had enticed him into her spare room for rent with the plot to snag a nice American Jew for matrimony. He sneaked out of her cozy trap, but somehow forgot to pay the fat phone bill. I had already discovered in the Promised Land that "all is fair in love and war!"

In a vindictive rage, the elderly lady reported "fraud" to her friend, the local police Chief. Without any further ado, because the policeman did not speak English and Barry could not access his Bar Mitzvah Hebrew, poor Barry was hauled off to the local jail. I had to go to the jailhouse and bargain with the Israelis in my limited Hebrew to secure his release!

"Listen," Barry interjected, "if you intend to continue with David, I must *warn* you." I shifted nervously in my chair. A somber tone resonated in his voice. "I've been through two divorces already. Both divorces were by mutual agreement, mind you, but divorces can become a *very dirty thing!"*

In each case, even though my wife stated that she wanted the divorce, too, I was rooked!" His eyelids narrowed in pain. "I did not begin dating my second wife until after separation from the first. Nevertheless, the first had a detective follow me, create stories and all that jazz that they fling at you, while I was dating the second. They tried to use this against me as evidence. Both wives subpoenaed the woman I was dating to court!"

I took a deep breath. I was compelled to listen and heed every word that crossed his lips. He continued. "The second was even worse. She was a sneak. She ripped off all my possessions and money and sent a detective after me to boot!"

"Was there infidelity on your part?" I questioned carefully.

"Absolutely not!" He denied emphatically. "I did not even look at another woman until after separation.

My heart began to pound. I felt that God was speaking to me through Barry. I must listen.

"Now, you must know that David's ex-wife sounds like the kind of woman that just might pull off some of the same tricks!" Barry warned.

"Oh, there is absolutely no question about it," I moaned in recognition. "Her behavior has been especially vicious and bizarre with him lately." I had already diagnosed her as "bipolar".

"So," he added, "please be careful. I'd hate to see you hurt in all this mudslinging."

"Do you think I should stop seeing him until all the particulars are arranged at the rabbinate?" I inquired.

"That's up to you. It would be safer for you to wait. However, if you decide to see him, then you must be very much on your guard!" He advised me.

"*"Oi weh!"* That was all I needed for fear to take over. My hyper imaginative powers were already busy conjuring up images of being accused as the "other woman"! I could see the slander of the local press with the help of my religious enemies, "American *'missionary'* Entices Poor Israeli and Wrecks Nice Jewish Home!" Back in the States it might read, "Israeli Jew Seduces Naïve American Christian Girl". Either way you read, from the "Jewish" or "Christian" side, I really preferred to run from any scandal. I could see David's kids hurt and awarded to the full custody of a deceitful sick mother!

Barry left on a happy cloud and I sorted out bits and pieces of our conversation. I determined I would choose "to march into hell for a heavenly cause." I loved David enough to bear all the reproach of Israel on his behalf! But what about those darling innocent daughters? God's love would not allow me to let them down. I decided to retreat. I resolved to discontinue my relationship with David until all the connections with the courts were completed.

TILL DEATH DO US PART

"Where you die, I will die, and there I will be buried. May the Lord deal with me, be it ever so severely, if anything but death separates you and me."
(Ruth 1:17)

Black, sinister clouds were rapidly gathering on the horizon to release their stormy wrath on the joy of two lives that merely longed for the freedom to love, and perhaps even become a bridge between their peoples. One after another they rolled in, each one dumping a strong and stunning blow. Each onslaught momentarily paralyzed me, and would have pulverized me had not the hand of God sent one angel after another to my rescue.

Efes was no longer at my side to whimper her warnings of discernment to me, but I was granted the privilege to visit her daily at her new home. Her new quarters had come via the miraculous once again. I had cried out for help from the Lord for a living arrangement for my best furry friend, and another apartment down the street from me opened up while I was praying the prayer itself!

Efes's new companion was an elderly, bearded man I had discovered one Sunday, oddly enough in the same church where I had met Frau Herz's son. He appeared as much out of place there as Golda Meir at a PLO meeting. Nevertheless, the theme of the hour for me had been "mercy." Daily I was learning just to what depths God's mercy would plummet to love, rescue, deliver, heal and save. Consequently, I maintained an open mind and heart when I met the questionable character who some might label a "street *mensch*". I quickly concluded that he needed Efes's love more than she needed his, and she was quite spontaneous in lavishing it upon him. He entrusted me with a key to his shabby little apartment. He had been a widower for many years. I was permitted to slip in when he was away and take Efes for our daily walks on the Tel Aviv beach.

Meanwhile, Naomi had heard a warning "siren" go off in her spirit. It must have been God's Spirit who impressed my dear Jewish mother that my life was in danger. Unbeknown to me, Naomi had sensed a great urgency to take it upon herself to visit David and request his copy of my book, which detailed my Communist imprisonment. She ascertained the necessity of removing it from his apartment. All of this happened at the same time I was desperately attempting to reach Naomi in order to tell her to remove my book from his house. The Lord's angels were several steps ahead of us!

Immediately after this disclosure, I received an unexpected visit from one of my Christian pastor friends in the city. I had been avoiding him intentionally because I was certain that Lana had been pouring poison into his ears, too! How could I ever explain to anyone else all of the events that were occurring in my life at this time? How would they understand when I did not? Every attempt at confiding in someone had boomeranged on me. Therefore, I remained tightly entwined in my three strand cord with Naomi, and David, and sealed my lips. Every time I opened them it was an invitation for an attack.

I sat under the swishing green trees in the park behind my apartment house. John, the friendly pastor who came to visit me, was of Jewish heritage and he had come to talk to me because in prayer, God's Spirit had alerted him to *danger* in my life. I sighed with relief when I saw that there were no venomous accusations, only loving concern for my present welfare.

I trusted this man, because I knew that he had been a prodigal before he had found his relationship with God. He was a genuine believer. He would be the last person to hurl stones or dictate doctrine to another. I unfolded my love story between David and myself to his listening heart. I wanted any godly counsel he had to offer. When I ceased the narrative, he replied. "Let's pray about all this."

When John slowly lifted his head, he spoke. "I cannot tell you what the will of God for your life is, because I don't know. However, I sense that there is great danger around you. I also know that you must remain true to God's Word in order to guarantee your protection. Otherwise, you will thrust yourself out from the umbrella of His grace."

I heeded his words with gratitude. Back inside my hiding place from the vicious world outside, I breathed deeply in thanksgiving. I read Psalm 91: ..."*He rescues you from every trap...for He orders his angels to protect you wherever you go... They will steady you with their hands to keep you from stumbling against the rocks on the trail...*" How faithful is the God of Israel and how great His mercy to me!

As I observed the tender care and protection of my Heavenly Father, I also began to see Him as the greatest Lover in the world. Very few persons dared to come close enough to Him to discover His Romance with His creation. I could visualize the delight that filled His infinite heart, as he pulled out Adam's rib and shaped a beautiful woman for him. A man and a woman was His idea in the first place. He was the One who stated "It is not good that man should be alone." How I delighted in His love, when He had shown me He was willing to dispatch his angels on my behalf—even though I fell far short of His holy character. Try as they might, not even the mightiest army of hell could keep David and me apart!

A couple of days following the postponement at the rabbinate I ran into David, of all places, at the Sunday service of the church I often frequented. He was there with his younger daughter whom he was keeping at the time, and had not told me he was coming. There was a new and beautiful light in his eyes which had been birthed through suffering. It was no longer the "wild, wounded" look but a peaceful presence of endurance and hope in suffering. We had no time to visit there, but he telephoned later.

When David called he shared that his present circumstances were worse than ever, and it would be impossible to meet me before the next upcoming concert. Would I be able to see him then? Of course! I cautioned him, though, that because of the incredible "darkness" spewing from his ex-wife, I felt it was especially dangerous to be seen with him in public. Great apprehension seized me as I even discussed the matter over the telephone. What if she had his telephone bugged? Such a move would fall in line with her latest actions. To make our "cloak and dagger drama" complete, I felt I should throw all enemies off guard. David had told me that Shula was well aware of his feelings for me and had begun to launch an all out maligning campaign against me. Therefore, to disguise any romantic intentions that were exchanged between us, I decided to invite a new friend, Bronson, to escort me to the concert. Bronson and I made a beautiful couple. He had a long gangly Anglo Saxon frame with sandy brown hair. He also had a lovely wife back in New Zealand, who had just given birth before Bronson had come to Israel on a business trip. Bronson was a genuine believer and loved his wife very much. We had become mutual friends as we shared our spiritual stories with each other. It was pure brother and sister fellowship in the Lord.

Bronson had been learning the price of putting God first in his life when he had to leave his wife and newly born son and come to Israel. There was nothing deceitful about Bronson, just the gentle compassionate heart of his best friend, Yeshua. Bronson made his stage entry into my life at the moment I most needed a big brother. No one around me knew Bronson, so he provided a perfect shield from any wagging tongues that might arise. Even without all the warnings, I felt the need to back away from public exposure with David until the time was right. No one in the world could be more perceptive than the Jewish people, and I felt that so much love flowed between David and me that a person would have to be blind and dull not to detect it. In the same manner that our eyes were the window to our soul, I felt that my open heart was transparent to any observer.

Back in Jerusalem on the night of the concert I stationed myself as close to the front as possible. David was performing on the piano, and I wanted to be as near to him as I could. I felt he needed my support and encouragement. With every iota of power within my soul I projected the most loving stare I knew that said "David, I love you!" He blinked with a knowing nod in return, and I discovered new excitement in our romantic intrigue. I sat at such an angle that no one else could see my face. There in the magnificent splendor of the courtyard of a grand plaza of antiquity in the Golden City, God was writing his own love story hidden from the fiery darts of misguided religious "Christians" and "Jews" alike. The true believers would have loved it! It was the way of the Spirit of God, and it all about *His mercy!*

After the program a coterie of concert lovers gathered at the back of the building to chat or have refreshments in the lounge. My heart was fluttering with the prospect of stealing a few moments in a corner with David. The little coffee klatch had just assembled with Clara at the serving table when the door swung open. My heart sank. There was Shula! There was a real head on collision!

David swallowed hard, never showing a single wrinkle of disapproval on his face. He graciously assisted his ex-wife who was still his actual partner in the eyes of the unknowing beholders. He had strictly kept his personal affairs private. There had been outer rumblings of marital discord through the eaves of the church community, but no one knew the particulars. Everyone was certain that the "playboy of the Middle East" was at fault. I choked down the last sips of my coffee with my most feminine submission and examined my watch, which told me it was past time to leave. Shula and I exchanged sugar smiles with each other, as I questioned in fleeting how she was getting along. No ripple of evidence manifested itself in her face. I surmised what I had been learning all along, that she was a "master of deceit".

As I walked away I felt great heaviness. Our little plot had been foiled. I had learned by this time, though, that I was not standing between a husband and wife, but Satan and God! This was great reassurance spiritually but little consolation to my heart. I longed to be with David.

As I drove back along the Mediterranean, I wondered just when I might see David again, although my better judgment militated against seeing him at all. There was too much danger. This woman was out to destroy us both. Finally, back in my little refuge with Frau Herz and emotionally exhausted, I arranged my bed for a long night of agony and turmoil.

The following day I had to return to Jerusalem to take care of some matters at the church where David had performed. While I was there the telephone rang and Clara informed me that the call was for me. "For me?" I asked Clara with raised eyebrows. "Who could possibly be calling me here?"

"It's David" she said. He said he needed to speak to you about something." She raised her brows. Stark terror and joyous jubilation mingled in my emotions. I took the receiver nonchalantly.

"Yael! I'm so sorry about last night....she never goes to any of my concerts. She only came to try and stop my happiness. I love you! I want you to know that!"

I could only mumble "uh huh" in the most casual tone possible. Clara was in hearing range, and it was no secret that all of the church phones in Israel were bugged. In fact, I picked up interference on the line while we were talking.

"I'll see you when I can."

"O.K." I hung up the receiver. Peace and fear were at war within me. Clara's reaction. Was it the religious underground that did the bugging or Israel security? I felt safe with the Israeli security and hoped that they were the ones. Had David lost his cool? Calling me like that right in the middle of complete exposure? Yes, I guessed he had, and I had, too. We were no longer sober adults, but passionate adolescents—just like Romeo and Juliet, inflamed with their first love. I was convinced that as an outsider to his culture, I could see many dangers he was not aware of.

By this time, I knew that I was not paranoid, but I sensed that phoning on my house phone was also dangerous. I thought I had detected some device on his end of the telephone. Now the way appeared blocked to see him at the concert. One alternative remained. He knew my address, and I left him free to drop by when he could. There was always a "chaperone" with me as well for any "enemies" to walk through before they got to me. Although I sometimes struggled with the rigid stubbornness of my ninety year old grandmother, I soon began to love and appreciate her attributes. She was my mother protector.

The fact that Frau Herz was hard of hearing left me free to entertain an infrequent guest in my room without disturbing her peace. The long narrow hallway from the front door to my room also provided a private passage for any visitor to bypass the rest of the apartment. However, she respected my privacy and wanted me to have guests.

The eve of the next concert I deliberately decided not to make an appearance, just to outfox the sly Shula. Just in case she was going to make a grand entry again I would provide no evidence to warrant any more warfare. In my cozy room, I was just arranging all the evening accoutrements, preparing for a long night's journey into day, when a loud "bang" occurred. The hair on my arms stood on end, and I stood motionless in suspense. Then, ever so faintly from the outside, a voice pierced the night. "Yael! Yael"

I rushed to the balcony, flung open the long glass doors, and there stood my beloved below! "Shhhhhhh!" I whispered, as David yelled up to the second story balcony. "Oh Romeo, Romeo, Wherefore art thou?" I was giggling inside. There was no trellis to climb, so I told him I would come down and meet him outside! I rushed down before anyone could see him.

"We *are* just like Romeo and Juliet," he remarked with a broad smile, "with balcony and all!"

"With them it was fiction, with us it is fact!" I was still giggling as quietly as I could. "Oh David, if our own personal drama were not such a life and death struggle, we could have had a good laugh together! Instead, we fell into each others arms at the entrance arch.

"David, it's been so long since we could really be together!" As soon as we showered each others face with kisses, we strolled down the beach in the dark. Gentle waves stroked the shoreline with tender throbbing pulsation. Then, we stopped at my very favorite bench overlook, tucked away in a colorful patch of green vegetation and wild flowers. We watched the warm waters of the Mediterranean dancing in the night from our own hidden hill.

I snuggled tightly into David's side. A burst of stars was proudly displayed against the pitch sky. As we breathed in the beauty of the night together, he confided distant intimacies to me. I learned that the only American girl friend he had ever had was from Tennessee—my home state! David said words that endeared him to me forever. "Oh how I wish I had met you when I was fifteen!"

"Why fifteen?" I wondered.

"If I were young and pure and had not married, I would have done to you exactly what my father did to my mother?"

"What was that?" He was teasing my curiosity.

"Oh, my mother had many admirers....they all talked a lot.... but my father acted! He merely went to her house; firmly told her to pack her bags; he was taking her with him!"

"Nothing would have thrilled me any more than that!" I announced. "But, David....it's not too late to start a second time!"

"I don't know," he sighed. A shadow crossed his eyes. I was stirred by his hopelessness. The war had intensified with Shula. "You don't know her," he sighed again. "She would pursue me all the way across this country and even the world to attempt to destroy me!"

I pulled his head down and brushed his eyelids with my lips. "Oh David, if Adam and Eve had never fallen from the garden, they would have remained children and naïve. The garden was beautiful but they did not know what they really possessed until they lost it. It's after you have known failure and loss, heartache and separation from God that discovering His love and redemption means so much more. It is richer, deeper, and fuller the second time around—after we have walked away and come back! It's the prodigal who can love deeply, because "*to whom much is forgiven, there is much love*."

David cast his eyes downward in discouragement. He related the evil events that his ex-wife had schemed against him. One of the neighbors who was making one of the regular security rounds in the building had definitely found a "bugging device" in the main telephone box. It was attached to David's telephone line! The news struck terror in my heart! My instinct was right. He did not realize the consequences her lies could have on child custody.

David continued to narrate a long string of malicious acts that Shula had instigated. She had telephoned many of the locations where he was to perform, announcing to them that he was a rotten musician and recommended his competition to them. She was continually using the children as pawns in a big chess game, to hurt him when she could, or block his plans when she felt like it. She was busy teaching the older daughter how to connive and lie and cheat and erecting a wall between her and her father. Many times she had barged into the apartment and stolen his things. She had used and aggravated his friends and slandered him to his competitors. He shared that some of the things were so bad that he had rather not even talk about them. I knew he was not maligning his ex-wife but had to share his pain and struggle with someone. I felt strong indignation as David reported his story to my ears. His marriage had been built on the wrong foundation in the first place. He confided that he had married with her pushing him hard, so that she would not have to serve in the Israeli army. She was attractive and had a nice body, so why not? But, oh, how his values had changed in the meantime, and, along with them, his understanding of marriage!

"You know, there is a hidden blessing in all of this," I uttered. "God is using all of this to prepare you for some task! Now, He is bringing you into His light, teaching you to take a stand against evil compromise and deceit. The way Shula is persecuting you reminds me of the story of King Saul and David. God used the tyranny of Saul to prepare David to rule in Israel!"

"The wonderful thing about you, Yael," David interjected, "is that with most women in Israel, you visit with them and they serve food. I visit with you and you serve truth!" His eyes twinkled with love as he said it.

We had hardly any opportunity to have time for food. I felt his heart was hungry for spiritual food—to be fed with truth! All his life he had been surrounded with the beautiful "people pleasers" who continually oiled one another's egos with flattery. I knew that truth is not always pleasing to the ego, but the spirit longs for it. In the depths, David was a man of the spirit! His own spirit had almost been buried by the deceit that had surrounded him, but the suffering was causing him to soar.

We ambled back to my "stone mansion" by the sea. David did not want to let me go back inside. It was long past midnight by this time. We stood in a clinging embrace at the doorstep, fearing that it might be the last time for a while. When I clicked the key in the lock, he nudged me inside. "Please let me kiss you 'good night' before I go. As we embraced it was difficult to pull away, knowing that a "while" of waiting might be a long time. One thing was certain, after every storm, the rainbow was becoming more beautiful.

As I unfolded the couch and prepared it for the night, I thought about just how much I missed my furry little companion. Previously, she had always snuggled up next to me in bed. My furry friend Efes had found her a real sugar daddy in the old man who adopted her. She used all of her irresistible charm to mooch him out of his last bite when he was eating. She was especially skillful in finagling him into buying her chicken. She would dance rapturous circles to obtain a bite. She thoroughly enjoyed being queen of his house and was sometimes arrogant when I visited her. We still took our strolls on the beach all the way out to the craggy rocks where the water crashed into big sprays over us both. For some strange reason while we shared every other pleasure together, Efes did not like the sea. One day out on the rocks together, independent little Efes pulled away from me and walked back to Shlomo's apartment all by herself with her leash trailing along behind her. I suspected that she feared the thundering waves, but she had also taken on an arrogant attitude since she moved in with Shlomo.

Old Shlomo was a character study by himself. Even in his seventies, he had the vitality to chase a skirt. I humorously played his game by holding him at bay. It was all in jest. At the same time, I offered him a motherly touch which his barren life greatly needed. I decorated one of his drab rooms with some of the leftover furniture from the deceased Arab lady's estate. Every stray human species that darkened his door, he proudly introduced to the room. It was there in "my honor", and he boasted to everyone about me. He exercised tyrannical control over his two sons and was possibly the root cause of one of his son's shattered marriage. I was confident I was the only person in the eccentric old man's life who had ever really loved him with God's unconditional love.

I could love Shlomo even though he had become a thorn in almost everyone's life around him. I saw beyond the glaring flaws that reeked from his spiritual pores. Inside, I viewed a lonely old man with a thwarted career and life. Music had been the life of his soul, but the Nazis stole that from him. After fleeing from Germany, he damaged his hands through the manual work of rebuilding his life in Israel and could no longer play the violin. Although he sought new hope in Zion, like many of the early pioneers, he met one tragic misfortune after another. In building the new frontier, he had to take up hammer and gun like all the rest. First, with the loss of a finger, his career as a violinist crumbled. Then, the mental breakdown of his second wife and years of living in the same household with insanity and her subsequent death fueled an irreconcilable bitterness which was buried in his soul. The climax came, when after devoting all his energies to rebuild Zion, he received no support from the nation in his time of need. Pity was a luxury that no one could afford in a Land where everyone was undergoing the same struggle for survival. His Zionist dream finally went up in smoke.

Those who love us the most, we often tend to hurt the most. Shlomo had reached out to some of the Christian community for acceptance and received what he was seeking. It unleashed all the demons of his soul, which made him dump his bitterness on them. I was certain that his experiences under the Nazis did not help. His behavior became so malicious that he forced everyone to back away from him. I became one of the few people who had the power to subdue him, but there were times when I had to retreat from his tirades against God and mankind.

Sometimes, I got boxed in with Shlomo's wrath on one side; Frau Herz's loving control on another; the fear of the tyranny of the religious extremists who had slandered me; and the unpredictable terror of a vindictive and deranged woman. Into the midst of all these *tsuras* the Israeli underworld must have moved into the apartment under my sheltered room.

Before dawn one morning, I awakened to a modern symphony of dissonant crashing, banging, howling and arguing. I heard shattering glass, screams, loud yelling, muffled sounds, and then silence. Cars screeched off. Loud knocking was heard followed by silence. My nerves were shattered.

The following morning the neighbors reported that a card game had resulted in a brawl which smashed out the window. The call girls flew like chickens from a coop with feathers flying everywhere! Oh well, at least we were in for a couple of days of peace until the storm blew over and the proper authorities had been rewarded for closing their eyes.

Every way I turned it seemed that someone or something was trying to get me out of there as fast as possible. I suspected that it was the power of the evil one wearing me down. Little sleep and constant conflict and turmoil began taking a toll on me. I decided to visit a Christian family I thought might be close to David because of their participation in his musical outreach. I trusted the pastor's wife who was always kind, gracious and sensitive to other's needs. I decided to test and see whether it was all right to trust her with my struggle. I told her the general outline of my dilemma without giving any names or locations. When I was sure I discerned a compassionate and nonjudgmental attitude, I continued to share more details.

Spontaneously I decided that this should be a matter for both her and her husband, the church pastor. My better judgment should have had a premonition of danger. This proud pastor was a stereotype of everything I felt was wrong in organized, institutional Christianity. In addition, his background was Germanic. He possessed all the correct theology, carefully compartmentalized in his computer mind, but there was no visible connection with his heart. He appeared able to think logically and theoretically enough, but not to feel. Truly if I had used my sober reason, and not my emotional trust, I never would have spoken openly with the man. As a true romantic, I seldom let reason usurp my heart. I made a tremendous mistake that was harmful to David.

I divulged my deepest spiritual secret with the man who was least qualified to counsel. It released an outburst of rage from him. If for no other reason, his reaction was enough to let me know he was alive inside. When I confided that David and I….."David!" he screamed and almost ejected from the chair. I could see his mental computer ticking away. "This poor, sweet, innocent girl is being seduced by the big, bad Jew!"

I recoiled in horror at what I had done. I immediately saw that this man was no friend of David's, nor even of the Jews! He manifested no evidence of the spiritual fruit of love, mercy, and compassion toward my beloved David. I knew he did not even know him with any depth at all. I secretly suspected him of being anti-Semitic, although he generally displayed an outward tolerance toward the Israelis. He adamantly advised me against such a relationship. I retreated from his office several rungs lower on my emotional ladder than when I had gone in. As soon as I arrived home, the phone was ringing.

"David!"

"Why did you talk to the pastor? He's not to be trusted! He will only create problems for us!" I had never heard David so disturbed.

"I'm so sorry." I replied. "I needed to talk with someone. I did not realize how he is....I'm really, really sorry."

"Well, the damage is done, but he told me not to see you!" David said.

I moaned, incredulous of what I was hearing. I sensed that David was as intimidated by the "religious" Christian legalists as I was by the Jewish ones. I had never realized just how threatening these Christian religionists could be toward Jews!

"You can be sure that I will not say another thing to anyone. Please forgive me." I begged.

"I'll see you when I can. Shalom." I felt terrible that I had upset David so much. I was most angry with myself and my own lack of judgment.

My own fears were magnified. Who could I really count on for protection in this jumbled maze of onslaught from every side? Of course, I trusted David, but we could no longer easily communicate with each other. It was David and Yael against the rest of the world, entwined with dear, defenseless Naomi, who could always be counted on to be loyal and understanding. It felt as if we had to dig a tunnel under the rest of the earth and meet in hiding at its core merely to love each other. We both had to walk outside the camp of our cultures and meet outside the walls in order to be free. But what a price! How could our worlds ever lie down together like the lion and the lamb?

"O God," I cried, "I know you will answer me—show me your strong love in wonderful ways, O savior of all those seeking your help against their foes. Protect me as you would the pupil of your eye; hide me in the shadow of your wings as you hover over me..." King David had written my prayer.

I had stirred up a hornet's nest by telling the pastor. Not only did I have a vision of the Jewish religious hierarchy rising up against me, but now, the Christian religious establishment as well. Many of them did not know God, either. They had religion, a lot of information about God, but they knew little of His Spirit, of His character, of His mercy.

Now I began to question whether the heat was becoming too intense to remain in Israel. A time abroad might grant a cooling period for all involved, where we could quietly build our relationship alone.

After the time when David called me on the church phone, which I knew was bugged, I overheard a story that brought me more apprehension. Clara told me that some strange Israeli had just dropped by the church house and proposed marriage to her, stating he was even willing to divorce his wife in order to marry her. He had never met her before but told her he thought she would make a wonderful wife. Would she be interested?

Dear prim and proper Clara rolled in indignant hilarity. Someone was having a big joke at her expense. She told the guy off without sparing any rhetoric. My analytical mind read between the lines. I was convinced that it was some religious investigator, trying to set a trap after he had overheard my conversation with David. All the Christians and Messianic Jews who had lived in Israel any amount of time learned to live with electronic listening devices on their telephones. Most had been subject to "tests" and "traps" when someone was sent to their doorstep with a request for help to "get out of the country." The favorite argument of the religious subversives was that "big, bad, foreign missionaries come and steal Jews from their country by paying them for conversion and helping them leave." In my entire sojourn in Israel, I had never learned of even a single case where this was true, and I had met people from every background. How amazing that the Jews had their own brand of lies and darkness against the Christians, as did the anti-Semites against the Jews.

The war raging around us served to drive us closer and closer into each other's arms. When we met in my room again for afternoon tea, David was still bemoaning the fact that I had destroyed his relationship with the pastor. I detected that in some way David must have also been looking to him for support. Initially, before David and I met he had sought counsel from this man. The minister was too busy with his own administrative trivia to find time for a human being in need. David also related how the same man had tried to cheat him out of some of the profit after one of the concerts. David had been deeply upset, more over the loss of confidence in the man than in the money he tried to take from him. When he told me about this incident, I knew he wanted to elicit my perception of just where God might be in the matter. Without even thinking, I blurted out to him, O David, *people will always let you down, but God never will!*

This answer had brought him such delight that he had spontaneously picked me up and spun me around on the street. It was as if he had heard this for the first time: God is faithful, even though the rest of the world is not!

When David was a boy of fifteen, he had begun to relate to God in a personal way through prayer. Naomi had told him that this was not in accord with Jewish religious tradition which only prescribed formal written prayers from their liturgical book—leaving no room for spontaneous utterances from the heart. Fifteen was the age that I had also begun to seek for God in my life.

The cultural wall between Jew and Gentile was sometimes an irritant to our harmony with each other though. Occasionally David insisted I was trying to make him see things "my way". There were still many riddles about God that were troubling his heart. "I must find my own way in everything," he announced from time to time. I reassured him I had given him freedom to do just that.

"David, did you know that every star has a different glow from its sister stars? Or that each snowflake tumbles from heaven with its own unique geometrical design? Such a Creator can contain both unity and diversity at the same time! He speaks to His creation in many different ways."

Sometimes when he became greatly discouraged, I had to remind him:

> "Oh David Satan does exist! He is the archenemy of God and mankind! He is the spiritual personification of all that is

malevolent. He must be recognized and fought against. His goal is to destroy all that is God's. God is indeed greater, but God has also given us humans a free will to choose. Here on earth we are all in the midst of a life and death struggle!"

YOUR GOD SHALL BE MY GOD

"Boaz replied, "I've been told all about…how you left your father and mother and your homeland and came to live with a people you did not know before. May you be richly rewarded by the Lord, the God of Israel under whose wings you have come to take refuge."
(Ruth 2:11-12)

It must have been on a Tuesday that the idea first struck my mind. It was at a time when Frau Herz lay snoring away at her afternoon nap in the adjoining room. David and I were quietly sharing in my large room. I had snuggled up to his side and he wound his strong arm around my shoulder. We sipped tea and discussed life on the firing line and more pleasant topics such as our affection for each other and the glories of music. Each time we had to be together was treasured, because we shared moments which were difficult to come by. I delighted to discover new nuggets about his life on every occasion.

"David, would you like a son?" I asked.

His eyes twinkled and he squeezed me tighter. "Of course I would."

David was definitely a family man. All my life I had longed to have a happy family where everyone loved God and each other. It had been "an impossible dream" which eluded me. I had prayed much that I might have a godly marriage one day. Of all the places I had been and all the people who had crossed my path, there simply had been no one I felt was "Mr. Right." There were numerous proposals, but not from a man who had a passion for God—not religious ritual! In the meantime, the evil one himself had sent some wrong candidates to divert me.

I had not yet spent forty years in the wilderness, but I had gone my own way on occasion. I was very fearful of marrying any man who was not a genuine believer. At best marriage was the most challenging relationship in anyone's life and I preferred to remain single rather than make a horrible mistake. Life in my own family as I was growing up had been painful and problematic. Both parents struggled with alcohol abuse, and my mother made me her scapegoat for emotional and verbal abuse. Neither of my parents had any religious commitment. I was left to find my own way. I had to come to the end of my own way to discover God's way. He found me before I found Him. As others had prayed for me, it was as if heaven was opened and the presence of Messiah was poured into me with immeasurable love. I was compelled to share this love with others and felt privileged when God directed me to Israel as a social worker. I did not know what a Christian Zionist was at the time, but that is actually what I became, as well as an intercessor that stands in the place of prayer for others.

I had prayed for God to give me a partner, and I felt that He was in the process. I had no doubt that the Almighty had brought David and myself together but it appeared that there was a mountain to climb before we could achieve our union. Inside I experienced a beautiful spiritual and emotional oneness unlike anything I had ever known. Now David had begun to wrestle with his career.

The tougher the battle became on the outside, the greater the flow of creativity streamed through his music. He was composing, conducting, playing and even writing poetry with a new quality of depth and sensitivity. He was rewarded with increased recognition. There were more programs, appearances, fame and honor before the world. I could sense that David was probably weighing these matters in regard to his relationship with me. There was an undercurrent of a spiritual tug of war going on inside his mind and heart.

David's heart was toward God, but he was not yet "married" to Him in his commitment. For that reason I was wondering if he would be willing to pay the price to be married to me. I had the scandal of severe slander attached to me in the highest religious circle, and that was an important consideration living in such a tiny land as Israel. I did not want to take him away from Israel. I was convinced God wanted him to serve his nation. I wanted to be at his side. "David," I said, "God wants to love Israel through you to help her become *the light she has been called to be for all the nations*!" David found as much excitement in my spiritual overtures as any of our embraces.

"Oh David, God would never give you anything to harm you—He will only give you those things that will make your life better, which will make you more like Himself! I know He has given you my love, and me, yours. You are the most beautiful gift He has given me next to Himself! We can trust in this love and the One who has given it to us. He is able to work out all the details we cannot yet understand." I could see that he really wanted to believe this but was still wrestling. "Remember, Jacob wrestled with God before he became Israel!" He smiled as he continued to contemplate. He said nothing.

I was confident that God wanted to bless his career because he was gifted. I shared how Naomi and I had gone to a performance of Handel's Messiah at the Mann auditorium in Tel Aviv, where Zubin Mehta was conducting. We both had prayed that God would pour His Spirit upon this beautiful work while it was being performed. Naomi and I sat in awe as we heard the most beautiful musical portrayal of this piece ever! The girl sitting next to me, a total stranger, cried the entire production. Other wet eyes were all around, and ecstatic "bravos" rang incessantly afterwards. Jews who were obviously religious by their *kipas* were standing clapping and shouting. Truly Messiah himself was there by his Spirit. The newspaper reported the next day that it was truly a "spiritual performance". David knew what that was about. He was experiencing it himself more and more with his own music and life. But fear had begun to creep in.

"David, I believe God is showing you not to be afraid about your career. For that reason He is blessing it more and more. I am praying for you many hours daily so that you will be blessed. You must know that *this is not happening by chance, but by the blessing of God*. Nor is it by your mere talent alone! God answers the prayers of His children! I pray because I love Him and have given Him everything. He's my husband, friend, and father. We discuss all of our decisions together! David, God has chosen you!"

"Yes, I know, but don't push me!" David replied. "I must get to know God my way." His words reminded me of Naomi. I had a stack of diaries she had written, where her own mind was arguing with her spirit. Her spirit saw the glory of her Messiah, but her Jewish mind was unable to accommodate him just yet! Finally, though, God's Spirit broke through from her heart to her mind, and she began to live with unceasing joy.

"Oh David," I pleaded, "I do not want you to go *my* way, but *us to go God's way together!* It is a new adventure for both of us! Just imagine, what would happen to the world *if the true Christians became one with the true Jews!* We believe in the same God. Our only real difference is that Christians believe that Messiah has already come, first as a servant to atone for sin, and then he will return to rule as King! Believing Jews who don't yet know Messiah are waiting for Messiah to come—as King. I have heard some say that if the Messiah is Yeshua when he comes, so be it. We will rejoice together!" That wall that divides us from each other has already been torn down through Messiah's death and resurrection. He has revealed the one true God to both Jews and Gentiles and given us an eternal hope.

David always appeared to delight in our spiritual discussions. It was like the sweetness of Baklava, though, one could only eat a bit at a time. He changed the subject. "What did you say about a son?" He squeezed me again tightly.

"I would love for us to have one," I announced. "I would show those extremist rabbis! I'd make a *true Jew* out of him! I would teach him to "love the Lord our God with all his heart and with all his soul and with all his strength!" If they would not let me list him as Jewish, I would list him as an Israeli, a *meschichi!....*"You know the Shushan dictionary of *the Hebrew language gives the definition of meschihi as 'a Jew who believes in Yeshua as the Messiah and is loyal to the State of Israel!'"*

David raised his eyebrows in surprise. He turned to me and scooped me up in his strong arms once again. We became dizzy with longing but we had agreed on "doing things God's way"—that meant any sexual relationship was reserved for marriage!

The following day I drove to the kibbutz to see Naomi. She informed me that she had spent an earnest time in prayer for me in which she had asked God once again about my relationship with David. She felt she had received a definite affirmation of our getting married.

I spent the next afternoon with Frau Herz. Her neighborhood coffee klatch companion had volunteered her input into my drama with David. The elderly lady was a true busybody. Her window overlooked my balcony. Not only was she able to observe the goings and comings of the underworld downstairs, but she had access to the romantic overtures when David and I made contact from the balcony. Most likely, she had heard David calling out "Yael" long before I did.

Frau Herz had informed her that I was not Jewish, and the neighbor took it upon herself to help me out—or "in", depending on which way one was looking at it. Frau Gold directed me to a group that met in the area to help work out any problems with conversion. This bit of news coming at the time it did warranted a serious investigation. As soon as I could I strode off to the hotel at the end of the street where these people met.

I walked into the middle of a "bull session" of a group of religious Jews. I marveled at my *chutzpah* in walking into a potential "enemy camp". They asked me to introduce myself, which I graciously did, almost choking over my name—lest it was lurking on some black list hidden away in some secret file. The newspapers had already published documented information that had been uncovered about the Interior Ministry keeping lists of "forbidden marriages". All sorts of juicy private details of people's lives were stashed away in secret. One Israeli Knesset member was challenging the principle of such behavior. When I read the news I felt grateful that God had protected me as much as He had!

I was sure that such a list would contain all marriages forbidden by Jewish law. It was ironic that a Supreme Court Justice of the Jewish State was not even legally able to get married in Israel. His surname denoted priestly origin according to Jewish law, and consequently marriage to a divorcee was illegal. He chose to fly to New York and marry his beloved there. One Jew was not even able to marry another Jew in Israel!

I proceeded to inform the council that I had attempted to undergo a conversion class, but had run into problems. They assured me that they would help me work it all out. "By the way, whose class were you in?"

When I spoke the Chief Rabbi's name their faces fell. That was the person they were working for! Everyone shifted around nervously, mumbling something about looking into it for me. I gave my sweetest smile and headed for the door as fast as I could. That was the final straw. Now I had even delivered my new address to the Chief Rabbi's office, and he probably thought I was going to try to publicly challenge him. I figured that I had been a "thorn in his flesh" just as much as he had in mine! I decided to leave well enough alone.

I had fear bubbles in my stomach when I arrived at the apartment. Would there ever be any let up? When Frau Herz saw how agitated I was, she invited me out to take her shopping.

Of all the terrors in the land of Zion, I believe that the Tel Aviv supermarkets are the worst! Vicious and bold, old and young, fat and skinny, they come whizzing at you from the right. They plow into you from the left. They bump you from the rear. All the aggressive ladies in the city bustling through the crowded aisles at the same time can be most dangerous! I thought we would even see a murder in the produce line one day, as a distraught senior citizen tore into some brave woman who had dared to crash in front of her basket. The former woman ripped away her bananas and cursed her. The latter lady insisted on going first in the line because of a heart condition. A third woman pushed her way forward because her husband was standing out front in a "no parking" zone, and she had to rush out. So goes the supermarket. I always lost my last trace of charity in that violent place and walked out enraged.

As Frau Herz and I were standing in the checkout line, I was about to assert myself, *a la Israeli*, when a demure little lady stole in front of us. "Ah ha! Caught you! No you don't!" I thought. Seething with frustration, I started to say something to the woman, especially to protect Frau Herz, who usually marched ahead of all the others. Frau Herz saw my body language and addressed me, "Why don't you just let this lady go ahead of us."

I cringed with conviction. Frau Herz was acting more like a "Christian" than I was! The gentle little woman in front of us responded with overwhelming gratitude, as if this had been the first act of human kindness in her life. Tears came to her eyes. Then she rolled up her sleeve and showed us the concentration camp number on her arm. It was my turn for the tears. I melted into a pool of sorrow at my arrogance and impatience. I had assimilated much too well in Israel! In fact, I had assimilated so well that suddenly Hebrew no longer became the chore it had been. I no longer forgot to open books from the wrong side. I knew how to defend my place in line better than all the rest. Israel and I had become one!

Later, for some time I had been longing to run into the arms of my Yiddish Mama, and I was awarded the surprise of spending her birthday with her. She had also been fighting bravely on another front, caring for her husband who still remained in a wheelchair after his stroke. Her hopes for his healing, and mine with David's and my relationship, rose and fell like the Mediterranean waves. We both encouraged each other in our mutual dilemmas with the comfort of God's Word. We read together "If we must keep on trusting God for something that hasn't happened yet, it teaches us to wait patiently and confidently....and we know that all that happens to us is working for our good, if we love God and are fitting into His plans....If God is on our side, who can ever be against us?" That was what I kept telling my friends, "One person with God is a majority!"

As I drifted into sleep that night, I prayed a feeble prayer, "Oh dear God, please, please don't let me down at this most difficult moment in my life....and don't let Israel down either....we are together, we are *one...*" The national horizon was equally as bleak as our own personal ones.

"The God of Israel never slumbers....never sleeps....He is your defense at your right hand....He will guard your going out and your coming in from this time forth and forever more....If He did not withhold his son, how much more will he freely give you everything else...." A sweet blanket of peace enveloped me.

As soon as I cleared one hurdle, another appeared in view. It was alarming enough to realize that I had alerted my archenemies to my whereabouts. Added to this, a shady character began to pursue me on Shula's behalf. He was apparently her good friend and neighbor, and one of those people who had dabbled into all sorts of questionable and forbidden practices of witchcraft and the occult. Having seen me in person at one of the concerts, he took it upon himself to "get next to" me. Behind my back it was obvious that he was spying for Shula, as well as filling David's ears with words that frightened him.

The evil man warned Shula that I was a "missionary," which might not have sounded so bad had he meant it in the purest sense of the Hebrew word, *shaliach*. However, he did not use it in that vein, but in the foreboding sense, which for some Jews was as bad as "Nazi". David was man enough to see for himself who I really was, but the cultural cloak that was draped around many Jews in his nation, especially from Eastern Europe, rose up with prejudice, superstition and lies. I was not a "missionary". I was a Christian Zionist, who had been called by God to come and stand with Israel in rebuilding her nation. I did have a mission to fulfill. From time to time David would let me in on some of the fiery darts of slander that were being flung behind my back by these wicked people. But, for the most part, he refused to fill my ears with the garbage.

Threatening phone calls began to come to the house. Fortunately, I never received a one, but dear old Frau Herz, who did not speak a word of Hebrew, always picked up the phone. The most she could make out was my name and some ugly animal sounds. David had reported that similar incidents were happening to him, too.

I had to laugh at Frau Herz's behavior on such occasions. She was a tough little German Jewish lady and intended to take no nonsense from anyone, least of all from such good-for-nothing scoundrels! When she detected such ugliness on the telephone, she shouted in her strongest German "*Fahre zum Teufel!*" Translated it meant "Go to the devil!" in German. Then, she slammed the receiver down. I appreciated the fact that God had planted me in this ninety year old lady's path for my protection!

I had to admire her will power and determination, for she had much to teach me. During one of my more intense periods I had unleashed a mini explosion, precipitated by her meddling—especially after Frau Gold had become involved. Frau Herz stiffened, sat up straight, and announced "I'm too old for this. I refuse to get upset. I will not react!" I needed her ironclad resolve!

Like a destructive cancer, growing wildly in the brain paranoid thinking began to try to seize control of my mind. I expected to be attacked at any moment and was looking for a demon to jump out at me from behind every bush. I felt like it was a matter of time until they destroyed me—whoever they were.

For refuge, I ran to the psalms, where King David had a much longer history than I with treachery and evil. A vast horde of enemies overwhelmed him on the day when he was weakest. "Help Lord, for the godly are no more; the faithful have vanished from among men," he cried, "everyone lies to his neighbor; their flattering lips speak with deception." The utter extremes to which King David swung in his spiritual walk had always bothered me. I had never seen anyone who lived with such intensity. Now, my own life began to be one long parade through similar experiences of those psalms. King David and I became best friends. I knew and felt with King David, the depths and heights of God and the reality of the utter depravity of man!

One postponement followed after another in the settlement for David at the Rabbinate. Half the time Shula failed to show up for the hearing, or when she did, she ridiculously tried to sue David for thousands of Israeli shekels. David's future was deadlocked by her tyranny. Like little foxes, discouragement and even dejection were trying to eat away at the confidence of our relationship. Would it ever work out with so much evil all around?

David and I began to talk about the idea that it might be best for me to go abroad a while and get some rest. I would be removed from all the stress while he was busy fighting the war with a demonic woman and the manipulation of the religious court. At such a time David confided a dream which he had. He had seen us both high in the mountains somewhere together. We were married. There was great bliss and peace around us. God had spoken in the night to encourage us both.

What was the mystery of an attraction so overpowering that it compelled us together despite all the obstacles? What was the secret to the mystique of such an unconquerable love between a Jew and a Christian? I concluded that it must have been that each of us had something the other needed to be complete. Not just David and Yael, but the true Jew and the true Christian. It was the very Spirit of a Jewish Messiah that burned in my heart. The motivation of my life came from God through a Jew, Yeshua. I needed to know, understand, and love His people before I could really know God.

It had come to me as a great revelation to learn that the word, "Messiah" simply meant "anointed one". "Anointed" with what? Why, with the Spirit of God Himself! It was a further insight to discover that "Christ" was the word of Greek origin for "Messiah". So, being a "Christian," literally meant "one who was anointed with the Spirit of Messiah," or "a follower of the Messiah." That was the key to a "Messianic era on earth" which believing Jews and Christians were waiting for. It would be a time when God ruled on the earth through the power of His Spirit! Then, harmony, peace, love, and brotherhood would prevail!

When I reflected on the matter, it struck me as ironic that so many Jews became indignant over the fact that the Gentiles had venerated and followed another Jew! In fact, some of my Jewish friends had humorously questioned me, "How on earth could *one Jew ever believe in another Jew?*" Without the Spirit of God in his heart, I was inclined to agree! Every Jewish person I had met was an individualist.

I needed David's deep loving heart. When children were dying in Viet Nam after the Americans pulled out, David was in tears of genuine compassion. He felt their hurt. He cared. Such a man, if yielded to God, could be used to heal the heartache of a broken and bruised world! I adored his gentleness. He was the only man I ever knew who was never harsh with me or if he had to correct me, I felt no need to defend myself. I only felt overwhelming gratitude and love that he cared enough to let me know something was wrong. In some ways, it seemed to me many Gentile Christians had "head knowledge" of God, while many Jews had "heart knowledge" of Him.

I decided to embark on another spiritual fast for David, so that he might have the power to break the deadlock that was holding him captive in a "kangaroo court." Every time I sacrificed myself for him in that way, he appeared to enter into a new level of spiritual strength. I was hanging on the last shreds of hope for a breakthrough with the complete settlement of the children. I engaged in an intense time of prayer with crying and repentance concerning my own life, and I knew that this would also impact him in some way, for we were truly one. It did. It impacted me even more.

Somehow God allowed me to touch His holiness. When that happened I felt with the Hebrew Prophet Isaiah that all my own righteousness was as filthy rags. All the selfish roots of my motives of heart began to be exposed to me. I identified with the Jewish Pharisee, Saul of Tarsus, who killed Christians in his religious zeal before he had an encounter with Yeshua on the road to Damascus. After this he was renamed Paul, the Apostle, and declared that Yeshua ha Maschiach came into the world to save sinners of whom he was the worst! This revelation was not as if I had even committed all of the worst sins outwardly, although many of them I had. No, it was the deep inward realization that within my humanity were selfish and wrong motives for even the good things I did.

When I saw David in the afternoon during one of our infrequent stolen visits, a new brightness glowed in his eyes. Something dark had disappeared from him. He intimated how he had sometimes felt like an outsider in his own culture, as I had in mine. He shared how he had made his way up in the world and his career alone, not engaging in all the games and compromises that many played. So had I. He laughed as he told me that many Jews wondered whether he was even Jewish.

"I guess I am even more 'Jewish' than you are," I declared. David nodded affirmatively. "God apparently gave me a Jewish soul at birth—wandering, restless, and inquisitive. Then when I touched Zion for the first time, when I set foot on the Israeli ship, *I felt I was really home!* David squeezed my hand and brushed my finger tips with his lips. "Now isn't that strange; I am not aware of any Jewish ancestry in my family tree!" But was I really home? Yes, I was connecting with the Jewish roots of my faith. I began to see that for all of God's people, Zion was also a heavenly place and not on this earth! It would be brought upon the earth when Messiah returned. Just as the *true Jew* was a heart matter with God and not just a mere tradition.

David suddenly changed the subject. "You cannot imagine what happened. I am going to have to write a novel!" he exclaimed. David narrated the details. His ex-wife had run off to Europe with a local Israeli gangster, unbeknown to David. While abroad they both lost their passports. Fortunately, the ambassador of the country where the documents disappeared knew David and mailed them to him. He was aghast. No matter how bad things had been, he had not seen the depth of degradation he had been yoked with in the past!

A couple of days after the first news arrived from abroad, it was only the beginning. Shula and her underworld friend had run up a huge hotel bill of over $1000, and they had mailed it to David to pay! Moreover, Shula had "out-conned" even the con man himself, who came running to David to help him get his money back! If two little children had not been involved, the story would have made a hilarious comedy

The mood of our discourse changed once again. I shared with him my greatest fear. It seemed that the "wrong man" had always crossed my path at the moment I was moving in the greatest spiritual power! David accepted my response as an overture. He wrapped his big furry arm around me and declared "I am the right man but the wrong circumstances!" I buried my head in his chest.

"God specializes in such cases!" I replied. "They are His response to the way of faith. Nothing is impossible for God! David," I pulled back and looked at him squarely, "how much longer can I take all this stress and warfare? How much longer can Israel go on like this? I know how Israel feels....I've been alone in the world, unprotected by people, tempest tossed, hurled from one blow to another....I hate to be a fighter....I'm tired....and yet, to survive....I must keep on!"

With the most gentle, loving determination I had ever seen in David's eyes, he repeated what he had said before, "*I will fight for you!*" Suddenly, I could breathe deeply once again. Our roles were reversed. His spiritual legs were strengthened and he was becoming Israel, the one who prevailed with God!

I recalled a dream that someone had told me in the past. In the imagery there was a Jew, beaten down, badgered and broken. A Christian came along, lifted him up, cleaned his wounds and helped him get back up on his feet again and walk. As he walked, he became stronger and stronger. Suddenly, the Jew then picked the Christian up and began to carry him in his arms and even run the rest of the way! This would be the spiritual direction of the future. The whole world would be shaken when the Jews fully come into their inheritance with God!

Israel would come back to her God as a faithful wife, and really know the Lord as her husband! The Lord would fight for her even if the rest of the world failed her! Israel would run after the Lord, chase him from her heart, and He would express His tender love in restoration. I read David one of my favorite passages of Israel's love story with God...

> But I will court her again, and bring her into the wilderness and speak to her tenderly there. There I will give back her vineyards to her and transform her Valley of Troubles into a Door of Hope. She will respond to me there, singing with joy as in days long ago in her youth, after I had freed her from her captivity in Egypt.
>
> In that coming day, says the Lord, she will call me "my Husband" instead of "my master...O Israel, I will cause you to forget your idols...and I will destroy all weapons and all wars will end....then, you will lie down in peace and safety, unafraid; and I will bind you to me forever with chains of righteousness and justice and love and mercy. I will betroth you to me in faithfulness and love, and you will really know me then as you never have before. (Hosea 2:14-20)

Her prophet Hosea knew the depth of her adultery against God, but he also knew the greater depth of the faithfulness and mercy of her God!

I was looking forward to the day when David would be "carrying me" and we would be running together! The Jews were the ones who gave their lives in martyrdom to bring the Gentiles into their covenant with the God of Israel through Messiah. Now, those Gentiles who had joined them in their covenant could bring God's mercy back to the rest of them. God had made no one of us independent without the other.

O, the depth of the riches of the wisdom and knowledge of God!
How unsearchable his judgments; and his paths beyond tracing out!
Who has known the mind of the Lord? That God should repay him?
For from him and through him and to him are all things.
To him is the glory forever! (Romans 11:33)

The glory of God continued to strike through our lives like lightning in a storm, displaying brilliance and power. Great peals of thunder always followed with fierce winds and raging rains. The Lord was mighty with us, but the enemy continued with greater frequency and consistency.

Ugly words continued to come through the phone lines, although I never once heard them. Frau Herz was always the angry recipient on such occurrences. With her stubborn German Jewish streak she continually refused intimidation even though she did not understand what was happening. She shouted "no" in Hebrew, slamming down the receiver each time it happened. She continued to tell them to "go to hell" in German.

Was it Shula's spy? The religious extremist underground? Or all of these? They were so dark and sinister that it felt like they were great evil principalities I was fighting against. Indeed, they were, but they were using blind, unsuspecting humans to do their evil work. David was growing stronger in his power to stand against them, while my strength was failing through exhaustion.

Each time we saw each other, we feared it might be the last time. We began to discuss my departure from the country, where I might go. To Europe and wait? Or home? What did God want for us?

Even when the final settlement would be granted, there needed to be a time for David's own restoration. Also, there was the question of the children. Initially I had a greater awareness of the emotional damage that was being wrought in their little lives than David did. Of late, he had begun to become more deeply aware of their needs—even to the point of sacrificing times with me which he longed for. As he was able to become more involved in their lives, another issue arose concerning us.

There was no question that I would make an excellent mother for them. Naomi had reassured David of this when he asked her opinion. However, the stigma of the national rejection of the Chief Rabbi that still hung over my head and would probably continue as long as I was in Israel. David had not paid too much attention to that until the more recent time. As long as that stood in the way, another stigma would be added to the children's lives. That was not fair to them.

The alternative was for both of us to live outside Israel. I felt that David belonged to his nation and I did not want to take him away from it. On one occasion the President of his country privately said to him, "I believe you are a prophet!" Certainly, he had such a role. He belonged there in the land with his people. To have to give up his children for me? To have to leave Israel for me? These were all questions that tore at our hearts and had no easy answers, no matter how great our love was for each other.

The only reassurance that there could be found was the words of Yeshua: "No one who has left home or wife or brothers or parents or children for the sake of the kingdom of God will fail to receive many times as much in this age and in the age to come eternal life!"(Luke 18:29-30)

Yes, it was scary to "sell out to God". First, one had to discern the line between one's own selfish desires and responsibility. Would it be selfish for him to leave all for the fulfillment with me? Not if God was asking him to go that way! Or, was God asking him to sacrifice me for his children's sake?

I had my own dilemma to discern at the same time. Was the overpowering fear that followed me like a cloud, something I was called upon to stand against with faith and courage, or was it a warning to get out before some danger destroyed me?

There was a fine line between fear and wisdom in spiritual danger. Only the discernment of God's Spirit could separate the two. I was tossed between the knowledge that with any shred of evidence, our enemies would attempt to make our relationship impossible. Or they would create a scandal that could hurt everyone. Even then, if David needed me, I was willing to suffer whatever shame I might endure for his sake—to love him recklessly, not caring about my name or what others might think. If Messiah laid down his life for me, so must I for him. While our hearts were being probed, I remembered that there were many occasions with God's people that there was a time of "flight" instead of "fight".

If the Lord had not been on our side, I also knew that for David there would be a deep tearing in his heart if his children had to suffer wrong. David was one of the most loving and beautiful fathers I had ever seen. Yet, more and more the reality of human love apart from the Spirit of God was being made evident to me. The dangers were greatest when human love equaled "control" of another's life. There was no unselfishness or humility in this love, because there was no recognition of the will and desire of the other. It was unlike God's love, which was liberating, freeing one to be the true self, not bowing to the wishes and tyranny of others, but choosing to bend to become a bridge. David was already three quarters of the way across the bridge that God wanted for him. What about the rest of the way? The last stretch was the hardest.

IF THE LORD HAD NOT BEEN ON OUR SIDE

"If the Lord had not been on our side when men attacked us, when their anger flared against us, they would have swallowed us alive."
(Psalm 124:1-3)

Swaying greenery outside my back window and a brisk sea breeze from the balcony blended with the exuberance and vitality of Schumann's Third Symphony throughout my room. For a few moments I was transported high above the seething struggle of the spiritual war that surrounded me. The tyranny of evil religious control and intimidation, the terrors of the spy intrigues of a vindictive woman, the barrage of threatening phone calls, and the clandestine operations of the underworld below me were all gone. I sat bathed in absolute peace unlike I had known in an immeasurable time. In such exalted moments, I knew that the time had arrived for me to depart the land of my love.

The very thought of leaving would have produced a terrible tearing of my soul, had I not held firmly to the knowledge and certain hope of reunion with David and also with Israel. Despite the grandiosity of our love and its power to elevate me above all grime and grit of a filthy spiritual world of darkness that assaulted me, I had been losing strength to keep standing. Even the best soldiers suffer from combat fatigue and need to depart the frontlines for a season of recuperation.

I was tired of stolen meetings in the night or afternoon snatches of delicate exchange in the secrecy of a lonely room. I was weary of the constant waiting with magnified emotions, and then continually missing the contact the moment I stepped out for a brief chore. I was exhausted from the intense longing to belong to my beloved freely without any outside interference from real or imagined enemies. I had reached my limitation of endurance. Now, the rest was left in the hands of the Almighty to resolve.

On the last occasion that David and I had discussed what plan was best, we decided that America and my family should be my destination. It would be too difficult to begin again in some European surrounding. Therefore, I chose to turn down the opportunity to work toward a doctorate in Israeli Studies in England, a prospect which thrilled me with possibilities. When David and I discussed my proposed departure, he tenderly declared, *"When the time is right, I'll come and get you!"*

What further confirmation could I need? But the thought of leaving him for an extended period also alarmed me. A multitude of evil surrounded his life still. We had withstood the onslaught together with our faith, love, and prayer. Of course this would continue even in separation, but other things could crowd in to harm. I had no doubt that he would succeed, but at what price?

I was besieged with a string of nightmares or warnings; I was unable to discern which. I saw a hideous, malicious anti-Christian spirit over a part of Israel. In the dream both Lana and Rachel stood by in silence while a Jewish man took advantage of me, just because I was a Christian. I was crushed by their disloyalty and passivity. I stormed out of the scene in anger, proclaiming that there was just as much anti-Christian feeling in the world as anti-Semitic! It never occurred to me that I was experiencing reverse discrimination, the same force that the Jews often experienced outside their land. Both anti-Semitic and anti-Christian forces were hatred against God!

Another night I had a dream about being betrayed. In the dream I was instructed to read Chapter 13 from the book of John. I turned and read the betrayal of Yeshua first by Judas and then the heart-breaking denial by Peter, his friend and companion. The words leapt out at me: "You do not understand now what I am doing, but you will understand later on…."

I began to fear the enemies on every side and began to wonder whether David had the strength to remain faithful in the face of so much evil. I was in such a mood of questioning and crying out for direction when I received a letter from Maureen. She quoted a verse from the book of Acts, "Keep up your courage, for I have faith—complete confidence in God—that it will be exactly as was told me!" It was the very word I needed to hold on to.

Maureen shared that she also needed to return to her native Scotland for a while in order to sort out some things in her own life. She planned on returning to Israel afterwards. Our lives appeared to be on a parallel course. Her words gave me the encouragement I desperately needed and I sought further direction in prayer. I trusted that God would prove faithful in pointing the way. In the meantime, I received an unexpected piece of news.

Lana, who had turned against me in her jealousy, called me. She wanted to see me.

While we sat together and talked, Lana apologized for her ugly behavior toward me. She was jubilant that she had just received an inner "liberation" through a Christian minister from Australia who prayed with her. This gentleman had a ministry of praying for people's deliverance from bondage to evil spirits. Lana claimed that she had just been released from a horde of them! It did not surprise me because before her encounter with Messiah, she had fallen into a lifestyle of orgies, drugs, and other despicable and destructive behavior. Her testimony reflected the events of the Bible. Yeshua stated that he had "come to destroy the works of the devil" and "set captives free." This was taking place in the current time through the power of God's Spirit!

Lana also announced her wedding to a Gentile Christian from America who loved Israel. She shared that everyone she knew, all her Messianic friends, had advised her against the wedding, but she was completely convinced that it was God's will! Lana also had learned to stand alone; it was ironic after she had misjudged my behavior! She apologized profusely for being so legalistic and judgmental with me. I appreciated her apology and forgave her.

I received an invitation to her wedding, along with the surprising news that our little "sister" Rachel had received the visa that I had so ardently fought for by writing letters to the Israeli government on her behalf. Together we had even gone to the foreign ministry. Shortly after her victory, she had turned around and felt a need to go back to her family in America for a season.

I was delighted with her news. I had also advised Rachel that she needed to go back to her family in America for the purpose of healing her relationship with them. I was then met with severe rejection from a very proud and deceived couple who had exercised great evil influence over Rachel's life. When they heard about my counsel, they telegraphed Rachel from America, where they had returned after being "thrown out of Israel" by government authorities. This was a justified expulsion according to my information. They condemned me in no uncertain terms to Rachel. They had also been the instrument of divisiveness between Rachel and her family. Moreover, I sensed that there must have somehow been a connection between Rachel's relationship with them and the fierce slander that had maligned me from the Chief Rabbi's office. I still felt grieved that that the Rabbi would not let me confront my accusers.

Daily I felt the clock ticking down to my departure. One by one all the people and events in my time in Israel were parading before me. A big surprise package arrived at my doorstep one afternoon. After the bell rang, I opened the door and before me stood Harriet and Barry! God had indeed sent her back to him as he prayed!

Barry had done some digging into his own soul. He discovered that he was guilty of treating her wrong in the past. His previous track record with women had left his trust in them at zero on the "Richter Scale." When he got some of the dirty linen out of his own closet, he decided to beg her for forgiveness. Her heart melted into wax and she hopped the next plane to Tel Aviv. I embraced them both at the same time.

My dear "buddy" Bronson came by and gave me a "sisterly" hug before his departure from the land. We both reviewed the brave rescue we had accomplished a couple of weeks before. Bronson had contacted me when he met a young European woman who needed help. I had previously met her as well. She was married to a Moslem and had lived in East Jerusalem for a couple of years. The husband had become violent with his wife, promising to leave her and take his young baby with him. When she met Bronson she asked him whether he knew of any way to help her get the child out of the house before her husband kidnapped him and left. She had arranged a safe place for herself and the child to go but she had no transportation. Bronson immediately thought of me and my car. Bronson and I launched out after dark late one evening and met her on the Mount of Olives at a designated place. We wrapped the baby in a large blanket, hiding him on the floor of the car and drove him to a safe location. Bronson had accomplished the task he set out to do in Israel and then planned to board an airliner to return to his wife and baby in New Zealand. Before he left he had dropped by for tea and the last goodbyes. While we sat sharing our stories of "cloak and dagger" drama which was being enacted in our lives, the doorbell rang. Old Shlomo surprised me with an unexpected visit. I invited him in to have tea with Bronson and myself. Efes was parked on her leash in the alley below. After five minutes of conversation between the three of us, Shlomo turned to Bronson. He asked him if he knew a certain person in New Zealand and named the name. Bronson lit up like a floodlight. "Why that's my best friend" he exclaimed!

"That's my brother," Shlomo declared. We all sat together amazed and speechless. We knew we were in the midst of "Divine Intervention."

The two men began to exchange lively conversation. Bronson learned that Shlomo had been rejected and cut off from his brother years ago. They had been estranged from each other for many years. Bronson gave Shlomo the hope of bringing reconciliation when he returned to his homeland. I had never seen the old man so happy.

I also learned about another wonderful surprise. Shlomo's grandson, whom I had befriended earlier, had received a miracle, too. Maureen and I had visited Shlomo and his grandson just before the young man was to be conscripted into the Israeli military. We had prayed for God's blessing upon his life, as well as protection during his time in the service. The boy was heartbroken because he was a concert pianist in the making; his military duty would postpone his musical career by a couple of years. A few days after we had prayed for him, he raced to his grandfather's apartment with a joyful declaration. "I believe in God now! I believe in God now! I have just received a letter from the army that they are postponing my entry for one year so I can go to a musical academy and get an automatic musical placement in the military!" We all felt that only God could have arranged that. It was generally unheard of for the military to postpone duty from the IDF's own initiative!

Each new event added excitement and joy before my dreaded departure date. A few more loose ends in other relationships needed adjustment before I left the country. One was my dearest friend and confidante, Naomi. I needed her as much as she needed me. I received a joyous invitation that would provide the turning point for us both.

Naomi had wrestled long and hard inside herself unbeknown to me about taking a step to be baptized in her newly found life in Messiah. There were two great stumbling blocks she dealt with. The first was her own brother who lived in Europe. He had been baptized to gain "acceptance in the Gentile business world around him," although he had no faith or relationship with God. Such hypocrisy Naomi abhorred. She would never succumb to such deception. However, in Israel there was no Gentile society to impress. Therefore, other motivation would be the pivot of her decision.

The second obstacle was more deadly. A Jew who was baptized as a "Christian," or actually a "Messianic believer," was labeled as a "traitor" to the Jewish people. Naomi would have died before she would betray her own people! There was not one disloyal bone in her body; she was the most ardent Zionist I had ever met. I had her diaries that she had given to me which proved it. She was unwilling to seek anyone's opinion but God's about this step.

When she prayed she fought a battle in her soul against a *"misguided national spirit"* in her nation, which separated her people from the rest of the world in fear and rejection. It represented the history of the Jews who had lived in the Diaspora. Finally, she felt she had received a revelation from God. The Lord impressed her with what a "true Hebrew" really is. The word "Hebrew" itself comes from a root which means "to cross over". It reflects Israel's history in building her nation when she was called out of Egypt to cross over the Red Sea and eventually enter the Land of Promise. Naomi realized that *water baptism was about "crossing over from her identification with the world's side in order to take her place on God's side"*. For her water baptism was the act of leaving an old life behind and receiving a new one from God's Spirit. The immersion was symbolic of a burial of the old life, and a resurrection into a new one. Naomi marveled when she realized that water baptism had come from the custom in Jewish law of the *Mikveh,* which was the Jewish ritual cleansing by immersion in water. She and many other Jews had been wrongly taught that it was a Gentile practice and betrayal of their Jewish identity. However, Naomi felt that God had shown her just the opposite—*-it was the entrance into her new identity in Messiah!*

When Lana had been baptized, she came up from the water speaking in an unknown language. Rachel had come up out of the water speaking "Arabic"! There were Arab Christians there at the time to hear it! (Rachel had never learned a word of Arabic!)

Most Christians have no idea that water baptism is a Jewish ceremony; Christians have inherited it from the practice of *Mikveh* laws of Jewish ritual religious cleansing. When Naomi discovered that baptism really originated from her own people, she delighted in taking the bold step that most of her people could misunderstand. I rejoiced in her courage.

Whenever anyone asked Naomi whether she was a Christian, she always said, "No, I am a Jew." She would call herself a "*meschichi*", "a Jew who believed in Yeshua as the Messiah and was loyal to the state of Israel!"

There was another relationship that needed resolution. Frau Herz was much on my heart. I would never leave the country until I had found a replacement for her companionship. Even though she had a will of granite, she could not fend for herself alone. She refused to burden her children. I wondered where in all of Israel I could find anyone who would work for a mere pittance of pocket money and spoke fluent German at the same time. A replacement for me was another of those impossibilities that only God could resolve.

Frau Herz and I had grown to love and appreciate one another. When I arrived she behaved like a German genteel lady who had been provided for and protected all her life, still living in the untarnished glory of the era before the Third Reich. I came along and was the "wounded Jew" working for my bread. The dear little lady with her grace and charm always had everything under control, except my nervous system!

Through all the haunting harassment we had undergone together in the apartment, a solid bond of friendship had been welded between us. I had dared to confide some of the ugly incidents that were happening in the backdrop of the drama. She wrinkled her prune face and told me to toughen my skin the way hers was. This little grandmother with her will of iron was willing to suffer with me and that gave me an anchor of hope!

I was very excited when I met an older German Christian lady at the church congregation house one Sunday. She had always loved the Jewish people, and from time to time she took off months from her retired life in Germany to come to Israel in order to serve the Jewish people. The sick, the lonely, and the dying in the Land had felt the nursing arms of this devoted lady holding them many times. When I presented the possibility of replacing me at Frau Herz's house, she was interested, but already involved in the care of a dying man. We put the proposition on the shelf until the time was right. Then, I received the news that the elderly gentleman had passed away and she was willing to take my place.

Another obstacle remained to be surmounted. My bank account had dwindled down to nothing. Where would I ever come up with such a big sum to purchase an airline ticket home? I prayed for this answer.

As I drove the steep spiral between Tel Aviv and Jerusalem, I realized that I had only enough gas for one way. By this time a gallon cost over two dollars. I had to decide whether to turn around and not make the trip at all, or risk it not knowing how I would return. Suddenly, I was reminded of the prophet Elijah. God had fed him by the ravens in a time of his need. God did not let him down and would even use the birds to help His child in need. I decided to make the trip and trust God. Another divine provision awaited me on the other end when someone handed me unexpected money! God did provide! King David had said, *"I've never seen the righteous begging for bread!"*

On such a day I was still pondering the matter of money. When I removed the mail from my box, I found a letter from a widow lady I barely knew in America. She was a lover of Israel, too. She lived on a modest pension, but she explained that God had moved on her heart to send me five dollars. On her check she had recorded two verses of scripture which I looked up.

> The Lord will surely comfort Zion and will look with compassion on all her ruins; he will make her deserts like Eden, her wastelands like the garden of the Lord. Joy and gladness will be found in her, thanksgiving and the sound of singing. Listen to me, my people; hear me, my nation: The law will go out from me; my justice will become a light to the nations. (Isaiah 51: 3-4)The third I will bring into the fire; I will refine them like silver and test them like gold. They will call on my name, and I will answer them; I will say, "They are my people," and they will say, "The Lord is our God." (Zechariah 13:9)

This precious lady's sacrifice reminded me of the story of the "widow's mite" in the New Testament—"this poor widow has put more into the treasury than all the others. They all gave of their wealth; but she, out of her poverty." The widow's check was a proclamation of the Lord's faithfulness and worth more than a thousand dollars! Somehow, my financial need for a ticket would be resolved. In the midst of such an atmosphere of divine intervention, there was another miracle that I greatly needed—David! I had a dream that my beloved was very discouraged and felt that there was no hope for us ever to get together. There were mountains of obstacles blocking our path still. In the dream I informed him that these thoughts came from the enemy and were not from God! Afterwards, I had the occasion to attend a concert. When I saw him perform, the wild, wounded spirit had returned to his eyes! My heart fell, though not so far this time. He would weather the storm again, although I was sure that my leaving was playing a role in the fear and pain he projected. It came at a time when the upheaval around us prevented our meeting. I wrote him a letter of encouragement, telling him that there must be a beautiful spiritual preparation for his life in the suffering he was undergoing. I reminded him of Joseph and the years of imprisonment. I reiterated the persecution of David by King Saul. I told him that each blow of suffering could be received as another stroke of beauty from the Master Sculptor's hand when we entrusted our lives to His care. God would make his faith into "gold" in the end. Above all, I loved him and I told him that I would wait many years for him!

It appeared that after each victory, another attack would follow. The enemy crept in to deal a low blow. Naomi's baptism brought several Christian denominations together in loving fellowship with each other. Immediately after this wonderful spiritual gathering, she discovered that her mail had been opened. Her own letter and the pastor's letter which he had written had been opened. Moreover, Barry found that his mail was also being examined. Then, the worst scenario happened.

One of all our dear Messianic Jewish friends Julia, a young immigrant from America, had a letter she had written to a friend intercepted by her own mother, who opposed her faith in Messiah. The mother marched straight to the military Chief Rabbi's office with the letter, which was a detailed description of the spiritual deliverance from demonic power, which Julia had received in her life at the same time as Lana! The mother was appalled and threw a tirade. The Rabbi enlisted an attorney. These hostile forces were boiling enough to go after the Christians involved in the girl's life in court at this point. So much for religious freedom in a democracy! In the area of religion, Israel was beginning to look like a totalitarian state!

Instead of the courts, the attorney turned the letter over to the press without the eighteen year old girl's permission. The scandalmonger reporter with the help of the attorney twisted the content to say the opposite of what the girl had written. The article stated that Christians were trying to "cast spirits *into* the girl, instead of out of her!" It sounded familiar. The evil religious extremists of Yeshua's day had accused him of "casting out demons in the name of Beelzebub!" It was always like Satan, the "Father of Lies," to twist the truth destructively.

All of this had no effect on my life until Julia decided to visit me on leave from the military! I was certain that my enemies were probably making me look like a guilty party in something I had absolutely no influence. It was guilt by association. No matter what I did to avoid trouble, it crossed oceans, climbed mountains, and tracked deserts to follow me!

I had truly shut myself away in my room, bothering no one, and adversity knocked on the front door. After I had first arrived in Israel, An American pilot friend of mine had decided to visit me on his trip to the Middle East. He planned to spend a couple of days in Israel and then go to Egypt, where his former wife and children were living. He had routinely arrived in Israel with an Egyptian visa in his passport. That was very rare in Israel at that time. After a two day visit and spending some of the time with me, he discovered that his visa had been stolen from his passport. He did not know what to make of it, but to go back to the States via Europe. He later wrote to me that a "charming Israeli man" had sat next to him on the way to Germany. "I told him all about you," he said, "and the man said you were going to have a difficult time in Israel!"

I had done enough time in a communist prison to learn a little about international intrigue. I supposed that my friend had sat with an Israeli agent and his visa had disappeared in order to get some Israeli into Egypt!

On one of the days when I indulged in self pity concerning my lot, I asked God why I must wait so long to come into His place of peace and blessing. The answer that came on such occasions was always the same: "You have need of patience."

More upheaval occurred in the nation. The newspapers told of another young Jew who was being called before the Chief Rabbi simply because he had a "miraculous revelation" of the Messiah. I knew nothing about that case. My eighteen year old friend Julia decided to stop by my place for a visit. Despite the fact that she had become a national scandal, her courage was an inspiration. She sensed my own great struggle and prayed aloud for me. This time it was not me praying for her, but the other way around. Julia knew nothing about David, but as she bowed her head in prayer, she spoke. "You are praying for someone who I sense will become your mate in the future in Israel, but that will happen after a period abroad first." How could she possibly know unless God had showed her?

After Julie left, I was resigned to a long afternoon stretched out on my couch in misery when suddenly my door flew open. David walked in with the brightest light I had ever seen in his eyes. He had gone away for a week to a monastery in the north, where he had fasted, prayed, and written music. He appeared to be more in touch with his own heart than before. He was obviously in touch with God. He told me it had been a very sacred time for him, and he deeply knew that he was supposed to do something for Israel, but he did not yet know exactly what that was!

His music was becoming filled with a more beautiful presence and it was clear that he had divine inspiration in what he was doing—so much so that I got to see him less and less. I was happy for him, but his success was stealing his time away from me. Each brief meeting we had felt like the last. Each time he had to leave, there was a desire for us to cling to each other.

The final settlement with Shula was still deadlocked, just like the current peace negotiations in the Middle East. All the confirmations were lining up for me to depart, step back and trust God to do the rest. My own dreams at night were supporting this conclusion as well. First, I dreamed one night about a girl who was going to America to visit her family and then return to get married. I awakened with joy.

The next night I had glorious dreams of being a mother to David's daughters. In the night I held his younger daughter in my arms, comforting her until she could sleep. In another scene, I was teaching her English and she was helping me with my Hebrew. I was receiving strong reassurances which would make my leaving easier. They could sustain me in time of separation.

The climax of hope in the midst of all the dark days came through an invitation to attend a Messianic conference on the Mount of Olives, in the same location where I had celebrated Passover. It was hosted by a former bodyguard of Ben Gurion, the first Prime Minister of Israel. The host had become a Messianic believer himself.

The convention met in a big outdoor tent overlooking the Golden City in all her glory. The speakers on the same platform included an Orthodox Rabbi from Bene Brak, a Reform Rabbi, a professor of the Hebrew University and scholar of the Bible, a Messianic Jew, a German Christian, and an Arab Christian! Only the Almighty could have brought all of this mélange of incongruent speakers to the same platform at the same time!

Out on the streets, none of the categories these people represented were on secure speaking terms with each other. In more radical cases, such as Arab and Jew, or Orthodox and Messianic, or German and Jew, they represented archenemies to each other. Yet God—- His Spirit could bring men together as brothers under the banner of His love, and true communication could come forth!

The first speaker was an Orthodox Rabbi. Since he represented the element whose extremists had sought my destruction, I paid very close attention to what this man had to say at a gathering of Christians and Jews from many countries. His text was from Ezekiel 37, the story of the prophet and the valley of the dry bones, which represented the House of Israel. He narrated how God had literally brought back to life all those dead bones of rotting skeletons and mangled humanity which had been annihilated during the Holocaust. It was the rebirth of the nation of Israel in 1948! The lame, crippled, wounded, homeless, broken lives were restored to life in the refuge of their ancient homeland. The bones had come together, with flesh and tendon and sinew and skin, but the Prophet said that "*there was no life in them.*"

The elderly rabbi, whose neck was rounded from years of poring over the ancient texts of *Torah and Tanach,* spoke words that brought great inspiration to me. He said that the "*rebirth of the Jewish State is the restoration of life to the dead, dry bones" of his people*. However, he continued, "The Lord told the prophet that although the bones had *life* in them, they had no *breath* in them."

Then the silver bearded rabbi lifted his head and stared heavenward. "I believe," he said, "that Israel has experienced her physical rebirth by being restored as a Jewish State in her homeland....but.... she has not received that *breath* from the Almighty, yet. She has not received her *spiritual rebirth*."

At the moment he spoke the words, great joy burst into my heart. I never expected in my lifetime to hear an Orthodox rabbi speaking of matters of "spiritual rebirth"! Why that was a term that Christians used for their surrender to God and His Messiah! From the class I had on rabbinical Judaism I had been told that spiritual matters were irrelevant and such things as interpreting and obeying the Law central. In Hebrew "breath" and "spirit" were the same word. This Orthodox rabbi was saying that "*Israel had not been born again in her spirit!*" Her nation had been reborn out of the ashes of the Holocaust physically, but her relationship with God needed a "*new heart and a new spirit*" according to the prophets Jeremiah and Ezekiel!

The old man struck me as a true sage. He kept his eyes glued to his papers. He proceeded to quote one of the psalms, "*when the Gentiles (or "nations") see what God has done in His land, they will rejoice and proclaim it!" He continued by saying, "Not even the best Zionists in the Land of Israel realize that God has rebuilt this land. They believe that they did it themselves with their own sweat and blood," the rabbi declared. "But you Christians know and believe that God has done this for Israel! Therefore, you are called to rejoice and to proclaim it!*" Again great joy surged within me at the revelation of this meeting point of Christians and Jews! This Orthodox rabbi was telling a group of Christians that they had a responsibility to "stand in the gap" and proclaim the greatness of the God of Israel until Israel was "*born again in her spirit!*"

Of all the time I had spent in Israel, this old Orthodox sage brought me more hope for his country and people and reconciliation between Christians and Jews than I had heard coming from the religious leaders I had been in contact with. It was becoming more evident that *the spirit of exile and dispersion of the Jews had separated them not only from their Land, but from the true heart of their faith.* The spirit of their faith had been swallowed up in long lists of detailed regulations and exercises, all of which no human could ever keep.

It appeared to me that the religious Jews who had come in from the Diaspora were often more closed to the outside world than those born in the Land. Israel's future hope lay with her native born sons and daughters, if they were given the right leadership. *Sabras* were not defensive about their Jewish identity. *Before a new spirit could be born in their nation, the baggage of their exile and dispersion needed to be discarded.*

I had previously read a collection of Israeli writings called "Unease in Zion," which animated me with more insight into Israel's national dilemma. It recorded some of her thinkers' different critical approaches to Israel's problems. First, there was Pinhas Sadeh, with his realization of the emptiness of Jewish *traditional* religion in contrast to the Jew, Jesus. Then, Yonatan Ratosh, with his "Canaanite Outlook" exposed me to the search for the Hebrew task of embracing others with light and brotherhood. These men were searching for the spirit of true Jewish identity in contrast to the exile mentality of the Diaspora.

Historical Judaism of the Diaspora was a necessary institution to maintain the cohesion of the Jewish nation and people when they were outside of their homeland. Now that the nation had been partially reestablished, in her God-given Land of Israel, the structural purpose and form of her Diaspora traditions had been fulfilled. It was time for her *"new heart and new spirit to be reborn."* However, many of the ultra Orthodox still wore the traditional Jewish garb of medieval Poland, and there was absolutely nothing Hebraic about that! Restored to their land, Israelis needed a new spirit! They needed a living spiritual relationship with God as the source of their power, not just ceremonies and rituals. That appeared to me to be the meaning of the true Jew—*"one who was circumcised in his heart by God, and was filled with and lead by the Spirit of God!*

The prophet, Jeremiah, had announced the way when he called out to the Jews to *"Circumcise yourselves to the LORD, circumcise your hearts, you men of Judah and people of Jerusalem."*(Jeremiah 4:4)

The conference had brought tears to dear old Shlomo, as well as me. I had invited the old man to come along with me. He had joined me out of curiosity. When a German Christian stood up and began to speak, Shlomo broke down and wept. In his mind all Germans were Jew-killers and Nazis. As Shlomo heard with his own ears a German Gentile Christian man announce his avowed love for Israel and the Jewish people, his defenses crumbled and he began sobbing. This same German Christian made another interesting point. He maintained that the consequences of God's promises to Ishmael in the Bible resulted in the *"riches of the oil from below"* to the Arab states. Whereas, the promises of God to Israel brought the "oil from above. This is the Spirit of God!"

I was disappointed with the Reform Rabbi, who said all the "right" things, using the same text as the Orthodox, but it felt as if he spoke from his intellect and not his heart. The last speaker greatly disturbed me. He was an Arab Christian pastor who spewed out fiery political overtones in his presentation. Many in the audience stormed out in anger when he spoke. Probably, their departure was a protest because he used the name of "Palestine," instead of Israel! Beyond the Arab's national and political militancy, I could see wounded pride and deep hurt. His tone marred the beautiful unity we had experienced until he spoke.

After the Arab's presentation, he immediately rushed out of the conference. I jumped up and ran after him. "I just want you to know, dear brother, we love you, too." I was compelled to tell him that even though we disagreed on Arab claims to God's Covenant Land with Israel, he was loved as a person. Arab Christians were hurting deeply. They were rejected by the Arab Moslems whether they were true believers or not. In addition, their lack of acceptance of Israel's right to her land, made them suspect among both Jews and Christians.

I had held my own "mini peace conference" at my breakfast table in Jaffe one morning some months before. An ardent American Messianic Jewish Zionist dropped by to spend the weekend with me. At the same time a lovely Arab Christian I previously had met came by for a visit. She was invited to spend the weekend, too. While we were having coffee and toast together the next morning, both young women received the same revelation at the same time. "Hey, we are sisters! The Jewish Messiah has joined us together! We can both still love and identify with our own people, but we can also love each other." True reconciliation had occurred at my breakfast table, and both of them left with a new revelation of what genuine peace is all about. The crown jewel of the conference came when

I met an Israeli soldier at lunch. I discovered that he was a relative of Naomi's. Moreover, he had met his Messiah in the Six Day War while he was hanging from a tree in a parachute! The beauty of the ways of the God of Israel never ceased to amaze me!

Back on my tiny balcony in Tel Aviv, Frau Herz and I were sipping afternoon tea and watching the swelling tide of the Mediterranean and making small talk. My mind was recording everything. "It is Rosh Hashanah, Jewish New Year 5736. David is somewhere in the Golan Heights on reserve duty. He is scheduled to return and take me with him to Ashkelon for an excursion. His call comes. It is *best not to go*....still too much danger in the air."

My ninety year old Jewish grandmother shifts the topic to marriage and wedding ceremonies. What will the coming year bring? I had just finished my morning reading in the *Tanach:*

"Who can be compared with God enthroned on high? Far below him are the heavens and the earth; he stoops to look, and lifts the poor from the dirt, and the hungry from the garbage dump and sets them among princes! *He makes the barren woman to be a home-maker, and a joyful mother of children."*

"Are you speaking to me, Father?" I wonder. "Is this going to be Your year of mercy for the poor and hungry? The brokenhearted and mourning? O God, it must be!"

Frau Herz smiles her loving approval to me. I notice how I have been planted in the Land. A Jewish mother in Naomi, a father in Barry, multiple sisters in Lana, Rachel, Julie, and a brother in Yossi, a grandmother in Frau Herz, and even a grandfather in old Shlomo. "Lord, when can my husband and I remain together?"

The bright blue Mediterranean sky smiles back in silence. My father has telegraphed the money for my return ticket. I have booked the beginning of October to depart when my visa expires. My mind rolls backwards. My own journey to Zion had first brought me through Spain, where I had a taste of the Sephardic culture. From there, I discovered the Ashkenazi influence through my sojourn in Germany. Finally, I encountered the heart of my faith, when I came to Israel and met my own "King David—a man after God's heart. "Oh God, when will you arise and show your mercy upon Zion?"

IF I FORGET YOU, O JERUSALEM

"If forget you, O Jerusalem may my right hand forget its skill. May my tongue cling to the roof of my mouth, if I do not remember you. If I do not consider Jerusalem my highest joy."(Psalm 137:5-6)

The touchdown of the giant El Al bird in New York was bitter-sweet. Half of my soul had been ripped away from me and was being taunted with uncertainty of its future restoration. It remained behind me, wedded to the land and people of the patriarchs, the Book, and the beautiful man, my beloved David. They had become a deeper part of me than the rolling foothills of East Tennessee, now splashed with brilliant autumn outbursts of color, which I had missed in my far away land of stones, sand and desert. I was looking forward, though, to the quiet refuge and retreat in the friendly community tucked away beside the huge lake and a warm reunion of family ties, which had been unraveled for years. Three years was a long span to be away from parents and country, and the abundance of freedom and material prosperity I had enjoyed in America. I sighed deeply as I set foot on my native soil and welcomed the upcoming months of peace and recuperation.

The flight itself, which had been my first with El Al, was an adventure and study in culture at the same time! I was packed in with the Brooklyn religious neighborhood on its return across half the world back to the little Jerusalem of New York. I had been planted down in a busy beehive of activity from the moment the aircraft closed its door for flight. The bearded black suited men marching up and down the aisles with dangling curls, rocking back and forth, davening all the while, were a mixture of delight and terror. They symbolized everything that wanted to destroy me; yet, it was evident that their rocking prayers were sincere efforts to honor their prescribed ritual—no matter how it affected others.

The departure had been delayed two hours because of maneuvers of the Israeli Air Force. The passengers had squirmed in their seats in a hot airplane munching lox and bagels and reading "The Jerusalem Post". I was daydreaming about a refreshing space which lay just across the Mediterranean and Atlantic when the flight attendant rushed through the plane with controlled panic, holding a briefcase in the air and shouting, "Who does this belong to?"

In Israel no one feared theft of personal articles left standing alone, because they were prime suspects of terrorist bombs. The little town in Tennessee where my folks had resettled after I departed knew nothing of this world of violence and bloodshed. The passengers relaxed when they saw the owner claim ownership of his briefcase. He had been an "uninitiated" American Jewish businessman who had not fully discovered the hazards of life in Israel.

As the big bird soared through the sky, I zipped up my invisible shell around me in order to ward off the outside world and contemplated what lay ahead. I noticed that in my last weeks in Israel, I had felt a growing sense of my loss of need to justify all of Israel's actions, as every ardent lover did in the beginning. I could still love her, perhaps less passionately and more maturely, even though I had been victimized by her faults. I had seen her probably more from her worse side than the wonderful vibrant nation of hope that had emerged out of the ashes. I would remain faithful to her no matter what. It was clearly a choice of my will, not always my emotion when she hurt me so deeply. To continue to love someone who keeps on hurting you and rejecting you could only be divine. I had already given my all to her and would continue to do so as I gained strength and endurance.

My father was visibly relieved to see me alive and well at the Knoxville airport. He knew my departure was wrought with urgency, which I had been unable to elaborate through the telephone wires, and certainly not in writing. The haggard lines of his face revealed a weariness which was the result of long stress from my mother's illness. My first steps inside the front door provided a rude awakening, though, as I learned that my mother had taken sleeping medication and gone to bed before my midnight arrival. I knew that she had not been well for some time, but I could not help but read the message with grave concern.

Despite drugs, my mother got out of bed and greeted me with limp acceptance. My heart was crushed to note that my real mother was not even there and I was embracing a shell. Long ago, she had give up the fight and fallen into the quicksand of addiction to alcohol, pills and passivity. She first seemed beyond reach, but a ray of hope glimmered through her eyes as she tightened her hold on me. Instantly, I saw that I was her spiritual lifeline. I was the connection to the spiritual strength that she needed to survive.

From the Jews I had already learned one of the most important lessons in my life—*the responsibility to my own family!* I greatly admired the depth and devotion of Jewish family bonds, but also understood that carried too far, they were equally a source of destruction. The kibbutzniks had found that by taking children away from smothering parents and housing them in another area, they could expand family ties to include all of society. Even though this had produced the most socially responsible citizens in Israel, it was not without its emotional scars.

My own mobile jet age American upbringing had allowed our family to be scattered to the four winds with independent lives flying in different directions; now was the time to shift gears into reverse. I, who had been willing to "lay down my life" for Israel, was now being challenged to "lay down my life" for my own flesh and blood. As I understood Jesus' command for his disciples to lay down their lives for one another, it was evident that he did not mean going to the firing squad on one another's behalf. That was much easier to do than to put aside one's own selfish needs and desires on a daily basis for one's family. To do that on a continuing basis was far more difficult than getting killed for your family. It was no simple task to give my time, energy, and myself unselfishly to those around me, when the first half of my life they had lived to serve me. I could see that my parents needed my help. However, I was uncertain whether they wanted it.

A more hopeful note rang in my heart as my mother and I later shared about the joys and sorrows of Israel. From the limited Bible knowledge she had accepted from her rigidly fundamentalist parents, she had an unwavering conviction that the Jews are "God's chosen people." However, her own religious upbringing had been more focused on a god of rules and regulations, instead of a God of *relationship with His children.* She knew more about "thou shalt nots" than she did of His love and mercy. Consequently, she never felt she could measure up to being good enough to be accepted by a loving personal God who was so demanding. My mother ran as far away as she could get from the God of "hell fire and damnation" she had learned about from her overzealous mother. I blamed her religious upbringing for the destruction of my mother's ability to know a loving heavenly Father, instead of an angry sovereign Potentate, who wielded a big, wicked stick. She had never really met the true savior who said, "*I have come to give you life, and that more abundantly!*" Instead, she had inherited harsh religion and death to her soul through rebellion!

While I spoke with her, I was moved to see that she was just one of many simple believers in the truth of the Bible who were part of America's backbone. They represented the basic core of America's populace until the "moral majority" created a controversial climate around them. She loved and supported Israel in her heart and was willing for America to stand at Israel's side because she believed the Bible. She had read little of it or had never really met its Author Himself, but she knew it was true. There were multitudes of people like her in the "Bible Belt" of America. They believed Israel had a special plan in God's eternal purposes. Most of these people had never met a Jewish person, either.

I also discovered a new side to my father. He had always been a secular man with no outward inclination toward religion or churches, he, too, stood on Israel's side. For him, his identification was always on the side of the underdog, and I felt that my own sense and fervor for justice in the world must have been birthed through his heart.

I really marveled that these two Gentiles who had seldom stepped outside of their provincial circle had embraced some vision toward Zion.

My new neighborhood was wrapped in dying autumn brown and crackling leaves. It gave a friendly welcome for my transition. I discovered that the neighbors next door had moved into a smaller portion of their house and chopped wood for fuel to beat the energy crunch. Never did I hear a word of complaint from them. Nor did I hear murmuring when the state speed limit was reduced to save fuel. These were beautiful homefolk I had forgotten about. They brought my parents covered dishes when they were ill. They provided shuttle service to the hospital in their own vehicles if need be, or fed the pets when the family was away.

Although many of the decent homefolk of Tennessee stood with Israel, they knew nothing of her reality, her problems, and her heartaches. Holocaust was a word that the older generation knew, but very few of the younger generation could tell you anything about it. I felt a strong desire to bring Israel's reality to the heartland, because Israel needed America, and America needed Israel, more than she may have realized.

No one thought it strange when I announced that the great love of my life was an Israeli. Neither were there any burial ceremonies, hysteria, or expulsion from the family clan. Long before I left home, my family had recognized that their high-spirited little girl had a mind of her own and an unyielding determination to accomplish what she set before herself. From the moment I learned to crawl, I crashed into every new discovery from dresser drawers to bookshelves, and continually moved around with "black eyes." I received the nickname that never left me, "Blackie". My father tagged me with it very early in life.

The thing that troubled my parents was not that some exotic Israeli was going to steal their middle child to the seething cauldron of the Middle East. They wondered when that little girl who kept running after the exciting toys she saw across the room would stop tripping over all the obstacles on the way to her goal. She had never seen any hurdles in her path. As a distant seer, she spotted something far away, headed straight for it, and continually tumbled over all the reality and circumstances which lay in her path. Never mind! God was the God of the impossible, and the circumstances were insignificant when one recognized the grandeur of the Almighty. Performing supernatural feats for His people was no problem.

Soon I saw that my own mother was a tiny microcosm of Israel. She had fallen prey to constant bombardment of an array of enemy forces that sought to destroy her. Divine liberation was her only hope. These forces hurled their hatred at me with intense hostility. Although my mother and I engaged in much clashing, there were moments of bright breakthroughs. I saw that she was too weak to withstand emotional and physical onslaught on her mind and body. I made her my next prayer assignment.

One day she confided her dream of the previous night to me. It had been identical to my own. In my dream I was trying to get ready for my wedding. The hour was approaching. I had my dress on, but had not finished zipping it and combing my hair. People continued to arrive and enter the room interrupting my urgent preparations. I felt frustrated that there was no one to help me. The same night my mother dreamed that she was trying to get dressed for my wedding, but because she had gained weight, she was having trouble. The people all around were disturbing her, too.

My mother's dream showed me that in her heart she really was standing with me, no matter how fiercely she fought against me. I felt compassion that she had little control over her own behavior because of the prescription medication she was taking, but I had little power to respond to any onslaught in love. I always fought back and lost in the end becoming very discouraged at my own lack of patience and love.

While we were engaged in frequent warfare, I was avidly pursuing the other half of my soul. I had subscribed to "The Jerusalem Post" and had fallen into the same addiction as all the Israelis. I lived from newscast to newscast. When life was poised on the pinnacle of a powder keg one had to be chained to current events to keep abreast of the action. I devoured every article about my beloved land and rose and fell with her moods of hope and despair concerning any peace settlement that she might accord.

At the same time, I was afraid to let the local mail box out of sight, lest I miss some change in my David's personal peace settlement. We both knew that the news would be sparse, and I had even advised him to write me under another name, since both Barry's and Naomi's mail had been monitored before my departure. For certain I knew that our enemies would do anything to destroy our love, so I wanted to make sure that he did not bring my name to the attention of the religious underground!

David was unaccustomed to the cloak and dagger precautions I advised. David had never been under the totalitarian control of Communism, nor gone through the Holocaust, or probably even been bothered by Israel's religious control until the real possibility of involving his life with mine occurred. I had told him that I had been severely slandered from somewhere through the Chief Rabbi's office. He listened but he did not understand. I also doubted that as a secular kibbutz Israeli, he had really had much contact with religious extremists. Every single Christian or Messianic Jew I met in Israel had encountered some harassment or attempted control over their lives! Many even lost their jobs when it was discovered that they were Messianic!

I had heard numerous incidents about religious harassment. In one religious neighborhood they smashed up the home of a non-Sabbath keeper while the man was away. They made impossible laws to hinder Reform and Conservative Jews from gaining any stronghold in Israel. Everyone was afraid of their tyranny. Sadly for Israel, it was tolerated out of fear of "rocking the boat."

David's divorce proceedings with his ex-wife had begun to open his eyes to both political and religious corruption, manipulation, and deceit in the religious political power used to usurp the people's freedom. This recognition had led David to take a stand and begin to speak out in Israel about these issues. At this time, Israel's President had called him a "prophet". David had begun to have his eyes opened to many such things before I left Israel. I was afraid that the intensity of some of these pressures might cause him to "compromise" his truth or values or even cause his persecution.

While news was limited between David and me on purpose, it was regular from Naomi. I received a weekly letter from her. She also wrote to me under another name, since I was aware that she was under surveillance. My own mother became interested in my "Jewish mother" as well and soon loved to hear the news. My mother was still having a struggle with alcohol addiction at the time, and I decided to go away for a few days to a neighboring community to fast and pray for her. I bought her a new dress with the little money I had and returned home. I could never get her to set foot inside a church. Her excuse was always that she "had nothing appropriate to wear". This time I knew that a little church in the community was having a special meeting by a traveling evangelist from California. I presented the dress to my mother and invited her to go. I was shocked when she agreed. She was also pleased with the dress.

My mother and I found ourselves seated in the second row of the church with great expectation. She loved the music and the worship which she had not known from her own background. After finishing his sermon, the minister called for anyone who wanted to respond to God to receive the forgiveness that Jesus had provided on the cross for their sins and receive him as their personal savior. My mother rushed up to the altar, kneeled down and invited Jesus into her life to receive forgiveness of her sins!

Then the minister felt he should pray for me. He spoke the words, *"you need a miracle in your life, and if you believe, God is going to do it!"* When we went home, we both felt reassured. There was a new beginning for my mother and the family. However, spiritual rebirth is only in seed form in one's spirit at conception. As in all growth, a process is required in maturing. My mother had been ill and depressed for a long time. She needed much encouragement and help to rise up and begin living a new life. She needed fellowship with other believers, but she also needed to be taught in the Bible. A person must choose daily whom he will serve. Therefore, a greater task was still necessary to help my mother grow.

The days were fleeting quickly. David had my prayers in abundance. Our letters were sparse, as we had planned until the settlement was over. Sometimes when he wrote the name I had given him, I sensed he was fighting fear. Other times he wrote in my own name. I was unsure just how much all these precautions were necessary, but when one had been slandered as severely as I had without any recourse to resolution, I did not trust some of the powers which were in control. I was really getting homesick for Israel the more the time elapsed.

Shlomo wrote me a sad letter telling me he had gone to a concert and left Efes on the leash outside. When he came out she was gone. That news really hurt. My little furry friend and I had weathered many storms. My mother asked me why I had not brought her home to America. I had not even realized that it was an option!

About the time I felt I would be unable to survive any longer in exile from Israel, I discovered a television program that brought me hope. I never watched TV in the morning hours, but my father had flipped it on before leaving for work. I was amazed to see familiar faces. Why I had even been interviewed by the host of the show on the program. The program was focused on what God was doing in the world in people's lives. People's needs were also prayed for on the air and miraculous answers were occurring.

I quickly became addicted to watching the show as a spiritual support in my life. One day while the host was praying, he spoke out that there was someone by my first name that needed a specific amount of money, and God was going to provide it. It was the exact amount I needed! It was the sum I owed my father for my airline ticket to return to the States! I rejoiced in the faithfulness of God!

The next afternoon a local attorney and his wife both offered to give me some money. They had felt prompted to do so independently of each other. I had been sharing in local churches about Israel and I had met them there. At the time this gift arrived, I thought to myself, "I wonder if I should ask the attorney to help me incorporate a foundation to help Israel?" I said nothing because I wanted to make it a matter of further prayer to be sure I was taking the right step.

The following Sunday, when the same gentleman offered me a ride home from the church where I had spoken, he turned to me as I was climbing out of the car. "Oh, by the way, have you thought about incorporating your work? I'd be glad to help you if you would like!" Overnight, HOPE FOR ISRAEL was born!

HOPE FOR ISRAEL was the vision that had long been germinating in my heart to become a loving bridge between Christians and Israel. Through speaking, writing, distribution of literature, exchange, and all other avenues of communication and interaction I wanted to provide an outlet to bless Israel both spiritually and materially, as well as *build a bridge of reconciliation between Christians and Jews*. No matter how much extremists in Israel had badgered and rejected me, I still loved Israel and held her welfare at heart.

Perhaps, I had gone about my relationship with her in the wrong way. I was certain that no matter what she did to me, I would still love her and daily I was learning the depth of this kind of divine, unconditional love in the face of fierce rejections, accusations, fears, and misunderstandings of my mother. In her heart, she meant well, but her mind was blinded by great darkness. No matter whether I argued with her, fought with her, I still loved her. In fact, because I cared deeply, I was always wounded more.

In those moments when I was least secure in my connection with Israel's future, I would pull out my old diary, and flip through the prayers that I knew were from God's heart.

> *You have made Israel for Yourself. Your people will one day honor you before the world. No one can oppose what you have purposed. You are the Lord, who opens a way through the waters. You promised that many will join themselves to Israel and the nations will help them return to their land. Those foreigners living in the land will serve them. LORD, I DESIRE TO SERVE YOUR PEOPLE!*

I was reminded that I had personally petitioned God with such a request, but I had no inkling of the price of the fulfillment.

As the time clock continued to tick away, I waged a war with whether God was really going to do what I had been convinced He said he was. I was longing for the vital heartbeat of Zion and the comfort of David's strong arms. I knew he could use some encouragement himself. "Oh God, why is it taking so long?" I asked.

A welcomed interruption in the snail routine of the small town in the South arrived. We had received an invitation to go over to the other side of the Smoky Mountains for a visit with friends at a spiritual retreat. Wonder of wonders, my mother agreed to go along. By this time her dependence on alcohol had also become almost nonexistent, and I was beginning to see tiny new buds blossom on the fruit tree of her life.

Hidden away on the side of a majestic North Carolina mountain, was a rustic retreat located far from the maddening crowd. Bible teachers and ministers from all around the country frequented the place to instruct those who came for spiritual refreshment. A visiting minister had come to teach and pray for us. When he prayed for me he said, "I may be wrong," he began, "but I believe that there is a marriage for you, just down the road. You are to be a helpmate to this person." Once again, the Lord in his faithfulness had strengthened me. Not only that, but after a short while on the speaking circuit, my entire financial debt was paid off!

All the while I was adjusting to the painful transition on the western side of the world; I had been corresponding with another "adopted" mother friend, Nana. She was a Gentile Christian who also had a genuine heart for the Jewish people. I had met her before I had ever sailed for distant shores. Our hearts had linked eternally at the time for "Zion's sake" and when I told her I was going, she wanted to come with me, for it had been her heart's desire for years.

This little grandmother had more zeal than an Orthodox army and the ironclad will of Frau Herz to the ultimate degree. She was a real fighter in the best sense of the word, because she was a "survivor". Once she set her mind on something, none of the forces of hell could stop her, and sometimes not even the ones of heaven! She had been liberated from "religion" late in life, when she discovered a real relationship with the living God! Nana decided to come and help me in Tennessee on behalf of Israel. I decided to go out to California to get her. Driving back from California, we kept the radio on all the way to follow Israel's glorious "Raid on Entebbe". Nana and I knew, because we regularly prayed for Israel, that this was "America's birthday present" from Israel! Israel later announced that it was, since it transpired at that time.

From the moment we set foot in Tennessee at my parents' home, my mother's blood pressure skyrocketed. Three "strong" women under one roof were too many. My mother chose to get rid of one by announcing that either I leave, or she would leave. My resources were scarce and inconsistent. I sent up one of my heavenly SOS's for the Lord's help, and got a miracle in return. A local leader in the community who had taken an interest in the work I was organizing for Israel offered Nana and me a rent free apartment. The Lord proved His faithfulness once again.

The glorious, long awaited news arrived. David's settlement had been forever resolved! He was completely free from the powerful chain that had held his life captive. It appeared that it might be smooth sailing ahead as far as our relationship was concerned. We kept the telephone wires hot between Israel and America with the latest victory and our avowed love.

"David, do you think you could come to America and give a concert over here if HOPE FOR ISRAEL would foot the bill?" America was the only option between our two lands where we could be married. I felt that this was the time for it.

"Why yes, of course. I'm free in August. You arrange the ticketing over there, sending a letter of request, and I'll arrange the time."

The dates in August were only some weeks away. Round trip fare for Israelis with the extra travel tax and other expenses would run to about two thousand dollars. Nana and I both realized that we needed another miracle for that supply to come in a short amount of time. We did what we always did. We asked our heavenly Father.

My next phone conversation with David was tender, loving, and close but "Yael," he groped for words, "I want you to know....I don't think it is yet *time for us*...... to...be...married."

"Oh David." My heart sank. "We'll talk about it in America!" As I hung up the receiver, I realized that David was *afraid*. He was coming out of a traumatic marriage, and our relationship had experienced some tumultuous moments also. He was certain to feel different once we were in each other's arms again.

The zero hour finally approached. I jumped into Nana's old Ford sedan and kept a heavy foot on the accelerator the entire forty miles to the airport. I felt weaker and weaker the closer I got to my goal. A myriad of questions after long separation burst across my brain like popcorn. Would he still feel the same?

As I posted myself against a supporting pillar at the arrival gate of the United Flight in Knoxville, a gnawing anxiety was welling up inside. The first passengers streamed through the doorway, and I overheard an olive complexioned man greet a petite dark skinned woman in Arabic! That certainly was symbolic. Suddenly, out strode the gentle giant with his warm glowing smile. I lunged forward at the same time he dropped his carry on and extended his arms.

"David!"

"Yael!" We melted together. I must have felt weak because he asked me if I needed to sit down.

"No, I'll be all right". I felt my legs wobbling. "You have made it, David! What a miracle to see you here! I can hardly believe it!"

As soon as David got his baggage, we ambled out to the car with our arms entwined. "How good it is to see you, David. I can hardly believe that you are really here!"

"A TIME FOR US"

"A time when dreams so long denied can flourish,
as we unveil the love we now must hide."
("Theme from Romeo and Juliet")

The humid summer air was sweltering in the East Tennessee hills. In the distance the constant drone of motor boats racing up and down the mouth of the lake was humming in the background. From my window I could see bare legged children sliding down the long drive on their skate boards. Swarms of honey suckle perfumed the air all around, and bright red cardinals pecked for bugs in the back yard.

The miracle of the whereabouts of $2000 had been fully resolved, and we had enough to cover the travel expense. I also needed to prepare a group of my Christian friends with the news of my soon departure back to Israel. Till Nana had arrived I had been clandestine and shy about letting anyone in on the details of my personal life. Her presence had injected me with a strong shot of boldness, and I began to feel somewhat freer to speak about my future hope with David. However, I felt the need to be cautious until David and I had the opportunity to discuss everything together. I was excited, but I feared that Nana was releasing too much information too quickly to the broader community. I was met with first one, and then another fiery dart of opposition. It even sounded like anti-Semitism in disguise.

"Is this Jew 'saved?" Some challengers wanted to know. My parents' residence was situated deep in the waistline of the Bible belt where it was of utmost importance that my theology was lined up with the letter of the law of God's word as the legalists perceived it! Otherwise, David would never receive a stamp of approval from them. Some of them were probably the Christian counterpart of the Jewish religious extremists. I was also aware that for some the fact that he was divorced was enough to disqualify him as a suitable partner for me. According to some of these religious law keepers, divorce was not a redeemable sin. There was no second chance according to the way they read the Book.

When some interrogated me about David's spiritual credentials, I really did not know how to answer. Our relationship was one of faith, trusting the Spirit of God who had drawn us together to fulfill His purposes. David had been in the midst of a great wooing process with the Almighty when I met him. There was no question he was a believer, but his culture and heritage were worlds apart from the small community in the South. His faith had grown unceasingly the entire time of our relationship in Israel. I trusted that since God had been leading us this far, He would complete what He had begun.

Some of the local Christians were very interested in the Jewish people because of their knowledge of the Bible. Nana and I had visited various groups to share about Israel, and we found many who wanted to learn more. They also gave generously of their resources to help HOPE FOR ISRAEL. The night before I had to pay for the ticket for David to come to America, the money was all there!

Some days before David had arrived, a lovely Christian lady from another city who had heard me speak before a women's group had taken a special liking to me. She had offered to make my wedding dress for me at no charge. In fact, she felt that this was her real God ordained mission to do so. While I pondered the offer, another dear woman who owned a fabric shop, felt she was to give me some fabric for no cost. Everyone seemed eager to play some role in this drama that was occurring before their eyes!

As for me, I was taking one step at a time and still unsure how the visit would unfold. David and I needed time to talk, and everyone seemed to be running ahead of where we really were. Moreover, David had called before he left Israel to come. He had clearly stated, *"Yael, it is not time for us to be married.* I have come to the attention of the Israeli government, and some of the leaders feel that I have a prophetic mission to fulfill here at this time.

"Oh, David, we can talk about it when you come!" I felt our wedding would be a symbol of God's mercy to His people—the union of Jew and Gentile in the Spirit of Messiah. Our lives were destined be a bridge between the two worlds.

I had already instructed all of my friends to be in prayer for us. David had expressed on the phone that he felt it was not "*the time for us*" to be married just yet, since much was happening in Israel. I was especially concerned about David's fears, which I knew were heightened by the warfare that surrounded his life in Israel. Everyone who was praying for us felt that God was certainly in this relationship and the marriage was his plan. However, most of them knew nothing of the incredible spiritual warfare that had surrounded our lives. Possibly many of them knew little about "spiritual warfare" at all. (Ephesians 6:12) Especially where strategic events were concerned in God's purposes, there was always a spiritual war to be fought in prayer and action. Now that David was coming to America, I sensed a greater dimension of opposition than I had known heretofore. I was not sure how to handle it!

Nana and the other ladies she was in touch with in the community had mobilized many to go to prayer on our behalf. I still had many meticulous details to arrange concerning the concert and a presentation in a local church. We needed an accompanist, a location and publicity. With a couple of weeks to organize all these details, we would need lots of support to carry us through. Yet, our heavenly Father was faithful! A local businessman who thrived on public relations and organizational opportunities went to work. Overnight we had the nice lounge of a community college, a newspaper story, and a potential accompanist!

The atmosphere tingled in anticipation. All of my lady friends were elated to play some part in this adventuresome romance, and some of their husbands jumped on the bandwagon, too. Another area businessman begged for the opportunity to take David out to lunch while the ladies got together with me for a going away party, assuming that I would be going back with David. They were assuming that I would be going back with David. That was not yet established, but I did not feel free to talk about this yet, since I did not know what was happening.

At the last minute my mother and I had fought over my using her best bed sheets for David's bed in my country cottage apartment. I had decided to give him a rest in the quiet little cove, alone with the birds and trees, while I stayed in town with my family. My mother finally gave in and allowed me to use the bed linens, and she even softened by offering me some of her best towels.

My mother's behavior was one of my gravest concerns, whether my gentle, compassionate David would be able to tolerate her contrariness. I knew that he felt very strongly about one's family background after all the anguish and torment he had undergone. Many times he had told me that he felt one's family training was crucial. It was. I had screamed out to God more than once for not giving me God-fearing parents. Along the way I had learned that God does not make mistakes! I could be certain that the Creator had chosen just the correct clay and all the right elements to combine when he began to mold me on His big potter's wheel! The Almighty always knows what He is busy doing, even though I frequently questioned the process.

The morning I was to go and pick out the material and pattern for my evening dress for the big event, my body felt limp and faint as I walked into the shop. I even felt like screaming and running. A terrible foreboding hung over my head. I forced myself to ignore it, shoving past its heaviness and making a selection. I chose a beige eyelet for material, and for a pattern, I chose a dress with long flowing sleeves and empire waist. It had a square necked bodice trimmed with tiny purple flowers, as well as matching trim on the skirt. The dress had a distinct flair of the Middle Eastern world about it. Underneath all of these preparations, though I kept feeling a resistance. Something was wrong. When I expressed it to Nana, she felt that I needed more faith, instead of fear. I had no doubt, that an enormous battle of spiritual warfare was underway. More and more people were getting involved, and I was losing control of what was going on around me. I did not yet have clarity on the agenda. However, Nana was running ahead in great confidence. If

I questioned anything, she insisted I needed to hang on "in faith". I had faith, but I did not yet see what God was doing, and what David had on his agenda. Also many young believers who surrounded me at the time knew very little about *"spiritual warfare!"* There was a wonderful verse in the Bible that said *"For our struggle is not against flesh and blood, but against the rulers, against the authorities, against the powers of this dark world and* against *the spiritual forces of evil in the heavenly realms."* David had clearly said on the phone *that it was not time for us to get married*! Nevertheless, I made sure that all details were covered for any possibility for a change in venue, because we had so little time.

In the midst of the beehive of last minute organization, I had been seized with overwhelming fear. With all the opposition David and I had known, I was sure that there would be more to come. A hurricane was headed straight for the path of the Kennedy Airport in New York City and was scheduled to arrive about the same time as David's plane! Of course everyone was praying.

Visions of cancelled flights and wreckages of aircraft swirled before my eyes. Later, after much prayer, a news cast flashed that the hurricane had bypassed the landing strip and the entire area they had projected. We had overcome all those obstacles and he had finally arrived.

As I was driving David and myself to the nice cozy cottage in the country, David caught me up on the details of his last days before departure. Then he began to engage in serious conversation.

"Yael." His eyes captured mine. They sparkled with beautiful clarity, but I could also see great fear in them. He held a long breathless pause. Where to begin? Then a torrent of words began to tumble. I clearly saw that his suffering had purified him. I felt flooded with peace as we sat there.

"Yael." His tone became serious. "I want you to know....this is not the *time* for us to get married...." He struggled for the words. "In Israel I have come to the attention of the Prime Minister, the President, and I was even met by the Israeli Ambassador in America at the airport in New York when I arrived...." David did not continue. Something terribly wrong was attempting to mar our joy. Although I heard the words, nothing in this world would allow me to believe what I was hearing. I was convinced that God had shown us otherwise.

"Yael, I want you to know....I'm very sorry....but you see, a couple of days before I left the country, *the Chief Rabbi came to my apartment....*"

"Oh God, no!" I moaned in disbelief. "*They have struck again!*"

"Yes, he just dropped in on me." David said.

"*How irregular*!" I responded bitterly, "The Chief Rabbi never *just drops in* on people."

David proceeded with his narrative. "You see, I have been speaking out on some of the evil practices of the religious extremists in the country, which has brought me to the attention of the government."

I sighed as he continued, feeling more and more dejected.

"The Rabbi said he just wanted to know my beliefs, and so forth....Well, *I talked to him about Israel going the way of love, and of God's Spirit...*that this was the only hope for peace with our neighbors and each other....Then, the rabbi said '*what you are telling me reminds me of a woman I met a couple of years ago*. Then he named your name. "And I want to know that *no one has ever upset me as much as she has!* After I spoke with her I could not sleep for three nights! She is an *enemy of our country!*" David dropped his eyes.

"Oh God," I groaned in agony. "*They bugged your phone, too, before you came*. That's how he knew!" I announced adamantly.

"No," David contradicted. "I think it was just a *coincidence.*"

"There is no such thing as a ***'coincidence,'*** I blurted back to him. I was abhorred at how *naïve* he was, although I was sure that many Israelis did not know what was going on in a part of their country with religious extremists.

David ignored my remark and elaborated. "The Chief Rabbi has *slandered you very severely!* You must have really upset the man! He questioned me three hours in my own apartment. I had vaguely known him when I was in the army, but never called on him."

It was obvious that we had been dealt a mortal blow. I kept convincing myself that God is greater. He could do something about it. God had opened the door for me to enter Israel in the past, in spite of misunderstanding and rejection from the Interior Ministry. I was convinced the top "religious army" of Israeli authority had been mobilized against us through the slander of the Chief Rabbi. I was indignant that the Rabbi did not even follow his own Jewish Law. Jews were never supposed to treat the stranger in the land unjustly. Moreover, the prophets had said "Woe to those who call evil good and those who call good evil!" David had been severely intimidated. His fear had to be dislodged. Did he not remember all the various signs God had given us that He was blessing our relationship? Moreover, some of the godly rabbis equated slander with murder! My character had been murdered! "It is obvious that they bugged your phone, too, David!"

We pulled up to the little cottage out in the country. As soon as I opened the door, he spun around and took me into his arms.

"Yael." It is soooo good to see you," he said. "I want you to know that *I have been faithful to you*! *All this time*!" I ached at the knowledge that this man really loved me and I could trust him completely. I had already observed him in the public arena and saw how some women approached him seductively. The fact that he had stood firm against these assaults proved his love for God and me.

It was already very late and we were to have a full day ahead of us. After making a simple evening snack, I informed him that I was leaving him alone in the cozy cottage, and I would be staying with my parents. We talked for a while, and he saw how devastated I was. I could see that he felt helpless. I had been severely *slandered* and he had been *severely intimidated*! I tucked him in with a goodnight kiss. David pulled me toward him. Spontaneously I said, "No we have to wait until God's time! "I do not want to disappoint the Lord." I rushed to the door and stopped. "I'll be back to prepare your breakfast in the morning, and then you'll meet Nana and my parents. '*Laila tov*. It felt good to say "Good night" in Hebrew for the first time I had spoken the language in ten months.

David was still asleep when I clicked the key in the lock the next morning. As I entered, the noise startled him and he sat upright with his face frozen in fear. I ran to him and sat on the side of the bed, wrapping my arms around his broad shoulders. "Oh David, it is all right! There are no *terrorists* here! We have no *Chief Rabbis*!

You can just relax and unwind! It is o.k. No one will harm you. You can stay in bed as long as you like and I will prepare us some breakfast."

I scrambled a generous portion of eggs and jokingly asked him whether he ate "unkosher" bacon, which he quickly "pooh-poohed." I tossed him a set of clean towels for the shower. When we sat at the little table, David stationed me as close to himself as possible. Across the table was too much distance. He gobbled the American honey wheat bread as if it would soon be going out of style. I loved to feed a man with a hearty appetite, and I had more pleasure in watching him than in eating myself.

The agenda for the day? "Well," I said, "First, we'll go over to my parents' house to meet everyone. Then, we'll take a little trip out to the college where we'll hold the concert. Sometime, you have to rehearse with the accompanist, too! How does that sound?"

"I'm completely yours...whatever you want to do is fine with me."

My stomach was gurgling in apprehension as I drove David to my family's house. In the car, though, I found myself humming the melody to the theme song of "Romeo and Juliet". The song was titled "*A Time for Us*". I only knew the tune and not the text, so I just hummed the melody. For weeks before his arrival, the melody had been floating through my mind, and no single day passed without my humming it spontaneously. It was a beautifully haunting melody.

When David walked into the front door of the modest little house on the hill and met my parents, it was love at first sight for all concerned. I was overwhelmed at the goodness of God because of the beautiful cooperative loving spirit that flowed through my mother. I had never seen my mother so gracious. She was absolutely charmed by the gentle, compassionate Israeli man she had just met, and the radiance I saw on her face showed it.

My father, when he had a chance to take me aside, chuckled warmly and stated confidently, "I think our daughter has met her match!" He, too, loved this man right away, and the two men became instant friends. Nana and David also immediately struck up a special bond with each other. Later, when David found Nana alone for a few minutes, he asked her, "Nana, will you come and join us in Israel later on?" Nana was intoxicated with rapture. Nothing in this wide world would have thrilled her heart any more than being a strand in the cord that wound David and Yael together! Here, too, was another son she wanted to mother.

I could never remember when so much light and life filled the little house on the hilltop. Even the two small dogs of my parents raced around in excitement. "You know what?" David asked as we all sat down at the kitchen table for a bologna sandwich together. "Your house is just exactly like my own parents' house! Even the yard and the trees outside!" No wonder he made himself so completely at home, as if he had always known them.

"That's amazing, isn't it? Your parents are Russian immigrants, living in Israel. My parents are English, French, Dutch and Cherokee Indian who are provincial southern Americans. I am so astounded that our two families' lives from different ends of the world spectrum have so much in common!" David nodded agreement.

After joyous conversation, David and I rode around the little community making all the final arrangements for the upcoming event. We also got coverage in the local press. Although I was excited about the concert for the community, I was really looking forward to the program we had booked in an area church. I had decided to read from the prophets, sharing God's vision and burden for the nation of Israel. My segments would be interspersed with musical interludes from David on different instruments. It would be our first opportunity to share God's vision of Israel together!

In the afternoon at my parents' house, David and I were discussing which portions from the prophets would be most appropriate, and marvelously we coincided. His suggestions were identical with the selections I had already chosen. That is, all except one. He loved the story of David and Jonathan and insisted I read it, too. The passage was a favorite one of mine, also, but I felt it was inappropriate for the type of program we were presenting. Like a bulldog, David stubbornly determined that this portion should be read, while I fought in ardent disagreement. Since I was winning, he ran to Nana for support.

Nana, who had already tucked David under her mother's wing like a Yiddish mama, weighed the issue at once, trying to decide which side to take. At the same time I eyed her, a brilliant idea struck, which corresponded to her resolution to the stalemate. "I'll tell you what, why don't you, David just read that portion in Hebrew to the people?"

"Yes," I applauded, "that's a wonderful idea. Then, they can also get a feeling for the Hebrew language." David mumbled something about their not understanding, but finally resigned himself to this alternative as the best solution.

Meanwhile, I had alerted all of the local and national prayer warriors I knew to engage in the prayer battle to conquer David's fears of the Chief Rabbi's rejection and slander of me. Powerful intercessors began storming heaven for victory for this pair of lovers to find their God given fulfillment. As they prayed, petitioned, and pled with God, they all received many impressions which they reported back to me.

One faithful friend saw the heavens opened and the angels singing and heard the words, "once again God is moving in the affairs of men and nations!" Another young woman who walked close to God discerned many fears surrounding David—"fear of his mother's disapproval, fear of rejection from his fellow Israelis, and fear of his tradition." She also saw powerfully ugly evil spirits raging against David. One was a hideously repulsive creature, which she associated with the religious-political powers behind tradition and influencing the Chief Rabbi.

As another woman interceded in prayer, she received a verse from Mark in the New Testament which stated, "He is a prophet, like one of the prophets long ago." Still another, after a raging battle against evil forces, saw hindrances being removed and there before her stood a hill of gold with a glimmering cross. It got higher and mightier.

I then received two long distance calls from some Christian women who were praying for us. The word to David was "If you are reproached for the name of Messiah, happy are you, for the Spirit of glory rests upon you. Salvation is found in no one else, for there is no other name under heaven given to men by whom we must be saved."

The other call was from a woman who had been awakened with three verses in the night. From Proverbs, "The *fear of man* brings a snare, but whosoever puts his trust in the Lord shall be safe." Then, from the Jewish writer, John, "when the disciples were assembled with the doors locked, *for fear of the Jews,* Jesus came and stood among them and said, "Peace be with you!" Finally, from Paul, the Jewish leader "....for you did not receive a spirit that makes you a slave again to fear, but you received the Spirit of sonship. And by him we cry, *Abba,* Father."

From all the flurry of words that were coming to me from the outsiders, I concluded what I already knew. David was called to be a strategic person in God's plan for his people, Israel, and he was presently in combat with *fear*! I shared all the verses with him and attempted to assuage his fears. We buried each other in loving embraces and each time I asked him about our wedding, he groaned in pain. "I've told you that you have been *severely slandered.* They said many more things which I cannot even repeat to you, because I don't want to hurt you. Now is not the *time* to take you back to Israel—they would *never* accept you there!"

The words stung more deeply than before, but I insisted I would listen to God and not David's fears. God would surely prevail somehow. He would. While leaving David to the quiet of his bungalow, I was silently pouting about the lack of courage in David to stand up to evil. I offered him a cool departure at the doorway and disregarded the deep hurt I saw flash across his face.

The next morning when I arrived to get David for the preparation of the presentation in the church, he shared a dream that he had the previous night. In the dream, the music of King David's harp was sweetly flowing out from Jerusalem, and drawing many to come and enjoy its sound. People were streaming in from many places. Even my own mother entered in to receive the beauty of the music. But I refused to go in.

His words hit me hard. I had a bitter recognition of my own pride. Because things were not going the way I thought they should, I balked against cooperation. As David and I drove to the church to share together for the people, we were barely speaking.

Like a rod of steel run through my backbone, I felt a pride so rigid and unyielding that I was on the brink of despairing at our having to present a spiritual program together. At the very last minute, up on the platform, seated across the aisle and facing each other, I cried to God for mercy. Instantly, I felt a breaking inside and I stared across to David. "I love you," I mouthed to him before the entire congregation. A knowing nod answered back. I knew everything was all right. I could stand up in confidence and expect God's presence to be with us.

I first read the passage of the dry bones from Ezekiel and shared the story of the resurrection of the Jewish state. The evil one had tried to destroy the people of Israel in the Holocaust, and the nations had time and again brought destruction to her people. However, God Himself resurrected her in 1948 in her homeland.

David played his own composition on the piano. Then, I rejoiced in the future glory of Zion from Isaiah in a recitation:

> Sing, O barren woman, you who never bore a child; burst into song, shout for joy, you who were never in labor because more are the children of the desolate woman than of her who has a husband, says the Lord....
>
> Do not be afraid; you will not suffer shame. Do not fear disgrace; you will not be humiliated. You will forget the shame of your youth and remember no more the reproach of your widowhood. For your Maker is your husband—the Lord Almighty is his name—the Holy One of Israel is your redeemer; he is called the God of all the earth. The Lord will call you back as if you were a wife, deserted and distressed in spirit—a wife who married young, only to be rejected, says your God. For a brief moment I abandoned you, but with deep compassion I will bring you back. In a surge of anger I hid my face from you for a moment, but with everlasting kindness I will have compassion on you, says the Lord, your Redeemer....
>
> O, afflicted city, lashed by storms and not comforted,
>
> I will build you with stones of turquoise, and your foundations of sapphires....

> All your sons will be taught by the Lord, and great will be your children's peace. In righteousness you will be established; tyranny will be far from you; you will have nothing to fear. Terror will be far removed; it will not come near you....
>
> No weapon forged against you will prevail and you will refute every tongue that accuses you. This is the heritage of the servants of the Lord, and this is their vindication from me. (Isaiah 54)

I elaborated on the rich, passionate love between the Lord as the husband and His deep pain over the infidelity of His wife, Israel, and her broken heart over His alienation. She had suffered misery, but He promised in the end that Israel, His wife, would come back to Him through His comfort and the ardor of His love for her, He would woo her back to Himself in fidelity and purity, in trust and love.

David's music was sweeter than ever before. I remembered the harp, flowing out its sonorous honey from Jerusalem. I looked at the faces of the audience. Not a single stirring was seen in the congregation, which was completely captivated by the sublime experience that was moving their hearts.

I concluded with the declaration, promise, and challenge of Isaiah 62. With my whole heart, I stated my vow to Zion before the sanctuary filled with Christians:

> For Zion's sake I will not keep silent, for Jerusalem's sake, I will not remain quiet, till her righteousness shines out like the dawn, her salvation like a blazing torch. The nations will see your righteousness, and all kings your glory; you will be called by a new name that the mouth of the Lord will bestow. You will be a crown of splendor in the Lord's hand, a royal diadem in the hand of your God. No longer will they call you Deserted, or name your land Desolate. But you will be called Hephzibah and your land Beulah; for the Lord will take delight in you and your land will be married. As a young

man marries a maiden, so will your sons marry you. As a bridegroom rejoices over his bride, so will your God rejoice over you.

I have posted watchmen on your walls, O Jerusalem; they will never be silent day or night. You who call on the Lord, give yourselves no rest, and give Him no rest till he establishes Jerusalem and makes her the praise of the earth.

I challenged all those who love Israel and her Messiah to become a *watchman on her walls,* to stand watch and warn of impending danger, and to remind God of His promises to her land day and night. They were yet to be fulfilled in greater ways.

When David and I finished, there was barely a dry eye in the crowd of people before us. Seldom had I felt the presence of the Spirit's power as I had on that occasion. When we walked out the door, David turned to me and said, "You *have a spirit like Moses*!" All Jewish pride was dissolved in the glory of God that was present that day. Both Nana and my mother had been deeply moved as the hand of God had touched their hearts, as well.

Late in the evening, as I was returning David to his hideaway for the night, I was again humming the melody of the love song of "Romeo and Juliet". Suddenly David perked up and turned to me, humming the same melody, with the words in English, *"It shall be done."* I instantly saw that David was not even cognizant of the significance of his actions. God was giving him the spiritual interpretation of what I was singing and reassuring me that it would be accomplished!

The next concert in the community center had its glory, too. Although I chose not to incorporate the recitation and turn the evening over to him, the performance also experienced another visitation of God's presence. In the intermission, the lady behind me tapped me on the shoulder and announced with surprise, "Why, he is just like King David, a poet and a musician!" Recalling my prayer years before, I smiled inside. "God, please give me a man with a heart like King David!"

David afterwards confided that while he was performing he saw a brilliant white light over Nana and me. This was a phenomenon he had never experienced. We informed him that this was a visual manifestation of God's presence. The entire evening met with great success. We received glowing reports all around.

Only one barb was slung, when one of the Bible Belters had been perturbed that David had not "preached a sermon" or shared a testimony. He had concluded with a prayer. The cloud of fear that hung over him would in no way allow him any public profession of his faith at this time. (I of all people understood. I also wanted to protect him.)

When it came time to exchange our embraces for the night and depart to our separate abodes, David shyly disclosed that he had peeped into the drawer in the bedside nightstand. "I read your letter to the Chief Rabbi, 'Ruth Yael'. It stirred me powerfully." His arm squeezed me tightly. "I also saw your other letters to the government...."

"God must have meant for you to see that correspondence!" I answered, pressing my head against his shoulder. "It's all right."

"You know," David whispered softly, "the beautiful thing about you is that you *can receive love as well as give it!* In fact, that is what drew me to you in the first place! I saw that you were reaching out to everyone around you, sensitive to their needs. No one was reaching out to you or even caring about your needs!"

"Thank you, David, for those beautiful words. Are you still so adamant about our not getting married now?"

"Yael....I've told you....no matter what I *feel* like....it's not the *time*. I could never take you back to Israel with me now. They would never accept you."

I felt torn apart inside. I drove the lonely two miles to my parents' house. Nana had encouraged me to stand my ground by holding on to faith. I refused to budge. God had the last word.

David could not return to Israel without paying a visit to his father's brother in a religious ghetto of New York. He begged me to go along with him, but I was undergoing cataclysmic emotional upheaval about his fear and stubbornness concerning our wedding. Unbeknown to David, I had already verbally announced to some of my friends that we had intended to be getting married before he returned to Israel. On the one hand, I knew that this could be greatly presumptuous on my part. It certainly was our original plan. However, that was before the Chief Rabbi had intimidated him and poisoned our love with his lies. I also knew that real faith must be expressed and acknowledged. I tried to hold on to my faith even in the absence of evidence to the contrary! My women friends were already busy arranging a going away party for the departure.

Every time I was about to announce the reality of what was really happening, those who were praying for me kept bringing me encouragement that God was going to see all this through. Some even had visions of us getting married. I concluded that maybe God was planning a last minute miracle before David's departure, although I could not see it. David and I shared delicate and beautiful moments alone, exuberant exchange with friends and neighbors, and lively, happy hours with my parents. *We belonged together, and how could all the forces of hell stop us?*

The afternoon of the party the ladies had prepared for me, I had agreed to dispatch David to the care of a friendly young Christian businessman, who wanted to drive him around the countryside and expose him to the beauties of East Tennessee's rolling green landscape. David clung to my hand like a lost child when I left him with the total stranger, a man I barely knew myself. I was tightlipped about my whereabouts for the afternoon, which incited his curiosity even more. Something felt very wrong about all this, but Nana kept insisting I should just "hold on" and let God do what He wanted.

I did not dare call off the event lest I be guilty of not "standing in faith" in this most crucial hour. Faith without action is dead, and I was expressing my faith by going to the ladies "good-bye party for me, even though David and I had not worked out any change.

All the local ladies could not have been lovelier in their generosity and caring. Somehow, though, I felt very squeamish doing all this scheming behind David's back. I knew something that he did not. Nana was expecting "divine intervention," which I deeply questioned. When David returned from his little excursion with Brad, there was a funny look in his eyes, which I could not define. I passed it over, along with other strange signals which were trying to capture my attention.

David had almost talked Nana and me into driving up to New York with him, when one of my praying friends called me on the phone. I have a message for you, she stated with her voice quivering. This came to me as I prayed:

> Oh, you are deceived! A great warfare has built up around you. It has been raging mightily. I have not instructed anyone to accompany David to New York. A great plan is in progress. Many things are being done. All is ready for a great awakening among my people. I will accomplish this and I will use my children in it. You must be careful. You must not do anything that would hinder. Watch more carefully for the timing, and I will assure you of the right time to join him.

Another prayer partner called also. She said, when I pray for you, I see a whole satanic army coming against you spiritually. But I also see the Lord rising up like a mighty warrior and casting his sword through the angry hoard. They are scattered to the four winds in tiny pieces! And....oh, I do see you in a wedding dress.

God was obviously slowing me down but still encouraging me about marriage. David decided to fly to New York alone, and the three of us would meet in Virginia, where he would depart the country. He, too, had been captivated by the same television program which had been my spiritual lifeline during my most difficult period. He wanted to visit their studios before he returned to Israel.

As I deposited David at the air terminal for his New York flight, I ran into some people who had heard me speak some time before. "Oh, I want you to meet my husband," the lovely lady from Gatlinburg announced, turning to the quiet man at her side. "Honey, she's a *missionary* in Israel."

Oh, Lord, help me!" I groaned. "Well I'm not a missionary, but a *servant....*" I muttered and stumbled. "There's a difference, you know...." I pulled David down to the departure gate. Those people had no earthly idea of the ugliness or the significance of that word to any Jew. Nor could they ever conceive of the inner realities of life in the contemporary Promised Land, but I knew that if anything could reinforce David's terror, it was that "m" word. David had already warned me that I was too outspoken. Israel was not quite ready for that, and this trait which he perceived in me absolutely terrified him in light of all the dangers on the other side. To be a secret believer in one's heart was all right in Israel, but to confide this in other Jews was *national treason!*

I wished I could explain the difference between a Christian Zionist and a missionary to him. I had not sought trouble in Israel, but it had knocked on my front door. Words could not have removed his fears at this point. I became queasy with dejection. I said nothing. Kissing him goodbye, we promised to meet at the Norfolk airport. *I was convinced that very few people in Israel and in the West realized what kind of totalitarian hold the religious extremes held on the freedom of thought and speech in Israel!*

The moment I arrived back on my own doorstep, a roaring twister of turbulence and confusion knocked me to the ground. I was ready to let him go back without me, but Nana kept pumping me up to "believe God and not him." We had three more days for a miracle to occur—if it was going to. I personally did not see the possibility at this point. None of these people knew or understood the power of intimidation and control that ruled through religious extremism in Israel! The drama was not finished yet!

On the drive to Virginia, I tossed all my belongings into the trunk....all prepared for that marvelous release from fear I expected to come upon David should it happen. We were to meet at one of the most spiritually dynamic ministries in the country at that time, and if he got no breakthrough there. Well....I had not decided just what I would do. When I again greeted David at the arrival gate, asking him about his visit with his uncle, his smile disappeared. He confided that this uncle was a practicing Ultra Orthodox Jew, and he had felt grossly uncomfortable in his home! He had not seen him since he was a little boy, so he really had no idea what to expect. He appeared happy to be back with me and sighed in relief. Nana and I decided to let David make his debut at the premises of the Christian Broadcasting Network alone. If God was going to perform a miracle, we wanted to step out of the way. He had already spent several days with us, and it was time for another to take over. We all checked into the same Holiday Inn together, and Nana and I waited and prayed while David toured. When David returned in the afternoon, I had never seen him so radiant. I dared not ask any questions but waited until he was ready to let me know just where we stood. We stopped at his door. Yes, it would be all right to have a few minutes alone to share our hearts with each other. As he closed the door behind him, I knew that this was the last occasion I would bear my heart with this man for a long time, unless he had been released from the control of fear over his life and was ready to take an open stand by taking me back with him.

David gently took me in his arms. I looked at him with the strongest plea I knew how. "Yael, I cannot take you with me no matter how deeply I desire to do so." I felt wet drops falling down my cheeks. They were not my tears, but his. I had never seen him cry. We both ached with an incredible longing to be together.

"No, my beloved, we do not completely belong to each other yet." I tore myself away and walked over to the door. "*Laila tov, David.*" I heard no answer, only soft sobs as I closed the door behind me.

Later, as we walked through the Norfolk air terminal together, I exclaimed "Listen, David, there's our song!" The haunting melody of the theme song of "Romeo and Juliet" was playing on the speaker system. The song's title, **"A Time for Us"** hinted of a future time for us together with a distant promise. "God is giving us a sign!" David listened attentively, pondering deep within his own heart.

"Oh God, how I love that man!" I thought as I watched his jet black hair disappear in the crowd that moved down the jet way to the departing plane.

IT IS ZION FOR WHOM NO ONE CARES

"Your wound is incurable, your injury beyond healing. There is no one to plead your cause, no remedy for your sore, no healing for you. All your allies have forgotten you....But I will restore you to health and heal your wounds," declares the Lord. "Because you are called an outcast, Zion for whom no one cares." (Jeremiah 30:12-14)

The rubble and ruins of what had once been my soul lay shattered into splinters and scattered throughout the tiny Tennessee community. Like the sawdust flying away from the buzzing saw, bits and pieces of whispers whizzed past me behind closed doors. No one dared approach me openly in such a small town that had held its head high for generations in the starched robes of fundamental legalistic theology. Many represented the religious extremists of the Christian world. As a public advocate of the freedom, gifts, and power of the Spirit of God for the day in which we lived, I had stood up boldly to the local Pharisees and failed miserably. Anyone could see that all my proclamations and confessions of faith lay wrecked in shambles as a living monument to the utter deception of my beliefs in their eyes.

There did remain a small band of believers, themselves secretly followers of the way of God's Spirit, in contrast to "religion", but most of them met in hiding in the security of private homes. Many of them had weathered a few storms of their own. They had been looking to me for encouragement and support. I had crumbled before their very eyes, feeding their worst fears about this much maligned route of faith they had been taking themselves.

One little group had been so captivated by Nana's vitality and spiritual track record, that they had asked her to teach them at their weekly meetings, knowing that I would soon be departing to Israel with David. On my first visit with them after my day of disaster, I was deeply looking for comfort and support, still licking my wounds and asking a thousand questions about God's *timing*! There was still much for me to learn about God's ways, which were "so much higher" than my own ways.

It had been impossible through all the flurry of events when David was visiting to find time to slow down long enough to weigh certain matters. For example, it had never occurred to me that daring presumption and bold faith were identical twin sisters on the outside, but were worlds apart on the inside. In the case of actual faith, where God had really spoken, neither hell nor high water could stop the performance of His purposes! On the other hand, presumption assumed that God had said something He never uttered. Learning to hear the voice of God was a delicate balancing act, like walking on tiptoes through egg shells. Above all, purity of heart was a requirement. Of course, *the timing of His answers* was also often a test of faith! However, His ways are not man's ways.

Simply stated, David had not overcome the great fear which had been placed on him through intimidation. Moreover, he had believed the lie that had been spoken that "*they would never accept me*" in Israel. I was not sure of the "they", but I knew that I had loving acceptance from some of the people I had met in high places. While I was greatly concerned about David's fear, God showed me about my pride. Everything had not been as we had expected. What the future of our relationship held at this point was a mystery which would only be solved in God's time and my sorting out the pieces of the puzzle. *Timing* appeared to be the keynote. Even David had said, "*It is not time for us*. That was hard for me to accept, because so many things had fallen in place, but as I quietly thought about it, I felt perhaps he was right. God was using him in a powerful way for his nation at this time. Several of the leaders had recognized his prophetic gifting in addressing the extremism and hypocrisy of some religious circles. However, I knew that the Chief Rabbi had made me out to be the villain, before other leaders of the government before David left Israel to come to America.

Nana and I arrived at the next weekly meeting of the little clan of believers. They were running scared because of the spiritual pride and fundamental theology of the Bible belt. We received a cool reception. Nana began her usual sharing, and I gave a report on the warfare on David's behalf as I had perceived it. I had hardly gotten the last words out of my mouth, when Brad interrupted. He was the young businessman who had served as a tour guide for David, while I had sneaked away to the women's party.

Brad launched the most scathing attack of accusations and charges against me I had ever experienced from another believer! I could scarcely believe my ears and I looked around me to make sure I was in the right location! Surely he was mistaken in what he was saying, but I was helpless to defend myself against him.

There in a room filled with fellow believers who had all received some measure of gifts and growth in learning to walk in God's Spirit, I was shredded through a meat grinder before all eyes. Brad first announced to the crowd that "no wonder it all happened the way it did, because David was not even a bona fide Christian!" Of course not! Naomi would never call herself a *Christian* either. They were *Jews*, who believed in a Jewish Messiah, and they did not want to become *Gentile Christians*. I did not blame them either. The big picture of Christendom had persecuted Jews mercilessly. Even as I had studied theology in Germany, I discovered that there were *Nazi officers, who professed to be Christians who prayed over their noonday meal and gassed Jews to death in the afternoon*. They dared to call themselves *Christians!* There existed gross hypocrisy and outright anti-Semitism among many segments of so-called Christianity who treated the Jewish people miserably all through history. No healthy Jew wanted to call himself by that name, nor should he ever have to do so! Generally, they referred to themselves as Messianic Jews, or in Hebrew, *meschichim*.

Brad related that on his trip to the mountains he had begun to pick poor David's brain, which by this time was very paranoid after the Israeli authorities had sent him off from his country with vicious intimidation from the Chief Rabbi.Brad had asked David when he became a Christian and David denied that he was one! None of the many Messianic Jews I knew would call themselves "Christian" either. They believed in the Jewish Messiah but never would identify themselves as "Christian." You had to be a Gentile to be a "Christian." Even my dear friend, Naomi, the most godly person I knew who believed in Yeshua, would not call herself a Christian. Brad was so stunned that he could not go on speaking. He turned around and brought David back to the house.

Brad continued to charge me with false teaching on the events I had shared about how God had been working in the hearts of the Jewish people. According to his theology, that was totally impossible because the gift of the Holy Spirit was only given to those who were already believers in Yeshua. Brad knew nothing about the "working of the Holy Spirit" in both the Old and New Testaments. Nor did he remember the story of Cornelius' conversion in the Bible. He obviously did not understand the sovereignty of God, or the prophets and priests who came under the anointing of God's Spirit all through the Old Testament.

I could have told him about a young Jewish man I knew in Miami who had been sovereignly visited by God's Spirit when he was smoking pot with some friends. It was the beginning of his conversion because he received a wonderful revelation of his Messiah and began to lead a new life! He realized his own spiritual emptiness and realized that Yeshua was standing above him, saying "Reach up, my son, and I will deliver you!" As he relinquished his life to the Lord, the Spirit of God filled him there on the spot and he began a new life!

Brad did not know that Naomi's cousin had met Messiah hanging from a tree in his parachute in the Yom Kippur War. I realized that Brad knew nothing about all the mighty miracles that only God could have done for His people in Israel's wars. As soon as Brad had finished crucifying me in the eyes of all the beholders, he turned and lashed out at Nana. Her prophetic revelation was "full of bologna and her visions had come from the pit!" Brad's behavior caused me to question whether he was a real Christian himself! He sounded more like a religious extremist— the Christian brand of religious extremists," who knew the letter of the Law, but not the ways of God's Spirit!

The blow knocked me breathless. I was stunned speechless. I feebly tried to defend myself. "Are you sure that you really understood David correctly?" I asked. "I sometimes have trouble with the way he expresses some things in English. By the way, Brad, I do not know a single Jew in Israel who believes in Messiah who would call himself a Christian! That is a "Gentile" word for them. It comes from Greek and not Hebrew!

Brad was adamant about his position. His steel pride and seething self righteousness smote me to the core. Even I, who knew David intimately and had spoken often with him, had misunderstood him many times because of the language barrier. Brad had drawn his own conclusions.

Brad, you have no idea of the enormous fear that is attacking him at this time...The Chief Rabbi told him that I was an enemy of the Jewish people before he left Israel. The Israeli ambassador met him at the airport with a warning not to marry me. A Jew never stops being a Jew, no matter what he believes about God. He would never call himself a Christian! Perhaps some Jews who live in Western cultures, like America might, but certainly not Israelis. You don't know what it means for an Israeli to take a stand for Yeshua as his Messiah. They have to give up everything! Israel is a nation of Holocaust survivors, out of the ashes of destruction from nations that they thought were Christians. *Jesus Christ had nothing to do with their persecution and destruction*, but some of the people who call themselves "Christians" did! Jesus commands his followers to *love everyone, even their enemies*. Moreover Israel is surrounded by hostile enemies on three sides. The sea is on her fourth side. If their own family, friends, and employers reject them, they have no place to go as we do in America!"

My words fell on a hard soil and did not penetrate the heart. Brad was self righteous with Bible knowledge, but knew very little about the sovereignty and ways of God. He was in total ignorance of the Jewish people and Israel. He knew nothing of the perils of David's world. Besides, should David have truly denied the Lord, so did the Apostle Peter, also Jewish, in his time out of *"fear of the Jews"*. I shifted the topic to the charge of "false teaching."

"If you will do a careful study of the Bible, you will find out that the Spirit of God came upon many lives in the Old Testament for God's purposes. They prophesized, they performed miracles. Moreover, in the New Testament the Holy Spirit came upon the elderly Jewish man, Simeon, to foretell the birth of Jesus. The Scripture says that he went up to the Temple for Jesus' dedication, "filled with the Spirit," and so on! Yes, God is able to put His Spirit upon His Covenant people, the Jews before they have a revelation of Messiah."

When Brad finished raking me over the hot coals, I knew that the others could only understand my defense if God revealed it to them. Some fundamentalist Christians had made a law book of the New Testament in the same way as some Jewish extremists had taken to the Old Testament. *"The letter of the law kills, but the Spirit gives life."* They were unable to understand God's Word unless God opened their blind eyes! Their real charge was not so much directed against David personally, but in my marrying a "non kosher believer" in their eyes! David and I both were unacceptable in the extremist communities of our own people. When I walked out of the meeting with Brad, I felt as if "Yael" had become the tent peg which they drove into the ground, instead of Sisera's head!

Brad was also young in his faith and probably knew very little about "spiritual warfare"! The Bible states that there are "principalities" and "powers" of wickedness in the spiritual realm that fight against the people and purposes of God. Even believers who seek God's will can be deceived or misguided at times. They can be turned aside from God's plan through the battle that rages over our minds and even faith in God. In our humanity we can easily confuse our personal desires and longings with the will of God for our lives. Our own emotions sometimes prevail over truth. There was a cadre of people pushing me in one direction, while David had said *"It is not the time."*

A whirlwind of terror swept across my mind once I arrived home. I had already heard rumblings of Nana being considered a "false prophet" by some frightened believers. I had images of the community spiritually "stoning me to death" with their tongues. I felt some of the same oppressive feelings that I had in Israel when I had any dealings with the religious extremists. There was little difference between Christian and Jewish extremists. Both groups were self righteous and filled with pride and hypocrisy and ruled over others through fear and control. In the midst of my personal storm, the Lord began to rise up to my defense. He animated my spirit with the verse from the Bible which stated if I would "humble myself before Him," He would provide me with a *"shelter from the strife of tongues and the intrigues of evil and wicked men."* God showed me that I had run ahead of Him in my *timing* in the community and I needed to be close to Him in order to hear His voice.

I failed to tell Brad that Jesus had forgiven dear old Peter, a Jew himself, and one of the spiritual founders of the Christian church, who *denied knowing Jesus out of the fear of the Jews.* Why could God not also forgive a modern day David, too, who had been challenged by the Chief Rabbi of his nation as well as other political leaders and had arrived in the States with that same fear? I had also felt the temptation to deny my Lord when I sat before the Chief Rabbi because of the overwhelming power of intimidation. My survival had been at stake.

Nevertheless, I became a *persona non grata* at the meetings of this Christian group. I knew of no other recourse than to retreat. To whom could I go, except to my loving Father in heaven? How much like a part of Israel this tiny community was with its religious darkness. Fortunately, these events had transpired in a neighboring town and not the place where my parents were living. The two places were like night and day in their atmosphere. My parents lived in a town that had a much higher educational level with a cross section of people from all over the nation. The small town that had made me their enemy was an old coal mining community where generations of families had lived all their lives. In fact, before my rejection, some of the believers who had moved there from other parts of the country had called the town "the armpit of Tennessee." One was more likely to find fierce regional pride, bigotry, and staunch self righteousness. Some of us from other parts of the nation who met there called it God's "humbling factory" for our lives!

The Lord wasted no time in dealing with the lives of those who had judged me wrongly. Many of them began to come under heavy judgments themselves. Brad's entire business failed not too long afterwards. The family who shut us out of their home fellowship had their roof cave in after a snowstorm. One of the more difficult things I had to do was send them some of the little money I had left to help repair their roof. They never acknowledged it, but one week after I mailed it someone gave me ten times the amount to help me. Another woman who had been viciously critical of us came under savage satanic attack.

The rejection had dealt me such a mortal wound that I had no more strength to rise up and fight again. On top of my character assassination before all the eyes of the area, I learned that I still had a number of bills to pay from David's visit. My resources were exhausted. I had a large phone bill to pay because of a multitude of long distance calls to Israel. I was even prone to be angry at David. However, my father, who truly adored David, stepped in and said, "Don't judge a guy until he has a right to a trial." All of these difficulties and lessons were teaching me how to forgive and to love others as God does!

Meanwhile, every time I was assailed with doubts and fears about the future of my relationship with David, Nana would run to prayer and always come back with the exhortation to "hang in there" and not give up. She was convinced that a miracle would take place. It appeared that each expected miracle would lie just over the next horizon.

Consequently, I withdrew to a tiny circle of Nana, my mother and myself and chose to seclude myself from the rest of the world. Nana and mother were very similar in their positive attributes; however, my mother lacked the faith, positive mental attitude, and tenacious fighting spirit of Nana. The three of us decided to go away to a meeting in a distant city where a well known minister was visiting. I felt numb and raw inside, and like my favorite prophet, Elijah, I longed for a cave where I could go and hide!

At the meeting in North Carolina, the minister prayed over different people concerning what he felt God was showing him. When he came to me, he burst forth in a prophetic word. "Oh," he declared, "you *really know* what life without Jesus is like! God has heard your cries for your beloved. He is going to do what you are asking Him! Now, He just wants you to *rest* in Him!" A wonderful spiritual release came upon me. I was energized once again to rise up and keep going.

My relationship with Nana was undergoing a fierce struggle. The strength of her personality overwhelmed me many times. Inside, I secretly blamed her for pushing me out ahead of God's timing. I had wanted to proceed more cautiously. Nana was also smothering me in her passion to mother a brokenhearted child, which I was at the time. At the same time, I was fighting like a wild cat to shut everyone out, because no one had proven worthy of my trust, except perhaps dear Naomi, who was too far away to get engaged in the heat of the battle.

A welcomed letter from Naomi had arrived on the day following a load of unpaid bills that were the result of David's visit. It was such a day when I desired to run away instead of addressing all of the tornadoes that were touching down in my life. I had reached the very last shred of the cord I was holding, and it was about to break. The letter from Naomi read: "*I had a vision of you, nailed to a cross, and you were shattered into a thousand tiny pieces*!" She continued to say, "*This was so that God could pour much more of His life through you!*"

Naomi never had "visions", but I knew that this one was of God, because it ministered great life to my own spirit. I understood that God had been present in my suffering with me, to crush me so that a much greater fragrance of His presence could flow through my life. That was the *way of the cross* that leads a believer from "strength to strength" and "glory to glory." If God had even *ordained* my suffering I could accept it. He was expanding my capacity to allow Him to love through my life! He was cleansing the vessel to use it for higher purposes. There was something very good and beautiful in the midst of all that was happening to me in spite of the incredible pain. Even in becoming an outcast! Messiah himself had suffered the rejection of his own people and the Gentile Romans as well.

As I continued to want to withdraw, Nana ran to my mother's arms for support. It was exactly where God wanted her to be. "I think your mother needs me more than you do," she announced on an emotionally stormy afternoon.

"So do I," I replied.

A few days later, we received the bittersweet news that my mother had cancer! That was the most horrid word in the English language to her ears. Underneath I felt that there was some spiritual blessing hidden in this tragic turn of events. It was destined to bring my mother closer in her relationship to God. Nana decided to thrust herself wholeheartedly into the task of being nursemaid, sister, and spiritual mother to my own mother.

As my mother faced the prospects of dying, her family's spiritual welfare became paramount to her, and she began to learn the power of prayer. She remained a difficult patient to care for. An entire cupboard of unmet needs in her life was opened up and all the broken toys spilled out upon the floor. The Spirit of God began to use Nana to help mend them.

At the same time, even though we related like cats and dogs a lot of the time, I discovered that my mother had a deep concern for my happiness. She wanted to see her single daughter blessed with a happy family before she departed earth. My mother, Nana and I sometimes spent long sessions in prayer together, sharing our own and others' needs. Fortunately, our friend who had allowed us to live in the little country apartment, now opened up a larger two bedroom duplex for us. It was located immediately down the street from my parents and furnished with beautiful old furniture.

One day when the three of us were in prayer together, my mother shouted joyously, "Oh, I see them! I see them!" Her eyes were closed in fervent intercession. I wondered what she had seen, for never in her life had my mother reported anything visual in prayer. She was doubtful about the validity of such things. Afterwards, I learned that she had seen David and me ministering together in some place. I was skeptical, but the fact that it came from my mother was miraculous in itself.

With the increasing passage of time, I got less and less news from David. His father had died just after his return. This mellowed my hurt and anger for leaving me behind, ridiculed before the outside world and with a heavy debt. Nevertheless, God was faithfully supplying the resources from unexpected places. All of the bills were paid on time! Whether David's lack of mail was his own hopelessness, his fear of the rabbinical establishment, or the gradual alienation of affection, I had no way of really knowing. When Naomi had snatches of conversation with him, his eyes would light up as he asked about news from me. He still cared deeply.

How long could anyone last, with no calls, no letters, no warm touch? I could continue indefinitely, as long as I kept on receiving assurances that this was God's plan for our lives. If it was God's plan, I would wait a lifetime for this man!

The season began changing from brilliant plush green to multicolored splashes of autumn leaves cloaking the mountainsides. Finally drab and barren brown dried leaves were canopied with gray skies all around. I thought about Israel's heart cry when she was in exile in Babylon. "By the rivers of Babylon, we sat and wept when we remembered Zion...." I felt the same way, because life in exile was becoming unbearable. I was terribly afraid to take the matter into my own hands. If it was not God's time, there was a possibility that they would not even let me in the country. I knew of others who had encountered such an experience because of religious persecution. I would hate to have to face such embarrassment. If it had to happen that way, I would fight to the end like a wounded tiger. In my imagination I had pictures of the airport officials bodily carrying me away to an airplane to ship me out! My survival was at stake! If there was no one else in the world to stand up for me, I would have to fight for myself....but; of course God would fight for me if I was walking in His plan.

Not only did I devour each weekly edition of The Jerusalem Post, but I religiously lived from newscast to newscast. Somehow, there must be a hidden clue to David's and my coming together with all those roller coaster peace negotiations in the Middle East. I rode up and down them for a while until I finally fell exhausted on the floor. I could take no more. A change in the peace status in the Middle

East could mean everything for David and me. It would signify that Israel would be free to fight her own internal cultural war between the religionists and secularists. That was long overdue. The most democratic nation in the Middle East was forced into living with an aborted theocracy!

I began to mark my calendar by seasons instead of days. I watched my mother progress from lung surgery to cobalt treatment. Then, she went to radiation of the brain with complete hair loss. Her spirit mellowed more and more and many were praying for her healing. She said that if God chose to spare her life, she would use it to serve the lonely, brokenhearted and downtrodden. Yet, if it cost her death to spare her family spiritually, she was willing to go. Although a beautiful hidden work was being done inside her heart, she could still get her hackles up readily.

My own inability to conquer myself with loving kindness and patience with my mother was a sore spot for my spirit. Into this wound flowed the bitter poison of watching those around me find joy, bliss, and victory in the midst of happy families when I had none. The gangrene of envy at other's happiness and my own sorrow began to infect my body. On numerous occasions when others prayed for my welfare, they announced that they felt I had a "*wounded spirit*". I could find no cure. At times I continued to be the victim of verbal abuse and rejection from my mother's own unhappiness. Bitterness filled my spirit like gall, and no matter what Nana said, I was angry at God for allowing me to be treated this way!

I had forsaken all to follow God, but it seemed that all I received was much heartache in return. I had no steady employment but I was surviving financially. My infrequent communication with David sometimes found him distant. I felt like an outcast except for a few people who lived in my parents' community. It seemed that Nana also began to take over my friends, my work, and my own mother. I was pushed aside.

A big test entered into this gloom. I was tempted to compromise. A Christian girl friend from Europe, whom I had met in Israel, was undergoing a parallel relationship with an Israeli musician in New York. She lived in England and he was a student in America. They were also having difficulty bringing their relationship together.

When I heard that Marla was going to visit Avi in the States, I determined to meet with them together. The money came through just in time from an unexpected source.

Two local friends wanted me to help them drive their car to New York, and I saw this as a great opportunity for transportation. As we were driving upstate New York, a fierce thunderstorm hit. We could barely see and the highway was covered with much water. I had a sudden urge to pray. All at once the car hydroplaned at fifty five miles an hour. It spun into the grassy median that divided the double highway and was headed into the direction of the oncoming traffic! Suddenly, it spun around again and stopped on the median. Once again I had been spared a terrible accident or imminent death! *God was still with me!*

When I arrived in New York, I befriended Avi, Marla's friend, and she returned to England. I was able to share with him about spiritual matters and in the subsequent days I began to note some wonderful changes that were taking place in his attitude. The great test came when we both recognized that we needed *visas*—he, in order to remain in America, and I, if I returned to Israel. He was Israeli and I was American. At this time, Israeli young men had difficulty in securing permission for an extended stay abroad by order of their own government, mainly because of military commitments. As for me, I could not be sure that I would even be allowed back in Israel because of the hideous slander against me. Both Avi and I attempted to find a mutual solution to our problem through our own reasoning. If he was married to an American, he would have no problems staying in the U.S. He wanted to set up his own orchestra here.

As for me, if I was legally married to an Israeli, they could no longer intimidate me out of the country in Israel. It really sounded appealing "Jacob style", for us to manipulate our lives in the direction we felt we needed to go. Or, I could try to act as Abraham and try to fulfill the promise with my own actions.

I never seriously considered this project, although it certainly sounded tempting. As long as nothing was happening, Avi and I could "make it happen". I dropped David a letter about this proposal, assuring him that if I married Avi, it was only in order to be accepted in Israel and be closer to David himself. When he felt the time was right, we could legalize our bond. Never would I have entertained the possibility of consummating a marriage with Avi. This little trick had been used by the pioneers who immigrated to Israel in the 1800's and 1900's when they could not get visas from the British to return to their homeland or bring other Jews out of their countries of exile and into early Palestine. So why not now?

I was again broken when David neither found the proposition amusing, nor did it rock him into action. "You do what you believe God leads you to do," was his gentle retort. How could he possibly tell me to marry another man, when I was waiting for him to come and get me and take me back?

Meanwhile, it looked as if a wonderful door was being opened for us. A very large city near where I lived in Tennessee was looking for a conductor position in their symphony orchestra. I felt David would be perfect for the position. While visiting two friends who lived close by in the neighboring community, I met one of the people on the selection committee of the board that was hiring for the position.

David was eager to explore the possibility. He sent resumes, telegrams, and letters, but got no response. The more I plunged right into the middle of the matter, the clearer it became that music was a severely political position. Because of keen competition in the field, it was necessary to play politics to get the best positions.

A friend of mine came along about this time, who knew the party who was leaving the position. He offered to arrange a meeting with him. It looked as if there was a real possibility for David. I thought perhaps God would give us a time of respite together outside of Israel and then send us back into the land for His purposes. David really wanted the position, too. He also made several calls to the States concerning the opportunity.

We both rode the crest of the wave for a few months until it came crashing down on the shore. I read in the local paper that the symphony had hired a Russian to fill the post. Once again my expectations were dashed.

While I was flying high with hope, I decided to write the Chief Rabbi of Israel a letter of apology for my strong reaction of comparing his false accusations to "Nazis". I did not apologize for my beliefs but for my overreaction to his false accusations and for my naiveté concerning the religious situation in Israel. How could I possibly understand the depth of hurt, heartache, suffering, and above all, *fear* that was upon his nation because of past history? As my own trials were multiplied, I felt I was experiencing reverse discrimination. I began to have an inkling of the deep, dark mistrust of the rest of the world that pervaded such thinking because of the Jews' past history. I concluded by asking him what *he suggested* I do to express my loving identification with the Jewish people! I never received an answer. Nor even an acknowledgment.

I finally reached my saturation point with suffering. All around me was raging war. There was opposition on all sides. Most of the time, I felt like the prophet, Elijah, when he wanted to die I could take no more rejection and disappointment. I would welcome almost anything that would help me escape from the overwhelming pain that filled my soul. The mercy of the Almighty spared me from completely giving up and falling into deep despair when I was tempted to overdose on my mother's sleeping pills, or even escaping to my own wilderness in the mountains. One bleak day, I had marched out of the house with the intense desire to get away from it all, without any transportation. I assumed some nice stranger would give me a ride to my friends who lived just over the mountain. When one of the local men of the area saw me standing at the side of the road, he offered me a ride. Most of the people in the community were trustworthy. However, as soon as I climbed into his pickup truck, I knew I was riding with an evil person! This was certainly a sobering wake up call when he propositioned me and I adamantly announced my Christian conviction to him. He continued driving to the next town and suddenly a snow storm began with furious flurry. I did not have a jacket. It was late March—I had never seen it snow at this time. I was sure that this was my "rescue call" from the Lord and announced that I wanted out at once! I had a Christian friend who lived nearby, whom I immediately called to come and pick me up! The Lord revived me with deep gratitude that "his mercies never cease!"

I believe it is either nonexistent or rare in the annals of state history to have a snowstorm in Tennessee in late March. In any case, it stopped snowing as soon as I stepped out of that truck! When I got back to my family's house, I learned that Nana and my mother had been on their knees in prayer as soon as I had left! God had sent that snowstorm to turn me around! I praised Him in gratitude and relief.

My friend in the neighboring town had called a Christian pastor we both knew to come and pray with me. I had reached the bottom with my pain and despair. From the incident, I learned again that forgiveness of others and even my own self is not optional. One must always forgive, if we expect to receive forgiveness.

The Christian pastor who came to my aid offered me no pity. "Yes, you can forgive," he admonished firmly. He sat with me and with his help I chose to forgive all those who had hurt me most deeply, including the rabbinical authorities in Israel. Pastor Jack then warmly reassured me that "even though we are sometimes faithless in our relationship with God, He will remain faithful to us" because he cannot not disown His own character. Those strong words from the little book of Timothy in the Bible spoke great comfort and assurance to my broken heart.

I set aside a time with each of my parents to ask them for forgiveness where I had failed them. I also told them that I forgave them where I felt they had hurt or failed me. It opened up a new relationship with each other, and it certainly freed me from some of the pain I was carrying.

At this time I found great solace from the book of Daniel in the Bible. I came across the passage "*many who are strong in God will stumble and fall in the time of the end, but this would only be in order to refine, purify, and make them spotless*" (Daniel 11:35). I turned to God and begged for mercy to deliver me from all the broken heartedness, pain, and evil forces which had invaded my soul at this most trying time of my life. They had been too strong for me. As the Psalmist said, "they invaded when I was weakest!"

My own unforgiveness and rebellion had been a door for my despairing. God remained faithful and beyond. He continued to be merciful to me. Somehow a message for Israel was born out of this event. Just as Satan wanted to destroy Israel before God could fulfill

His faithful promises to her people and nation, God had promised mercy to His chosen Covenant children. Many of them were still hurting and angry over all they had suffered in the Holocaust. This made it difficult, if not impossible, to place their trust in Israel's God.

Israel was not strong enough to stand alone against the vast horde of evil forces that sought her destruction in the world, but God Himself had promised to step in to her rescue. Not because she deserved it, or had earned it, but because of His mercy! Israel was *indestructible* because of the promise of God! Jeremiah spoke to the nation…*I will restore you to health and heal your wounds, declares the Lord, because you are called an outcast, Zion for whom no one cares.* (Jeremiah 30:12-17)

> And the prophet Ezekiel promised….*I will give you a new heart and put a new spirit in you; I will remove from you your heart of stone and give you a heart of flesh. And I will put my Spirit in you and move you to follow my decrees and be careful to keep my laws. You will live in the land I gave your forefathers; you will be my people, and I will be your God. (Ezekiel 36:26-28)*

Israel, my beloved, needed to forgive those who had hurt her in order to open up a healing fountain in her heart. I also forgave David for breaking my heart, begging God to have mercy on us both. I asked for God to give me a new heart and a new spirit. My deepest cry, though, was "God, why have You allowed me to be so broken, bruised, and betrayed? You are strong enough to stop it—especially since I am your servant. I already knew the answer. I had asked God *to allow me to identify with the Jewish people—even in their suffering!* I had asked this out of love—that wanted to understand and bring healing to their hearts from all the horrors they had suffered from those who had called themselves Christians! I wanted to bring reconciliation between those in the family of God who worshiped the same God! Jews and Christians belonged together.

Unexpectedly, the opportunity opened up for me to go to California. I received it with the realization that it would be a time of healing, restoration, hope, and of spiritual renewal for my life.

SING, O BARREN ONE

"'Sing, O barren woman, you who never bore a child. Burst into joy, you who were never in labor because more are the children of the desolate woman than of her who has a husband, says the Lord."
(Isaiah 54:1)

"Marriages are made in heaven," I always believed if you'll only give the Lord the time to do His job!" This was not some glib saying I had picked up from the gems of ancient wisdom, but a deep and overwhelming conviction. Hence each onslaught against the perfect designs of God for David and Yael served only to drive the roots of conviction deeper into the soil of faith and perseverance! The ways of God are beyond understanding.

I looked at David's and my relationship from the dramatic, poetic, beautiful gift he had given to us. It must be evident to anyone who knew all the details of the story that the heavenly Matchmaker Himself had gone to His pattern books and after careful deliberation, bellowed with holy laughter and made His decision. He picked out a visionary young woman from the pioneer frontier of the big Moabite melting pot of Western culture, gave her a Jewish heart and international vision, and ejected her halfway around the world. There in His personal pressure cooker, He was working on the complement of her soul, the poet and musician, her own David the King, who would inspire her heart and give emotional power to her vision. He shaped them just the right size for each other, too.

The Almighty must have really gotten carried away with His romantic imagination while he was preparing these two in His workshop, with its infinite variety of creative handiwork. He decided to decree a law, stating the magnetic power of attraction between opposites. He chuckled as He planted a desire in the woman's heart for a tall handsome foreigner, and in the man's heart, for a fair haired, statuesque loving lady. Her quest for truth to conquer and his desire for compassion and mercy to prevail were the perfect balance of harmony the world needed.

God was able to overcome all the obstacles that might stand in their path. It delighted the Almighty's generous heart to give this pair parallel preparation in their lives. In his youth the towering *sabra* of Eastern European origin had wandered to the United States with sixty dollars in his pocket and a heart of faith to pioneer his musical career in the West. He survived by mere faith, with unexplainable miraculous events. On the other hand, the American girl had met a marvelous Jew, named Yeshua, and had fallen in love with his Land and people. She set out as a spiritual pioneer in Zion with two hundred dollars in her pocket and much faith in her heart.

These two had an identical love for music and language and nature and the sea and dogs and travel and the way of the Spirit! The Almighty gave them both a faithful friend together in Naomi. Together they were able to inspire others hearts toward a nobler vision of Zion. This couple loved each other with transparency in their souls. And they both had a passion and yearning for the same God, who is the God of Israel. Why even their parents lived in identical houses, one in a small town in Tennessee, and the other in a kibbutz community in the Galilee. How could anyone possibly question the Almighty's wisdom and workings with these two? There was a great problem, though. Israel's God had many earthly enemies who had their rules, regulations, and formulas which did not fit the special mold He had chosen for the design of this pair. Their cultures, through long histories of alienation and misunderstanding did not trust each other, and sometimes considered each other enemies.

Would these two be able to prevail, leap over all the walls of suspicion, fear, persecution and hatred which generations had erected? All of the angels in heaven were standing on their tiptoes looking down in anticipation for the outcome! Yes, the Almighty had given the people below some of His guidelines, formulas, decrees and laws, but in the end, He wanted *everyone to know that His ways are not man's ways!* He is the Sovereign Lord, who does what He pleases! He is very emphatic about that!

Who was puny man to question His choosing a Moses, a shy spokesman, who was married to a Gentile who refused to circumcise her children, outside the camp of Israel's rule book? Or how dare man argue with His putting the lovely Jewish Esther in the court of a Gentile king, to rescue her own nation in a time of national annihilation? Why how could anyone argue with his choice of an adulterer and murderer, King David, to be considered the king of Israel and a "man after God's own heart?" Why should he choose Jacob, a conniver, over the breadwinner, Esau? Or even honor Rehab, the harlot, in the annals of sacred history? Or take the man, Saul, who massacred more Christians than any other in his Jewish zeal, and make him the main spokesman of the Christian faith? Or even select one of the despised materialistic Moabites to be the grandmother of the king of Israel?

The Almighty is always a God of mercy. Was His great sovereign mercy the reason Yeshua said that the "harlots would enter the kingdom of heaven" before the religious rule keepers? Was this the reason why the Almighty Himself was writing the love story of David and Yael? I pondered all these things from a rustic wooded cabin high in the upper regions of the Sierras. I was hidden away from the outside world in the heights of majesty and beauty of nature. I had come apart for a while to inhale the fresh, free air of peace, healing and restoration. From the broad floor of the sun deck, I could sit outside and study the rich fir trimmed cones of the surrounding peaks, meditating on the skill of the Master Artist. I especially loved the snow capped crown on the distant point of the mountain range, royally seated high above all the inferior points surrounding it.

I marveled at how God had already delighted in displaying His sovereignty in my wandering life! He had taken a simple lump of clay from the provincial pots of southern America, setting it down in a communist prison and calling it unto Himself through a Marxist.

While this strange process was in operation, He had raised up a little Catholic nun in a convent, who had read about her captive life in the newspapers and had felt the call to bring spiritual liberation through her prayers! Then, just to show the world He was God, He allowed an "atheist" to secure her release from prison. He then dropped her into the midst of people who were experiencing the promise of Joel, the prophet, who told about God pouring His Spirit upon humanity, and finally united her heart with a very special Jew. He was the Sovereign of the entire world. He could choose whomever He wanted for His purposes.

In the quiet refuge of the Sierra slopes, the Lord began to mend some of the broken pieces of what once was my heart. He showed me that like Israel I often refused to listen to Him, even when He was longing to show me His mercy and compassion. I kept looking to humans for support and comfort and love. Every human would fail at some point or another. The Creator had not designed them to supply the totality of needs to one another, but had reserved that inner void to be filled with Himself. As long as I insisted on doing things my way and not His, my troubles were compounded. I was truly sorry that I was not able to trust him at times in the midst of all those fiery and tumultuous dealings. He informed me that He understood that; for in this regard I was like Israel when He had sent Moses to deliver the people from captivity in Egypt. The Exodus account stated that they did not listen to Moses, "because of their discouragement and the cruelty of the bondage" they had suffered. So, as much as I wanted to, I did not know whether I was even able to *hear* Him anymore. My confidence had been shattered, and my spirit still lay wounded and bleeding on the battlefield.

It was no wonder then, when that gentle, still, small voice spoke once again, I was not sure where it was coming from...my own imagination, a counterfeit...or my Lord.

"Abraham!

"Yes, Lord. Here I am!"

"I want you to rise up, and take your son, your only son, Isaac, whom you love, and go to the region of Moriah. Sacrifice him there as a burnt offering on one of the mountains I will tell you about!"

"And, early the next morning Abraham rose and went up the mountain...."

"Is that You, Lord?" I cried. "What are you telling me?"

"I want you to give your beloved back to me."

"Do you mean David, Lord?"

"Yes. I have given him to you, as the desire of your heart, as I promised I would do."

"Now, I want you to give him back to me."

"Oh Father!" I cried. "I've already told you that I will choose to put you first in my life, whether there is ever again a David or even an Israel for me!"

"But I want you to give him back to me completely. I have told you that if you seek your life in this world, you will lose it. But if you lose it in me, you will find it."

"But Lord, didn't you create us just for each other? Aren't we two halves of a whole?"

"I gave you what you asked for, now I want you to give him back to me!"

"All right, Lord, you can have him back." As I spoke, I felt a deep tearing in my heart.

David was the most precious gift God had given me in this life, next to Himself. I was saddened that I could not release him with the gentle trust of Abraham, but let go I must. In my mind's eye, I laid David on the altar of God.

If I really wanted David to become a true Jew, first I must allow the circumcision knife to cut the flesh from my own heart. For the heart to be truly circumcised by God, every other attachment that clung to God's rightful place had to be severed. The soul must first know the death of its own desires, so that God can entrust everything else into its keeping!

After a brief period of mourning my surrender, I was suddenly enlivened with the recollection that *God gave Isaac back to Abraham*, once his father was willing to sacrifice him.

Why God was just testing my heart strings for fidelity and trust in Him to have first place in my life! This thought brought me true hope for both of our lives.

"He is yours, Lord! I offer him and our love back to You!"

Daily I strolled through the winding roads of the California Sierra Mountains, keeping vigilant guard for wandering rattlesnakes; I waited and longed for some word from my beloved, which I knew would be forthcoming any day now. I wove my way through the woodlands that wound around the big lake down in the valley.

One night I dreamed that David needed my strength in the midst of much confusion, terror, and darkness. Although I had not written in such a long time, so as not to interfere in what God was doing, I began to take up my pen once again. I would encourage him to make the choice he was so fearful about. I wrote a long letter.

My dearest David,

For some time now I have wanted to write you this letter. You see, it has been about four years now, since we met each other. I am so very grateful for having met you....since that first evening when you openly shared your heart with me, I have prayed to God about you...and about His plan for your life...and about His plan for my life. I have told you what I believe that God desires...and for a long, lonely time now, I have held tightly to what I have believed was God's revelation to me concerning you. I have waited far away from you, because I have believed that you needed this time in order to find yourself alone. I wanted you to be free to think clearly, without any influence from me, and discover who you really are and what you really want from life....Now; I believe that the time has come for you to make a decision, a choice....

You see, God offers His children many beautiful promises, but He *never* forces them to accept them or His way for their lives. He leaves the choice to us. It is we who must make the decision whether to follow Him or not.

I deeply understand what your fears are about making this choice concerning me. I have great compassion and feel for you in this. However, I *know* that the love that God offers and the plan that He has for your life is far greater and much more beautiful than what you could try to arrange for yourself or what you might have to leave behind at this moment. When you choose God's way, He will give you more than a hundred fold back of what you have given to Him. For example, the Lord has said:

He who loves father or mother more than me is not worthy of me; and he who loves son or daughter more than me is not worthy of me. (Matt. 10:37)

And also,

Truly, I say to you, there is no one who has left house or wife or brothers or parents or children for the sake of the kingdom of God who shall not receive many times as much in this life and in the age to come eternal life. (Mark 10:29)

God has promised to give back much, much more than any of us could every give away if we choose to follow Him. Now I want to assure you that I will give all that I am and have to give you the most beautiful life you could ever know. I believe that God brought us together to fulfill His purposes together. I have already given up all of myself in this long, difficult period of waiting. I have been deeply faithful to you in body, soul, and spirit, and I shall continue to be, *if that is your desire*.

The *choice is now yours*. I am asking you to let me know your choice at this time. The waiting has been agony. I have much love to give to a family and much desire to begin. If you do not choose, I am sure that God wants to guide my life in another direction. He loves me and wants to see me fulfilled as a woman, and if you do not desire, He wants to give me a man who does.

Most of all, I do love you, and this is my desire:

"Do not urge me to leave you or turn back from following you; for where you go, I will go, and where you lodge, I will lodge. Your people will be my people and your God, my God. Where you die, I will die, and there I will be buried.

Thus may the Lord do to me, and worse, if anything but death parts you and me."(Ruth 1:16-17)

I dropped the letter into the mailbox. Never had I been so bold and assertive to express my love to any man in my life. Following my loving overture, I had a series of dreams concerning David. I dreamed that his mother was trying to get him to marry someone else. I saw him reaching out to me for help, but he was powerless to do anything.

I awakened with the startling realization that now was perhaps the time for me to rise up and fight for this man. He was not strong enough in his own spirit to overcome the forces he was dealing with. Till then, I had purposely remained in exile from my beloved Zion. I could only go in God's time, whenever that was. I was leaving the choice to David to call for my return or to come and get me as he said he would.

As I rambled on the roads of the Sierras, I experienced my first earthquake, which was a solid reminder that God had truly promised to "shake everything that could be shaken!" With each footstep through the dry brush, my urgency increased to "fight for David". I rushed home again, preparing another letter. No, this time I would send a tape with my own voice. The preceding day I had discovered a musical tape in the house where I was staying, with both the melody and the text of the Theme of Romeo and Juliet. I wrote:

A time for us, someday, there'll be
When chains are torn, by a courage born
Of a love that's free.
A time when dreams so long denied
Can flourish as we unveil the love
We now must hide.
A time for us, at last to see
A life worthwhile for you and me.
And with our love through tears and thorns
We will endure as we pass surely through
Every storm.
A time for us, someday there'll be

**A new world, a world of shining hope
For you and me!**

"Oh David, please believe that God is greater than all the obstacles! Please be willing to take a stand for what you know in your heart is right!" I prayed as I posted the tape at the post office.

As I wound my way through the breathtaking descent to Santa Cruz for an international spiritual conference, I knew that *I had to* have some message from the Lord concerning my bold decision to step out and return to the Land that had been the source of my deepest joys and sorrows. This was the first opportunity in many months to enjoy the fellowship of other believers, and a rich banquet of spiritual food was on the agenda with some of the top speakers from the four corners of America.

After having spent so much time out in the waste places of a spiritual wilderness, I felt like a sponge soaking up every word that was uttered at the conference. With each utterance, I felt new life entering my whole being, and ever so minutely the seeds of an inner resurrection taking place. While I sat welded to my chair, at once one of the leaders, an older saintly looking man, walked up to the platform. He was not scheduled to speak.

"I have just had a vision," he announced, "of a shattered glass!" There is someone here who has had a vision you felt was from the Lord. That vision has just been *shattered!* Now, if you put your hand in the hand of Jesus, he has something *far better* for your life! The Lord is also speaking to you from Jeremiah, chapter 18, concerning the potter and potter's wheel!"

The elderly man of God returned to his chair on the platform and the speaker began his talk.

My eyes blurred. My heart pounded. My body began shaking uncontrollably. A deluge of racking sobs began to erupt from the innermost chamber of my soul. I could not stop. I knew his word was for me. A part of me wanted to resist. "Don't let go of the promise!" it said. No matter how hard my mind fought tenaciously to hold on to the "promise," my inner being was trembling incessantly. No one in the world could help me in that moment. I rushed out of the audi torium and got into my car. I was barely able to see because of the flood of tears that were unceasing.

From Santa Cruz I drove the lonely spiral road back to the Sierras with confusion and dejection. How very much the drive reminded me of the winding rocky fir speckled cork screw road between Tel Aviv and Jerusalem. "Oh God, I really don't understand!" A thick shroud of black silence suffocated the atmosphere in the car.

When I returned to the house, which a friend of mine had arranged for me at one of the highest peaks in the mountains, I pulled out my Bible and pored over Jeremiah 18.

"Then the word of the Lord came to me, 'O house of Israel, can I not do with you as this potter does?' declares the Lord. Like clay in the hand of the potter, so are you in my hand, O house of Israel.'" When the clay was warped on the wheel, He had to remold it into another vessel.

God was telling me that *He has the right to change His mind, especially when we fail to choose Him on our part!* But what did it all mean for David and me?

For a couple of days, I paced around the house like a rat running in circles in a cage. One moment I felt I needed to rush to Israel and fight for our relationship. The next moment I wallowed in the sticky tar of self pity, which was a black substance that clung to my soul.

As I reached into the mail box one afternoon, I jerked my hand out instantly. A breakthrough had arrived. There was a letter from David! Both exhilaration and terror ran through me at the same time. This would be a turning point, no doubt.

I ran to the car. I wanted to sit down to read the news. I ripped open the envelope as quickly as I could. "Oh thank God. It is in English instead of Hebrew this time." I thought. I had spent hours trying to decipher the Hebrew.

I read the words. "Yael….I have made my *decision,* as you asked me to do….*I have already been married two days now….*

I dropped the blue sheet to the floor. Paralyzed, I could not continue. Like a huge claw, the words tore into my heart. Disbelief grabbed me. Maybe I misunderstood. I picked up the paper again. "I've already been *married two days now…."*

"My God! My God! Why have you forsaken me?" I screamed on the inside. "I don't understand! I don't understand!" Even though I had truly given David back to God, on the altar like Isaac, I had honestly expected God to return him to me, just as he had done with Abraham! That had not happened.

Mechanically, I drove back up to the top of the mountain. Inside I had descended to a state beyond any consolation. Back in the mountain cabin, I flung myself across the bed, numb, with shock.

I looked at the blue crumpled sheet again. I had not read past the words "married for two days". I proceeded onward. "I hope you will find someone, too, and I wish you happiness...I'll be looking forward to working with you in the future on behalf of Israel...."

I dropped the paper to the floor. How could he possibly...? I stopped. I had no more answers. No more questions. I knew nothing any longer. Not even God. I was even too dead inside to die.

The following days of mourning were spent in total oblivion. One glimmer of light penetrated the gloom, which I knew to be my own spirit. With a quiet assurance, it announced, "I don't *understand, but I trust You."* Somehow, in the farthermost corner of my soul, a victory had been won. It had to do with absolute trust in God. It transcended signs, scriptures, prophecies, visions, words, directions, human understanding, people, confirmations, and circumstances. It rested on the very character of God Himself!

"I am my beloved's and He is mine!" The Song of Solomon proclaimed. My beloved was God alone, who had just drawn me into an intimate revelation of Himself that few could understand. He was longing to be my husband, as He was longing to be Israel's husband. To occupy the first place in the hearts of His people. "All right, Lord," I said. "Let's get on with whatever business You have for my life!"

Although I was utterly and mortally wounded in my humanity, I was reminded "that those who sow in tears will reap in joy." I knew that behind all I had endured; God was speaking the same message to me that He was so ardently trying to tell Israel. "I, the *Lord, am your beloved, O Israel. Though all other people in the world fail you and let you down, I will never fail you... Come back to me and drink from the fountain of my love, and I have treasures to bless you with—even treasures of darkness. No mortal can satisfy as I can!"*

Once again, the Spirit of God broke through the barrier of darkness, to comfort my heart and the heart of Israel:

> Sing, O barren woman, you who never bore a child; burst into song, shout for joy, you who were never in labor; because more are the children of the desolate woman than of her who has a husband says the Lord.
>
> *For your Maker is your husband—the Lord Almighty is His name. The Holy One of Israel is your Redeemer; He is called the God of all the earth. The Lord will call you back as If you were a wife deserted and distressed in spirit—a wife who married young, only to be rejected, says your God. "For a brief moment I abandoned you, but with deep compassion I will bring you back. In a surge of anger I hid my face from you for a moment, but with everlasting kindness I will have compassion on you, says the Lord your Redeemer. (Isa 54:5-8),*
>
> *"Weeping endures for a night, but joy comes in the morning." Psalm 30:5*

With the sheer power of faith in God's words, and the determination of my will, I would stand up and walk forward once again out into the midst of an unknown direction and an uncertain future.

COMFORT IN JERUSALEM

"As a mother comforts her child, so will I comfort you; and you shall be comforted in Jerusalem." (Isaiah 66:13)

The seat belt sign lit up in the cabin of the huge El Al jumbo jet. The flight captain announced "Ladies and gentlemen, prepare for landing in Tel Aviv." Squealing curly topped youngsters bounced back into their seats, with their rotund mamas pushing them along the aisles. Here and there black topped, bearded men rocked their heads in their seats with prayer books held high. Yiddish and Hebrew dialogues were heard all around me like torrents of gurgling streams. The year was 1980 and I was about to land in Israel to celebrate the very first Christian celebration of the Feast of Tabcrnacles in Jerusalem. This was one of the most joyous of all the Jewish holidays, and it inaugurated my re-entry into Israel after four years in exile.

I glanced at the young woman on my right. She found great difficulty in heaving her head from her husband's shoulder and lifting her heavy eyelids. The all night flight and jet lag to boot were too much for her system to accommodate. I reached inside my handbag, making the last preparations of improvement to my sleep wrinkled face. Just minutes away, the streets of Jerusalem would become my footstool once again. How was Israel prepared to receive my homecoming?

Till that very moment deep peace had pervaded my crossing. Had not the Lord provided a miracle for my return? When my lady friend had handed me the brochure about the Feast of Tabernacles conference and tour to Jerusalem, my first inclination was to push it away. "I'm no glutton for punishment," I thought. "I've learned to run as fast as I can in the opposite direction at the slightest smell of trouble!" How could I ever set foot on the soil of the land that had bruised, badgered, and broken me? I felt no blame toward her or her native sons and daughters, but my wound was too deep to touch the hurt which her vital heartbeat would ignite in my soul.

For five long years I had nurtured a *wounded spirit*, which no amount of praying, pleading, repenting, or begging help from God or man could begin to heal. The wound had been too deep, even incurable, until God Himself would rise up in His mercy and heal me. I was not allowed the luxury of crawling into some dark hole in the earth, zipping up the cover over my head, and shutting away the outside world. Nor did I flee to the refuge of some hideaway which greatly tempted me. I had been forced to stand up on my crippled spiritual legs and face the world with the sheer determination of will power and the fragment of faith I had remaining.

Eventually, I had been planted down in the middle of one of the most dynamic, demanding and challenging jobs of a lifetime. I was praying, counseling, and training others to minister for an entire megalopolis. Who could possibly know the pain, disappointment and heartache of others through experience any better than I and share the hope and comfort that God promises for those who trust in Him? Job had become my favorite person, and the Book of Lamentations my greatest consolation! God did promise restoration *in the end.* This was my hope!

In the meantime, my dear mother had departed the earth. She had been ready to go when her time came. Our last visit together was tender enough to erase all the scars of a bruised past. The beauty of togetherness was enhanced by a moving insight from the Lord. I felt He was saying to me, "No longer view her as your mother; begin to see her as My precious daughter, whom I am calling home to be with Me." An incredibly great love had swept over me as I received this revelation. My mother belonged to God and she was going home to be with Him. Her death came on the eighth day of January—the biblical number of new beginnings and resurrection!

I had long since stopped reading The Jerusalem Post, or paying too much attention to the newscasts, even though Naomi and I both knew that it had been the Spirit of God who sent Anwar Sadat into Jerusalem! Everything that reminded me of Israel was filled with pain, heartache, and longing. I had no desire to die another death. Yet, when I saw the title of the conference, "Feast of Tabernacles", *Succoth,* in Hebrew, I knew the biblical significance of that feast day.

The Feast was the only Jewish festival which had not in some way been fulfilled in the New Covenant. Jesus had been crucified on Passover, as God's lamb for the sins of the world. The Spirit had been poured out on the Feast of Weeks, or Pentecost, the same time Israel had received the Law. Tabernacles, or Booths, as it was also called, had no fulfillment yet, which pointed it to the ingathering of the harvest and the return of the Messiah. Was it perhaps God's plan for me to be a participant in such a gathering in Israel? Fearfully and reluctantly I had prayed, "Lord, if you want me to go on this trip, please show me by providing the money." I was relieved, because I knew a trip to Israel was impossible without divine intervention.

As if He had been waiting for me to say the word, suddenly people began to offer me money for that trip. First, a loving family gave me $800, then another $100. In a short time the entire sum was there! Obviously, the Lord desired me to go.

As the rubber tires screeched on the runway and the sound system played "*Heh vey nu shalom aleichem.*" A pain stabbed my heart. I inhaled a deep breath. So far so good. I had received royal treatment at the El Al terminal in New York. There had been no problem in clearing the passport controls there. The religious underground probably dared not challenge a person outside of the borders of Israel, for it might ripple world indignation. But how would they treat me in Israel?

I was third in line behind the other women who had joined the trip from Miami. Their entry proceeded quickly. Suddenly, it was my turn. I took a deep breath and uttered a prayer. "God if they have me on any black list, please blind their eyes!" I had carefully chosen the least stern looking of all the officials, yet the young Israeli had a hard, militant air about him. I handed him the document with my nicest smile. He held it some seconds branding it with the entry stamp, and then returned it. I was free! I could enter my beloved land once again!

A fountain of joy welled up in my spirit. I skipped over to the baggage carts, and instantly spotted a sign that welcomed the Christian pilgrims who were arriving for the Feast of Tabernacles. I was being welcomed! "Oh, Lord, you are bringing a new spirit to Israel!" I met our warm, lovely hostess who was to lead us through customs and to the tour bus to Jerusalem. My feet were firmly standing on Israeli soil once again, and I could not believe my eyes!

The most fluent flow of Hebrew I had ever known began tumble from my lips, as if I had always been there and had never left. Light and joy surrounded me. I knew that great surprises were in store on this trip! In all my three previous years in Israel, I had never stayed in a hotel, so I had the distinct impression that I was about to see the Land of Promise from another side.

All along the gardens and balconies of Jerusalem, the *Succoth*, or booths or tabernacles, were seen with their palm thatched roofs and tenting. It was the season of joy and celebration, and the time Jesus had stood up in the Temple on the last day of the Feast and said in a loud voice, "If any man is thirsty, let him come to me and drink. Whoever believes in me, as the Scripture has said, streams of living water will flow from within him!" By this he meant *the Spirit whom those who believed in him would receive*. (John 7:37-39)

The arrival of over a thousand Christians from twenty or more nations in order to celebrate the Feast had already captured the headlines of the Israeli press. I laughed inside myself when I realized that this was the only Land in the world where Bible prophecy was printed in the newspaper as current news! The prophet Zechariah spoke of the nations coming up to Jerusalem to participate in the Feast of Tabernacles with the Jews, and many Israelis informed us of this upon arrival, while it was actually happening before the eyes of the ordinary man of the street.

There was a gathering of multitudes of Christians from the four corners of the earth. The gathering was encased in the festival atmosphere of a rapturous outburst of musical joy. The event was filled with challenging teaching for Zion to stand up and be seen by the world, as the light she was called to be. All of this provided a magnificent beginning for the annual celebration of the Feast of Tabernacles for Christians from the entire world in Jerusalem. The Jews were reminded that the God of Israel was also the God of the Christians. The Christians were told that their God was the God of the Jews.

Wrapped in the theme of festive joy, was also the call of Isaiah the prophet, which the Christian pilgrims were taking as their theme: *"Comfort, comfort my people,"* says your God. "Speak tenderly to Jerusalem, and proclaim to her that her hard service has been completed, that her sin has been paid for, and that she has received from the Lord's hand double for all her sins!" (Isaiah 40:1) Almost every speaker quoted the same verse from the Psalms, "*You shall arise and have mercy upon Zion; the time to favor her, the set time has come!"(Psalm 102:13)* Those were the words God had given me for HOPE FOR ISRAEL, the non profit organization I had established in America in order to bless Israel.

My first personal surprise package arrived as I was walking up King George Street to the Anglican School where all of our sessions were being held. I turned to the ladies accompanying me, "Oh there's a car that looks just like my old VW." It was my car! The proud new owner was a Messianic Jewish immigrant from the States, and she was walking in front of me. Although I had given her my car when it became evident that my return to Israel was not impending in the near future, I had never met her. She beamed as she related how it had come as a great answer to prayer in a difficult time and place of struggle. I saw how my own death had brought life to another. When I had left, all of my worldly belongings had remained behind to eventually be given away. I had started my life all over in the States with only one suitcase of clothes.

Later, in the school courtyard, I met one familiar face after another, and each glowed in welcome reunion. Lana even telephoned the conference to give me an invitation to visit her in the south, for she had been unable to come! The people, the faces and the events reassured me that my suffering had not been in vain, for it was all bearing fruit.

The first highlight of the reunion with Jerusalem came at the opening of the International Christian Embassy, whose presence offered an expression of solidarity with the Jews' belief in Jerusalem as the "*eternal undivided capital*" *of their nation.* The Moslem world had pressured all of the nations to withdraw their embassies from Jerusalem. While most were succumbing to this pressure, denying the Jews the right to Jerusalem as their capital, a group of Christians, many who had been living in Israel, along with a large number who also came from other countries, joined together at the time of the Jewish holiday *Succoth,* (the Feast of Tabernacles), announcing their stand with Israel, and recognizing Jerusalem as her God given capital.

While the rest of the nations were withdrawing their embassies from Jerusalem, the Christians said "We will open an embassy in Jerusalem to let the world know that we are standing with Israel on behalf of Jerusalem as their "eternal undivided capital." The purpose of the Christian Embassy was identical with the vision God had given me for HOPE FOR ISRAEL! This realization was magnified above everything else. It was confirmation for me that I had truly been discerning God's purpose for Christian solidarity on behalf of Israel and Jerusalem as her capital and that this was to be a massive expression of solidarity of Christians from all over the world to express their loyal standing with Israel, both in their own nations and in an annual celebration at the time of the Feast of Tabernacles in Jerusalem.

The grand opening was accompanied with music, flags of the nations, and the dedication of each country's representative. It was spectacular. Everyone's heart was warmed when the mayor of Jerusalem, Teddy Kollek, told the people that those who had withdrawn their embassies because of political pressure represented their "governments", but the Christian pilgrims represented the "people!" I was especially moved by one Israeli political figure in the crowd. He had hurriedly painted his own sign with the words, *"We welcome the Embassy of all honest Christians to Jerusalem, the united, undivided capital.*" I stood with him and helped him hold the sign for the television cameras.

My next round of rejoicing came as I carried the American flag down a hill to the starting point of the annual Jerusalem parade, which had not been held for some years because of costs. The parade had been reinstituted at the report of the news of Christians coming from twenty-one nations of the world. All the Christians were invited to participate in the annual Israeli parade, along with the Israelis. They were asked to march in a position of honor, directly behind the Israeli Army! As I carried the American flag down a long hill to the leader of the American Christians who would be marching, I heard shouts of "*kol ha kavod!*" "We honor you" for standing with us, America, our friend!" A group of Israeli women soldiers began to sing, "*He nee ma tov*" in Hebrew—"How good and pleasant when brothers ("sisters") dwell together in unity!" I was really delighted by their overture to friendship, and I remembered that it was the Israeli flag that I had carried in a Christian rally in Washington previously.

The highlight of my "reentry" into my beloved Israel came when the parade actually began. Someone had made a huge banner in Hebrew which stated "*Israel, you are not alone!*" They invited me to march with them. Nothing could have compared with the joy I felt from the experience of observing the faces of the Israelis as they read the sign. Tears, shouts of honor, joy, extended arms of welcome and handshakes, eyes filled with comfort and hope, warmth and friendly nods, all came from the hearts of the Israeli people as they read the sign. "Israel we love you!" I shouted. "Israel we love you!" Even the most rigid military officer who was guarding the parade relaxed his face muscles with a warm smile as he saw and heard our pronouncements of love for the Land and people. Israel was not alone. Their hearts embraced the love and comfort that was being extended to them.

Another sublime surprise from heaven awaited me after the parade. The Chief Rabbi of Israel, the very person who had slandered me to David, had invited the entire group of pilgrim Christians from all the nations represented into the main synagogue, *Hechal Shlomo,* in order to pronounce a blessing upon us from Jerusalem!.

Our large group was welcomed into an upper auditorium by an assistant to the Rabbi, who informed us that it was "faith and hope" which had sustained the Jews through 2000 years of horrible times."

He reminded us that Israel was the only Land that was called the "Promised Land". This kind man told us that the presence of this group of Christians with the opening of the Embassy, was a "ray of light in the midst of darkness," telling the Jews that they "were not alone!" He paused, as the Chief Rabbi entered, and introduced "His Eminence, the Chief Rabbi of Israel!"

My heart sank. The wheels began racing in my mind as I scrutinized the man who had slandered me and intimidated David. He had grayed considerably since I last saw him. I was sitting very far in the back of the auditorium along with the rest of the women, while the men took their places in the front. He began by welcoming us to the "holy, permanent, undivided capital of Jerusalem!"

The Rabbi then stated that for those who "believe in the vision of the Bible and prophets, it is important for non Jews to come to Israel and demonstrate their solidarity, according to the fulfillment of the prophecy of the last days." While he uttered the words, I noticed he used some of the same words I had spoken to him some years before.

"Living in Israel," the Rabbi continued, "a man who does not believe in miracles is not a *realist!*" I recalled how he had previously sounded skeptical when he had mentioned the "miracles" of Jesus or even the Jewish prophets in the first interview I had with him.

This learned man of many hats, proclaimed how Jews who lived in exile knew nothing but failure. However, in the land of Israel, they had not failed on any project they undertook. Then, he added, to be on the "safe side", one had to learn to pray. He related an account of a parachutist who refused to pray and broke his hands! That was an admonition to prayer!

He changed the tone of his discourse. He became somber. "Inevitably, any Jew who is bearing the heart of Israel to the outside world has to speak about the Holocaust. It is their way of crying out and saying, "We *have been hurt! We still feel the pain. We cannot trust till we are healed.*" The Rabbi then told us that one and a half million babies had died in the Holocaust. What would their contribution have been had they lived? Also, the fact that six million Jews had been massacred by the enmity of outsiders was a memory that haunted every mind in Israel!

Then, with proud proclamation, the Rabbi declared, "We are fulfilling the vision of the Bible. The national accomplishments have not failed in the vision of the prophets. The Bible is the charter of the Holy Land!" I immediately thought about just how much the Bible had been violated in the way I had been treated, but I had chosen to forgive. His tone softened, as if he might be uncovering his heart. "*I did not believe after such hatred in the world ever to see such a group come to demonstrate solidarity and belief in the future of Israel!*"

"May the Lord extend His blessings from Zion!" The Rabbi exclaimed with exuberance. "For," he explained, "it is a Jewish belief that the gates of Zion are open to every human in the world! You are a part of the accomplishment of the prophetic vision! Your presence here will always remain a golden page! May God bless you in your holy mission to Israel and the world!"

I rushed outside, knots twisting in my stomach. Tears were streaming down my cheeks. I could feel love for this little man who was hard as nails on the outside! For that reason, the pain cut me deeply. I could see beyond his military exterior, his rigid religious code, his Jewish national pride, and his absolute ignorance of what true biblical Christianity was all about. I caught a glimpse inside his heart. *Fear* had been the cancerous root that sapped up the deadly poison which had been directed against me! But why had he, of all people, *chosen to believe slander, Instead of giving me an opportunity to verify truth? H*ad he not allowed me to defend myself with truth by explaining myself? Or face my false accusers?

Now I could understand. The most poignant thing he said was the crux of the deep rift that occurred between us. "Inevitably any Jew who was bearing the heart of Israel to the outside world had to speak about the Holocaust. *It was their way* of crying out. It was their way of saying, 'Look how we have been hurt. We still feel the pain. We cannot trust until we are healed.'

That very wound was at the heart of Israel, a nation of holocaust survivors. Before they could trust a Christian, they needed to see and hear the deep humble apology for the abject failure of the Christians to love, support, and protect the Jewish people in their time of need. They needed to see genuine repentance from the Christian world for every act and attitude of anti-Semitism. How could they ever believe in the Messiah that Christians followed when His people had so miserably failed the Jews time and again for 2000 years? *The Jewish people had not seen His reality in us. A ministry of deep repentance in the hearts and minds of the Christian Church must precede reconciliation with their Jewish brethren*!

My heart was deeply broken. I had been slandered somewhere by someone unknown. There was no way I ever could have earned his trust. I had come with great sacrificial love to give to Israel; in fact, I was willing to give my own life, but I had been maligned and viewed with suspicion and rejection. There was absolutely nothing I could do to erase it for me, but when we came *as a group of international Christians, standing together in solidarity with Israel*, we had been received into the main synagogue in Jerusalem by the Chief Rabbi of Israel. He had given us his bona fide blessing! It was a major turning point in the history of Jewish and Christian relations, because Jesus had wept over Jerusalem and told them *"you will not see me again until you are ready to say "Blessed is he who comes in the Name of the Lord!" That blessing had just been pronounced by the leading Jewish authority in the Land!*

Every facet of our time together in Israel linked the heart of the Christians and Jews more deeply and released drops of healing to Jewish hearts. As I planted a tree on the hillside outside Jerusalem, uttering my prayer, I remembered how years earlier I had helped plant an entire orchard on my kibbutz. I felt it was a monument of my love for the Land, and I was looking forward to seeing its growth before my departure.

Later, as I wandered through the grim halls of *Yad Vashem*, the memorial of the tragedy of epic proportions of the Holocaust, I was deeply grieved once again by the depth of the scar on the Jewish national soul. Six million adults and children had been brutally and senselessly destroyed for no crime "other than being Jewish". How could any outsider fathom the pain and torment of those they left behind? It was an "incurable wound" that only Almighty God could heal. I began to realize that part of that healing had to come through the genuine Christian believers. We professed faith in Israel's God and Messiah. Now, we had to demonstrate it through deeds and not mere words. The Christians of the world had to rise up and be Israel's best and faithful friend. There was no other human way for her heart to be healed.

When our group gathered outside the grim monument, we sat down on a huge stone slab and held a repentance service together. "God forgive us for not showing mercy to the Jewish people. Forgive us for closing our eyes in their time of need. Forgive us for not hearing their cries of heartache and desperation. Forgive us for every act and attitude of anti-Semitism that any Christian anywhere, any time has ever perpetrated against the Jewish people. For, even the Messiah we believe in has said "As we treat the least of his brothers, so we treat him." Forgive us for not loving our God or loving our neighbor. Forgive us for our sins against God Himself by the way we have treated His Jewish people!" Please, Oh Lord, heal the hearts and minds of Your bruised and broken people!

We prayed for healing and restoration. We asked for the broken hearts of the Jewish people to be healed. We asked for genuine reconciliation to take place between Christians and Jews. How on earth could a real Christian hate or harm a Jew when God commanded us to love?

Our somber visit was followed by a gala dinner in the evening. The Jerusalem believers had outdone themselves in preparing a Yemenite specialty. There was lots of food, fun, and fellowship between the Christians and their honored Israeli guests by this time. A long standing Israeli friend of one of our leaders was asked to give her impressions to the gathering.

This pioneer was deeply rooted in Israel's restoration to nationhood. She stood up and spoke to the audience in gutsy candor. We were assembled under the starry canopy of the courtyard garden of the Anglican School in Jerusalem. The elderly woman poured out the anguish of her painful personal memories of her nation in danger of survival. She warned us that when someone is treating a patient in suffering or survival, he or she is in a precarious position. "*To touch the Jewish nation could be an 'episode' or a 'covenant'.*" She shared her own "*covenant*" with Israel with us, describing it as a greatly demanding commitment. "To form such a covenant with Israel would entail the very meaning of one's life!"

I felt she was unknowingly speaking to me. I had already suffered an "episode", but yet I was still committed to my covenant with Israel. It had cost me *everything*, including the loss of my reputation and the loss of the beautiful love of my life! Yet, I was determined to remain faithful and loyal. The courageous woman challenged all the Christians there to decide whether they were choosing to stand with Israel in a covenant relationship or were merely engaging in a beautiful memory which would be forgotten when they returned to their own home countries. "This is a heavy issue," she warned, "you must examine yourselves and determine whether what you are doing *is humble enough to* allow the Jews to find their own relationship with God! The relationship between the *Jews and God is between them and their God! You must have no hidden agenda in what you are doing!"* Then, as if she had exposed the root of her own heart, she announced, *"We have too many hurts for you to try to change us!"*

"Wow," I thought! There we go again with the "wounded heart of Israel". I felt that this brave woman was God's prophetic voice crying in the wilderness to us. She was the voice of her people "Don't push us! You don't understand how deeply we have been hurt. Let us find our own way at our own pace!"

Once again, big moist drops rolled down my cheeks. I wondered whether David had felt that I was pushing him. My heart ached for him to know what was the "height and depth and length and breadth" of God's love for him. I loved him so deeply I wanted that for him. But God loved him even more. I was also very grateful that the first Jewish disciples and followers of Messiah had brought me the news of their God and a relationship with Him. It was the greatest gift in the world in my life!

Gentile Christians are deeply indebted to the Jews, for all that we have in our faith comes through them. It is a Jew who has brought us life and love and hope and joy and peace and blessing and salvation! In gratitude we desire to bring blessing back to them. It is the nature of love to *give* to the beloved. *Yet when one is deeply wounded, it hurts to be loved.*

When the Israeli woman took her seat, the Arab Christian wife of the Dutch leader stood up to speak. She told us that she personally *knows* the price of walking in a covenant relationship with Israel. She has had to stand with Israel at the expense of the rejection of her own people! For, she was a Christian first, and then an Arab!" She was the living expression of just how much it cost for a Christian to love the Jewish people unconditionally.

Her words reminded me of the Arab Christian pastor I had heard at the conference on the Mount of Olives. He had said, "The best way to get rid of your enemies is to *love* them!" In his church congregation he was doing what the United Nations was unable to accomplish! Arabs and Jews loved each other and were fellowshipping together.

Our last days in Israel were packed with visits to hospitals and to Israeli homes. The goal of the conference was to touch the heart of the land, as well as provide comfort and rejoicing for the people. Lasting bonds were formed between Christians and Jews at this time, and I truly felt that the ancient wall of partition between our peoples was crumbling. At least in the Spirit!

The last day of our festivities wound up at the "Wailing Wall", the remaining piece of the last Temple wall. We watched observant Jews dancing with the Torah scrolls for the holiday of *Simchat Torah, "The Rejoicing of the Law"*. The Western Wall was a very special place for me, as for all the Jews, whether through historical significance or religious conviction. My very first visit there had brought an unexplainable deluge of tears tumbling down my cheeks. They had flowed unexplainably from my spirit.

"Pray for the peace of Jerusalem," they said to me as I examined wide cracks in the wall which were stuffed with a multitude of prayer requests that cried out with urgency and longing. Hidden there in the remnant of the remains of what was once Israel's glory, the most holy spot standing in her memorable history, were the pleas that expressed both the chains to her past and the hope for her future.

I sat upon a stone protrusion from the Wall, talking with another woman whom God had called to be a "watchman on the walls of Jerusalem," not unlike myself some years before. The traditional prayers at the conclusion of the great Feast of Tabernacles included a request for rain, which was a vital necessity in the Middle East. I looked up at the sky. A giant heavenly gray cloud hovered over the square below, just waiting to explode at any minute. While I stood watching the chanting men draped in their prayer shawls, and the circling of the Torah scrolls, the first big drops fell from the sky. It felt as if the Lord could not contain Himself any longer, waiting to pour out His blessing upon His people!

The young Israeli guide, who led our group walked over to our area, eager to engage us in conversation. His blunt and probing questions were kind in their intention, so I felt drawn to a hungry heart. I had been waiting like that cloud overhead, to break forth and share my own love story with Israel with someone. Moshe was all ears.

I began to relate how there were many Christians like myself and Martha who sat with me, who loved Israel, would sacrifice all for her, and come to stand at her side. While I narrated, Martha entwined bits and pieces of her own early widowhood and subsequent call of the Lord to come to the Land and People of the Book.

Moshe's eyes widened into two large circles. I've never heard these things before," he uttered in amazement. "No one has ever talked to me this way. Most people are so superficial....I did not know that Christians cared. I've always been told the opposite...." His heart was bursting, and he could not get enough details from us.

I glanced up over the big Wall to our right, to those stones that had heard the secrets and desires of generations. My attention was drawn by a beautiful white dove, graciously circling over the area, diving up and down with occasional aerobatics. Moshe was watching, too. "You know," he explained, "the dove is a symbol of God's Spirit to us Jews."

"And to us Christians," I replied, recalling how the dove had descended upon Jesus after his baptism. A heavenly voice had thundered, "This is my beloved son, in whom I am well pleased! Listen to him!"

As Moshe spoke, the wall between our two worlds got smaller and smaller. Suddenly, it was no longer there. We became two people, sharing our hearts with each other. For the first time, I felt free to empty my soul of the adventure and heartache of my personal love story with Israel, her people, and a man called David.

Moshe listened. with tender receptivity. "I will marry you!" He exclaimed. His deep brown eyes became more intense, and I knew he was speaking from his heart.

I smiled softly and shook my head. "That's beautiful, Moshe, I am really honored by your concern....and touched....but I know that God has a special plan for my life...and I have to let Him make that choice for me...."

"Maybe it's me?" He questioned sincerely. "I have not found anyone yet!"

"Moshe, I'll ask God to lead you to the right person."

As we wound our way through the packed passageways of the Old City, with its pungent smells and Arab beggar children, Moshe kept his hand on my shoulder. The unique blend of rugged aggressive masculinity and gentle, tender hearts in the Israeli sabra men still stirred me to the core. Once again, the Spirit of God was wooing the spirit of Israel, and I was reminded that this was where the story really began....

"Moshe, God promised to give Israel a *new heart and a new spirit*, and I am feeling the birth pangs in the air, even now. My beloved Israel has changed since I last saw her. She is softer in her heart, more open and more receptive. I have *great hope for her future!*"

HOPE! I had never heard a Christian sermon on "hope", but it was the fuel that had run my engine for the past few years. "*Hatikvah*"," *The Hope*" was the national anthem of Israel, and the byword of her longings and aspirations:

So long as still within our breasts
The Jewish heart beats true,
So long as still toward the East
To Zion looks the Jew,
So long our hope is not yet lost—
Which two thousand years we cherished
To be a free nation in our Land,
The Land of Zion and Jerusalem.

My eyes could never remain dry as I stood and sang Israel's national anthem with her people in Hebrew. While the military musicians had continued to proclaim the hope for Israel's future on a platform at the Western Wall with a dove flying over and a tender-hearted son of her native soil standing before me, I knew that my future with Israel was being resurrected, out of the ashes of my shattered heart. It had only passed through a dark night of death in order to soar like a phoenix with new life, depth, sensitivity, and hope for Israel's tomorrow.

I left Moshe with a new set of friends in Jerusalem, where he had just moved from the Tel Aviv area. The last crowds had dispersed to their tourist buses, or headed to the airports back in the direction of their homelands. I had a couple of more items on my agenda before Israel and I could separate from each other again. To Naomi and the kibbutz and to my old quarters in Jaffe, and also just one last peek into the big old church where the stormy winds of romance had begun.

Naomi and my old kibbutz home were first. Just as quickly as I left the security of the spiritual fold of the festival, I was back out into the world of *balagan,* the Hebrew word for confusion. As soon as I had left the heavenly heights of the Eternal City, I descended back into the Israeli world as I had remembered it. An irate passenger yelled at me on the bus, because I had no place to put my luggage, and when I arrived at my destination, the people in the sardine can would not even budge to let me out! Israel could be the regal queen of ancient art, culture and beauty, or she could act like the brazen hussy! Both could be in her heart!

Dear Naomi had not changed, but had become rather weak from a longstanding infirmity. Otherwise, we merely picked up the threads where we had left off. It was so good to see her again. There were many things I had been unable to share with her in our weekly letters, and hours of explanations and clarifications were exchanged. Then, as always, we hiked up the long hill behind the kibbutz, past the rusty metal sculpture, which reminded me of a twisted figure on a cross, through the olive trees to our favorite bench. The old log was no longer there, and the back fields had been freshly plowed.

We bowed our heads in prayer, in the only spot in the entire area where there was absolute freedom to do so.

The kibbutz had received the factory that Naomi and I had prayed for some years before. Annually, now a group of Christian volunteers came and worked on the kibbutz. The most heartwarming event of the visit was the loving acceptance by Naomi's husband. We all went to the dining hall together. After seven years, the people had not changed, but they all remembered me and gave the warmest welcome I received in Israel. I had not even known that they noticed me when I was there before, and with such an unending turnover of workers and volunteers, it appeared supernatural that they recalled me or even cared. I was touched by my reunion and had even returned full circle when I stayed in the little house of Naomi's cousin. She had been my first friend on the kibbutz and we both had weathered many storms!

The next stop on my journey was my old crumbling "mansion" in Jaffe. It had a multicolored past history when the British occupied the land. I had spent months of joyous hours with many different people there. I stopped to sign the guest book at the desk. The new manager had been present only some weeks from America. He was astonished when he read my name. He reached under the desk and pulled out a copy of my book about my communist imprisonment, Every Wall Shall Fall which he had found there and read. He was wondering what had happened to my life, and now I could tell him. I stood before him, as an evidence of being in the right place at the right time!

My visit would not have been complete without connecting with some of the Christians I had met in the area. I heard stories of heartache and discrimination from several of them about the ongoing fight with the religious extremist authorities. The latest battle was around the so-called "anti-mission legislation" which threatened to put people in prison for "influencing others to change their faith!" Did they not realize that only God could truly change another person's heart or belief?

I was touched by their plight and their status as "second class citizens". Although they had lived In Israel many years, they were denied the luxury of citizenship in the land where they had labored

They had birthed and raised their children there, but they remained as "outsiders" in the eyes of the authorities. I was even more moved at their struggle continually to keep their hearts free of bitterness and anti-Semitism in the face of the opposition and rejection they received. However, they maintained their gentle and loving posture as servants of the people. My heart went out to them, and for a moment I sighed in gratitude that God had plucked me out of the fire myself and into the free spiritual air where it was possible to worship and love as I pleased. Yet, Moses had suffered with God's people for their redemption and should that be God's plan I would gladly do so.

Two more visits were in order before the stage was set for my departure. I had not seen old Shlomo who had often been another kind of "thorn in the flesh" to those around him. On the run between two places, I knocked on his weather-beaten door. He was home with his grandson and friends. He lit up like a firework when he saw my face. "Seeing you has restored my faith in God!" he exclaimed. I knew that all of the rest of the Christian world had abandoned him, because no one could deal with some of his erratic ways. My little Efes had not been seen again after she disappeared from the concert. I hoped that she had found a good home. I could see that even crusty old Shlomo was mellowing as I hugged him and his grandson "good-bye". Now, the last part of the trip was back to Jerusalem and the most significant for me. I was returning to the old church where David and I had met. Perhaps there I would find some clue to the entire mystery of our lives.

I was amazed that there was no evidence that the time clock had moved at all in the place. The prim and cheerful Clara was her same industrious, ordered self. The pastor neither had the time nor interest to share any words with me. I asked the plump old sexton, who was always filled with the latest church gossip to guide me through the church building which had been renovated somewhat.

The sanctuary had lost its charm in modernization. It boasted a new organ. The sexton was busy mumbling stories while he led the way. First he mentioned this one and then that one. "Oh, by the way, you remember David, don't you? Well, he still plays here from time to time...there's really not much happening, though....you know, he divorced his wife? ..His new wife is really nice...they've just had their first child now...but David...you know how he is...."

I said nothing. The garrulous sexton ushered me out and I graciously thanked him for the tour. As I returned to my lodging, I meditated on his words. I became indignant. This man, who professed to be a believer, had never bothered to enter David's world. He spent his time judging externals. No wonder I felt no life when I had walked into the old church house, only *religion.* It had the pall of death upon it.

Naomi, on the other hand, had given me a different evaluation. Even though at one time she herself had felt David was not worthy of my love, David trusted her. He had confided that he loved me deeply, and had truly come to a place in his God that he had never known before. It sounded as if he was experiencing what it meant to be a "true Jew"— one whose very heart had been circumcised by God.

In the Torah before Joshua had been able to take Israel into Land of Promise, all the men had to stop at the Jordan and be circumcised. The nation could not receive her national inheritance until her heart had been cut and severed from the idols of her own flesh. Even then, when Israel had submitted to this painful rite, there were still many enemies to fight and drive from the Land in order to possess what God had promised her.

Shema, Israel, Adonai Elohenu, Adonai Echad.
Hear, O Israel: The Lord, our God, the Lord is One.
Love the Lord, your God with all your heart and with all
Your soul and with all your strength.

Israel has never fully kept this covenant as a nation, and neither have the Christians. When Israel's heart would be fully circumcised, she would know the fulfillment of all the blessings God had promised. Then she would become the light that the world is waiting for her to become. Her hope is not in America, although she wants and needs America's friendship. Her hope is in her God who promised her redemption and restoration.

I was deeply grateful for touching Israel's heart in some special way through David. I had brought him a beautiful foretaste of the Spirit of His God who is the Hope of Israel through Messiah. As Christians we are called upon to be the midwife in Israel's spiritual rebirth, to be her loving servant, and the bringer of mercy to her people. To judge Israel would bring God's judgment upon oneself. All those who love her are called to be "watchmen on her walls" to prayerfully stand guard against anything that tries to harm her, and to cry out for God to fully restore His breath to the dry bones which have assembled in the physical rebirth of her nation. As watchmen we are to stand watch upon our own nation's relationship toward Israel, not only for her welfare but ours as well. The prophet Isaiah said *"The nation and kingdom that will not serve you (Israel) will perish! It will be utterly ruined."*(Isaiah 60) Her Land has been given to her by the God of Israel, whom Christians worship. Hence *we have no right to demand her relinquishment of it!*

When I lived in Israel, many Arab Christians got along very well with the Jews and even some Arab Moslems, as well. However, since the growing number of Islamic terrorists, any Arab caught assisting the Jews in any way will be murdered by their own people. Under these circumstances, there is no possibility of building peaceful relations. I have always found the Israeli Jews willing to be peacemakers, but they lack the genuine partners in a peace process. Consequently, we Christians are commanded to *pray for the peace of Jerusalem*—and the nation of Israel.

I was deeply touched by a meeting I had with some Arab Christians in Israel some years ago. They shared their stories of persecution from Arab Moslems. A young Arab Christian had been attacked by some radical Moslems for his Christian faith. They split his arm open with a broken jar because of his faith, seeking to get him to renounce it. He had heard his mother cry out when they had attacked her, "*Father forgive them, they don't know what they are doing*!" He cried out these same words while they were ripping his arm open. He showed a group of us his scarred arm. There was genuine love in his eyes as he told us he had forgiven them! I was also amazed by the deep love he had for the Jewish people. He stated, along with his fellow Arab Christian friends:

"I don't care where the borders of Israel are, the Jews are my brothers and I want to live with them in harmony because I love them!"

There are others like him, but many have had to leave the country or be killed by the radical Moslems.

I never got to tell David "You and I are just little prototypes of our people. No matter where we are, there is no question in my mind or heart that soon there will be a *time for us to stand together as a Christian and Jew. The rest of the world needs to know and experience the power of reconciliation that we have experienced through our God and each other! The greatest comfort I have received for my broken heart is that there will be a time for us*! *It is on its way!*

A time for us, someday there'll be
When chains are torn by courage born
Of a love that's free.
A time when dreams so long denied
Can flourish as we unveil
The love we now must hide.
A time for us, at last to see
A life worthwhile for you and me.
And with our love through tears and thorns.
We will endure as we pass surely through
Every storm.
A time for us someday there'll be
A new world
A world of shining hope for you and me.

WATCHMEN ON THE WALLS

"I have posted watchmen on your walls, O Jerusalem;
They will never be silent day or night.
You who call on the Lord, give yourselves no rest
And give Him no rest till he establishes Jerusalem
And makes her the praise of the earth."
(Isaiah 62:6-7)

I buckled my belt in the spacious seat on the upper deck of a TowerAir 747. I had never flown in such a prestigious place directly behind the cockpit, and certainly not with my husband as one of the pilots flying the plane. I felt like a bit of royalty. The Israeli flight attendants were fussing over me as they would a celebrity. They had made special provision for my bags, and even placed them in the overhead bin for me. They were more courteous and accommodating than any American flight attendants had ever been to me. As I watched them with other passengers, I realized that my treatment was not unique just because my husband was the First officer of the plane, but it was their way of caring for the others as well. This was the best service I had ever had on any trip, and Tower Air was not known for its quality of operation. "Israel has really come a long way since I first set foot on her land in 1973," I thought. "These Israelis are doing a great job!"

I felt as if Gary and I were on our way to a "second honeymoon"! After seventeen years of marriage, this trip had popped up like an unexpected surprise. Both of our schedules had coincided, and it cost only twenty-five dollars round trip for me. Besides, he was getting paid for flying it! Our honeymoon in 1983 had been spent in Jerusalem. We had decided to go at the time of the Feast of Tabernacles celebration, in order to take advantage of the Christian celebration of the International Christian Embassy Jerusalem. After my heart had been broken over Israel and David, God had sent me into full time ministry to the brokenhearted in Miami and South Florida. I was the Area Director for the Christian Broadcasting Network South Florida region. My job involved overseeing The 700 Club television program's telephone counseling ministry and outreach in the community. Daily calls poured into the center requesting all kinds of help, —spiritual, financial, emotional and physical. I trained and led an army of prayer counselors who prayed and watched God heal hearts, families, and physical bodies. The ministry also made follow up connections with community assistance for those who needed it. My own broken heart gave me a capacity of loving empathy greater than I had heretofore known. Also, as I reached out to others, God was healing me. I had met my husband just through such ministry of prayer for our city. When I learned that he had a "heart for Israel", even though he was not Jewish, it certainly got my attention. One of my prayers had been that God would send me a husband who had such a heart!

God orchestrated another romantic overture in bringing our lives together. Our mutual attraction was first and foremost spiritual admiration and working together in God's work of healing and reconciliation with other's lives. We were helping restore troubled marriages and bruised personalities. One of our Jewish friends called our wedding ceremony a "Steven Spielberg production". We had a strong flavor of *yiddishkeit* and Israel in the midst of our Christian wedding. We wanted to make a statement that true Christians have a "love debt" to the Jewish people for bringing us our relationship with God. I walked around a *chupa* seven times, while Gary stood under it and a lovely soprano sang "Jerusalem of Gold". Another friend did a worshipful song and choreography to the *Shema Yisrael* prayer. We all held hands and sang the "Lord's Prayer" together at the end of the service. We had Israeli dancing afterwards. Both Jews and Christians said it was one of the best ceremonies they had ever attended! "*How good it is when brothers and sisters dwell together in unity!*"

The romantic spark was first ignited in our relationship when we accompanied a Jewish holocaust survivor to a huge Christian rally in West Berlin. Gary and I were not married at the time, but he was fasting and praying for our friend Rose on the Pan Am flight between Miami and Berlin. Rose had been invited to speak to thousands of Christians who would be gathered in the Olympic Stadium in West Berlin. She was terrified, because this was her first trip back to Germany since the Holocaust. Our support for her was crucial help to prepare the way for her going. Obviously, God had assigned us to accompany her. I will never forget the impact that one little Polish Jewish Holocaust survivor could have on an entire nation!

We learned that many of the German Christians who were gathered there had begged God to forgive them for their national sins and atrocities against the Jews during the Holocaust. The rally was being held in the same stadium where Hitler had declared some of his most heinous and repressive laws against the Jews. Perhaps this was the first time a Jewish survivor had the opportunity to address so many Germans together.

As Rose stood up to speak, it was raining all around the stadium, but not a single drop in it, and there was no roof over it! The sky boasted the brilliance of a huge double rainbow. Rose told the people of her arrest as a Jewish child and the atrocities that were committed against her while she was incarcerated in Dachau, a notorious German concentration camp. She then shared how she much later in life had fought vigorously against the revelation of Yeshua as her Messiah when her own child brought this news to her. The Prince of Peace finally won her over with His love to become His child, friend, and sister. Rose then announced "I cannot speak for other Jews and their suffering in the Holocaust, but only my own. Because God has loved me and forgiven me for my sins, I am here to tell the German people that *I forgive them for their sins against me!*"

After her heroic act, instantly loud moaning and wailing from grown men in the audience erupted. Some men seated behind me were shaking and sobbing violently. This one little Polish Jewish lady was releasing these men from their prisons of guilt and shame.

They were crying tears of repentance in the presence of thousands of people, an act that Germans never generally would display. As soon as Rose finished speaking, several older men rushed up to the platform to speak with her. Rose later told us what happened.

One elderly German man approached her and asked her, "Did you *really* mean what you said about *forgiveness*?"

"Yes," Rose answered without hesitation.

He stuttered, "Well....I was a prison guard at Dachau," he announced shamefully.

Rose said that she instantly saw scenes of torturous memories flash before her eyes. They were filled with pain and cruelty. These pictures stung her memory with horror. She was unsure whether she could say "yes" to the man. She took a deep breath and finally said, "Yes, *I do forgive you*...because Jesus has forgiven me for my sins against God."

The old man fell into Rose's arms, broken and sobbing uncontrollably. She had set a captive free. Rose had given him permission to receive the same forgiveness God had given her for her sins. Rose, the victim, had also given the victimizer forgiveness for his sins against her. Other Germans were also set free from their past that day! One little Jewish lady could bring healing to an entire nation, if they chose to receive it! *That was the significance of the atonement for sin that Yeshua brought to the entire world.*

That trip with Rose was the beginning of Gary's and my romance together. We later married and continued down the path of reconciliation, first with the Jews and then with all people. In our various encounters with Jewish people in America and Israel, when the opportunity affords and it is appropriate, we continue to ask them to forgive us Christians corporately for our sins against the Jewish people. There are many sins of omission—not coming to their aid in time of trial or standing against anti-Semitism, as well as sins of commission—all of the hatred and persecution historically in the "name of Christianity". We have tried to bring this vision, and the repentance that accompanies it, to the churches whenever we can.

We continue to stand up politically on behalf of Israel, as well. We have volunteered as regional liaison reps for the International Christian Embassy Jerusalem in different areas where possible.

We have many close Israeli friends, that we stay in touch with, and I continued to maintain a close relationship with my dear Jewish "mother", Naomi until she died in 2006. She was a beautiful gift from God to my life!

In the Bible, when the Jewish man, Boaz, met the Gentile woman, Ruth, a non Jew and Moabite, there had not been a full scale nightmare like the Holocaust to destroy their relationship. The Moabites had been a despised nation and enemies of Israel, though. Nevertheless, Ruth was destined to become the grandmother of King David through her union with Boaz. The Jewish nation had experienced the slaying of male Israelites by the Egyptians. Haman in Persia had plotted to destroy the Jews. Babylonian administrators, who were jealous of the Jew, Daniel, mounted a campaign against his religion. There was Herod and the Romans who opposed the Jews. On and on, the Jews have faced one rejection and persecution after another. It has continued even with so-called Christian cultures—the Crusader massacres in the Middle Ages, the Spanish Inquisition, brutal pillaging of pogroms in Eastern Europe, and the ravages of Nazi Germany, including the Communist abuses against the Russian *refuseniks*. Somehow, though, the stigma and harm of persecution from so-called Christians does carry a heavier weight, and should, because the perpetrators profess faith in the same God—the God of Israel and His Messiah. Each of these campaigns against the Jewish people which upheld some sort of banner of Christendom drove a deeper wedge into the hearts of their Jewish victims, obscuring the biblical beliefs of Christianity, which is truly a Jewish religion. For example, Hitler, one of the most demon driven men in history had his military wear "crosses" on their uniforms, making it the symbol of death and destruction to every Jew. The crusading zealots and the murderous Spanish Inquisition all were professing to be followers of the Jewish Man of Galilee, the Messiah. No wonder there was such terror hidden in the heart of every Jew who had suffered at their hands toward that name and those who proclaimed to be his followers. The symbol of the cross had been severely twisted. To the Christian the cross is the symbol of God's forgiveness of all mankind, both Jew and Gentile. It represents the atonement, born by Messiah, of the sins of all people.

The archenemy of God, Satan, sold the biggest lie in the world *to the nation that God has chosen for Himself, Israel. All Christians and especially those who are genuine believers and followers of Messiah did not kill the Jews!* Their leader, the Jew Yeshua, said that his followers would be known by their "fruits", and that his true disciples would love others, including their enemies. Indeed, when Jews accuse true Christians of killing them, it hurts and alienates them in the same way that Jews feel when they are all accused of killing Jesus. Real Christians by definition would not kill Jews; nor would they be anti-Semitic. However, the world is filled with both nominal Christians and nominal Jews; neither of which follow the teaching or the Spirit of their God!

The spirit of Israel and all Jews everywhere has been deeply wounded because of the malignant poison that spewed out of the demonic powers of evil through those who called themselves Christians. Those who believed satanic lies and acted on them have been perpetrators against the Jewish people, whether they are atheists, Moslems or "so-called Christians". The spiritual war is against all evil. However, true Christians have also failed Jews in many ways from ignorance or neglect as well as active persecution. Martin Luther with his own personal bitterness and anti-Semitism toward the end of his life was one such example of a believer who greatly harmed the Jewish people. His writings were used by Hitler to persecute and destroy Jews! There has been much repentance on the part of those Christians who are followers of Luther's teaching.

In the darkest hour of Jewish history, six million sons and daughters were massacred in the most violent, degrading and brutal manner. In those who experienced the loss of their families and loved ones through this dastardly cruelty, or even those who were able to survive it, there is a scream in the depths of their hearts "*My God, my God, why have you forsaken me?*" Many of those who were consumed in the blazing ovens of crematoria, gassed alive, or riddled with bullets of sadists and thrown into open trenches had been faithful to the light of God they had known. They were unable to understand "why."

Israel's heart has been consumed with a thousand screams in the darkness of night in their souls "why?" Many of her sons and daughters have completely fainted from this mortal blow and abandoned any belief in a God who could allow such raping, plunder, and ravaging of His own people. Israel has known the words of the Bible, which is a text in all her modern schools; she knows the miraculous feats of her own history; but she does not understand "why" a loving God could allow such depravity to come upon her. Her heart has been broken almost beyond healing. How could she ever completely *trust* such a God?

In my own experience in Israel, God allowed me to touch some of the pain and heart cry of *the wounded spirit of the nation.* I entered into the darkness of rejection, hurt, alienation, and bitterness against Christian's apparent abandonment and failure toward the Jewish people in their darkest hour. I had left everything to follow what I perceived as the mandate from God to go and help serve the Jewish people in their time of need. It felt and looked as if God had betrayed me. It appeared that He had allowed the enemy to take the upper hand over my life and happiness, with, slander, rejection and ultimate defeat. My hopes, dreams, and even God given promises were asphyxiated through the poisonous gas of *slander*, hatred, and fear from others. My spirit was mortally wounded, and I was thrust into a world of darkness. God became silent, or my pain did not allow me to hear Him anymore. My own heart screamed "why?" For some time, I was no longer able to *trust* completely in a God who could hurt me so deeply, by allowing my betrayal, especially when I was doing my best to love and serve Him! Yes, He had answered my prayer for *identification with the Jewish people—even in their suffering*! God alone understood the pain and depth of our human suffering, when His own servant willingly chose to die for the sins of all humanity, in order to "bear our grief, carry our sorrow, and to bear our sin. The Prophet Isaiah says that by "his rejection and torment, we are healed!" The Suffering Servant has born our grief and sorrow, as well as the penalty for our sins!

I remembered as I had come into my first bridal love for this God, I had asked to enter into the center of His heart, to love His people as He loved, and even to identify with them in their sufferings. *I had actually requested God to allow me to know the sufferings of Israel!* He had taken me at my word. To be inside the heart of

God is not only to know the limitless love He has for all humanity, but it is also to know the pain and the heartache of His own people as well. It is to experience the incredible longing and passion for union with His own people which He desires. It is to hate evil with fervency and despise injustice of any kind! It is to throb with the aching heartbeat of the Creator in His longing to be loved back by His own creation!

The wisest man who ever lived, King Solomon, said that there is a "time to break down" and a "time to build up", a "time to kill" and a "time to heal". God had allowed me to be broken in order to rebuild me more like Himself. In His time, He would arise and have great mercy upon Zion and restore His favor for a mightier purpose. The prophet Hosea said that God would both "wound and heal". In His infinite love, God has given humans the *freedom of will.* We are people who choose the evil, to believe the lie and act upon it, even bringing innocent victims into its path. God is ever busy continually dispelling darkness, overcoming evil and bringing good out of evil for those who choose Him. The modern nation of Israel was reborn out of the blood bath of the Holocaust! *God did not will the night of horror of the Holocaust; it came out of man's depravity.* God brought rebirth to the nation of Israel out of the ashes of man's depravity and promises her a glorious future!

Unfortunately, the behavior of the world of Christendom in regard to the Jewish people has left a malignant blight on history. Most of these perpetrators against the Jews were not Christian according to biblical definition, and those who professed to be have distorted and blasphemed the image of God by their behavior. Israel's heart has been broken and her spirit wounded in relationship with her God. The degradation and depravity she suffered at the hands of her tormentors was too much to bear. It made it difficult to rise up to her high spiritual calling to be the "head and not the tail" until her spirit is healed. The prophet Jeremiah lamented her cry:

> *What can I say for you? With what can I compare you, O daughter of Jerusalem? What can I liken you to that I may comfort you, O virgin daughter of Zion? Your wound is as deep as the sea. Who can heal you ....Yet this I call*

to mind and therefore I have hope: Because of the Lord's great love, we are not consumed, for his compassions never fail! They are new every morning; great is your faithfulness. (Lamentations 2:13, 3:21)

Israel's impassioned husband, her God, has promised great hope for her future in the beauty of reassuring promise of comfort through Jeremiah:

I will build you up and you will be rebuilt, O Virgin Israel. (Jeremiah 31:4) Even if I utterly destroy the nations where I scatter you, I will not exterminate you:

Israel's hope became my own hope, even as some of her painful suffering had been mine. The words of her prophet, Hosea proclaim:

Come let us return to the Lord. He has torn us to pieces, but He will heal us; He has injured us, but He will bind up our wounds. (Hosea 6:1)

The glory of Messiah is that he sends His Spirit to heal us. He is the "first born" of many sons and daughters of God who have received new hearts and new spirits as the prophets Ezekiel and Jeremiah promised to the House of Israel. They tell of the day that God's Law would be written on the hearts of His people. God's covenant people would know Him from their hearts and not just their heads. As we turn to God with humble and contrite hearts, He takes our sin and pain and gives us a new heart and new spirit.

He pours His Spirit into our spirit in order to empower us human beings with the Spirit of God Himself—to give humanity new hearts and new spirits that are born of God's own Spirit!

One does not have to be a prophet to recognize the impending threats on the horizon of a new "Hitler" who has already made bold proclamations about his intentions to annihilate Israel and even

America! He is rapidly assembling the weaponry and technology to do it.

On the other hand, there is also a mighty move of God's Spirit throughout the world. There are multitudes of young people in many countries who are discovering the power of God's Holy Spirit. *This is our greatest antidote to the evil in the world.* I have seen as well, evidence of a new awakening among Christians and Jews to their spiritual roots and a hunger for faith and spiritual power in their lives. The Spirit of God—the God of Elijah, the God of Messiah, is the antidote, not only to anti-Semitism, but to all evil.

The harsh religious extremism, which rejected and slandered me in Israel, has driven many Israelis further away from God than toward Him. The plastic ritualism with evil hearts is transparent to many secular Jews, and they want no part of it. Some of the Jews who want to love Israel the most, "the Messianic Jews", until recently have not even been accepted by their own nation as Jews. When I lived there, only a small number of such congregations existed. Today, I understand that there are possibly more than a hundred and some believe over two hundred of these small groups throughout Israel. It baffles me that after generations of persecution, Jews would persecute others—especially their own people who are seeking faith in God. Because the political power of the religious extremists is threatened by these Messianic Jews, until recently, they have denied them citizenship according to the Law of Return. I have just learned that there are now some new breakthroughs in this regard with legislation for the laws of citizenship. If either parent is a Jew, they have the right of citizenship in Israel. Many of the Messianic Jews are from generations of pure Jewish blood. What concerns me most is that in the past those who have seen these injustices clearly did nothing about it. There is new hope that freedom and justice for all will reign in Israel concerning religion. Even as I finish writing this book I have learned that when a young Jewish girl who had embraced Yeshua as her Messiah and wanted to enter a Bible contest in Israel, she was given permission until a couple of rabbis contested the decision, even though she was qualified. A former Prisoner of Zion from Russia had cancelled his participation and refused to participate because he was obviously prejudiced against Christians. He said, "I refuse to support an event which is being hijacked by Christian missionaries to support their agenda." Obviously the little girl was not a *"missionary."* "It's a matter of principle," the older man proclaimed.

Moreover, recently a young boy, whose father is a Christian minister, received a Passover gift in the mail which blew up when he opened it! Religious extremists are suspected.

These are examples of "Antichristian" behavior which is no different morally than anti-Semitism! I am grieved to discover that there are still Jews today that reject a Christian's freedom to express their faith. *I do not know a single Christian who would forbid a Jew to share his faith with others.* Religious extremists use the word *missionary* in a pejorative, evil sense. However, the emissaries for the Jewish Agency are called "missionaries" when translated from Hebrew. A true "missionary" from the Christian concept is a person who shares the good news of God's love and salvation for all mankind! *This word has been abused by extremists in Israel to label innocent people who are accustomed to speaking openly about their faith.* How can any democratic nation forbid freedom of speech? However, Many Western Christians do not realize that at the time of the Spanish Inquisition, the pogroms in Russia, and many other places of Jewish exile, where Jews were oppressed and persecuted, Jews were forced into "conversions" with the threat of death if they refused! Religious authorities tried to force Jews to believe in teachings they could not receive. *Many Jews lump this behavior into the category of "missionaries" which is a great distortion today, except in the Moslem world.* This is slanderous of genuine Christian believers who have lived their lives in countries where there is freedom of speech to talk about one's faith openly without fear of persecution! This slanderous accusation of Christians destroys the genuine reconciliation and fellowship between Christians and Jews. The more we Christians and Jews live by the "law of *osmosis"*—- the free respectful exchange of ideas in our relationships with each other, the more we will understand and appreciate each other and the mutual values we share together from the same God and the same Bible.

The young Jewish girl, who had won the Jerusalem region Bible contest for secular public schools, was legitimately qualified to participate in the Bible contest finals. Do some Jewish leaders in Israel want to encourage reverse discrimination with an Anti-Christian outlook? It is a big mistake, because there is an enormous Christian population in America and some 175 nations of the world who have many of their citizens standing with Israel and the Jewish people. These are people that love and support the Jewish people, the nation of Israel, and religious freedom of expression. The majority of Christians in America are against anti-Semitism.

Moreover, the overwhelming majority of Bible believing Christians in America insists that our country must be Israel's loyal friend and ally. We should not pressure or force Israel to any political concessions that dishonor God's covenant with her land or people. Jerusalem is her capital and should not be divided! Israel is the only nation in the Bible that God has called "My Land." He has the last word concerning its destiny. Woe to anyone who tries to harm it or divide it against His will.

Some years ago, before Prime Minister Sharon fell ill, the opening of the International Christian Embassy's celebration of the Feast of Tabernacles was televised on America's national television. Prime Minister Sharon was seen before the huge audience at the opening. Thousands of Christians from all over the world were giving him a standing ovation—not because he was Sharon, but because he was the Prime Minister of Israel, God's Land. He was obviously delighted and replied to the audience, *"We Israelis know that you love us, and we want you to know we love you, too."* How far the Israelis and the Christians have come together! There is more that unites us than divides us! As genuine Christian believers of the Bible as the recorded Word of the One True God the overwhelming majority stand with Israel in believing in God's everlasting Covenant with Israel and her future restoration. Some of us even call ourselves "Christian Zionists!"

Now, I believe I finally have discovered a clue to the mystery of the lies that created the great slander against me when I lived in Israel! Some time ago I had a long distance conversation with Rachel, whom I had met and befriended in Israel.

In talking with Rachel, I learned that perhaps the *source of the evil slander that was directed against me when I lived in Israel had begun when Rachel first arrived in Israel.* She had come to Israel many months before I met her. She confided in me that *she had fallen under the influence of an American couple who were greatly deceived about both God and Israel.* Rachel was naive, had little Bible knowledge, and was not a stable person herself. She had many emotional problems. This couple had said and done very many misguided and divisive things which had come to the attention of the religious authorities. Rachel had been present with them on such occasions and consequently had "participated" in whatever deceptive behavior was taking place. The couple was terribly misguided about both Judaism and Christianity. They had neither love, nor understanding of the Jewish people and sounded like a "cult" from what I concluded from Rachel's description. Consequently, Rachel had been removed from the absorption center where I lived before I even arrived in Israel. She had been forbidden to set foot there. Rachel was also very rebellious and ignored the authorities who forbade her entry to the Absorption Center.

I had met Rachel at a gathering of some Jewish and Christian friends I had just been introduced to in Israel. I knew nothing about her, but I tried to reach out and help her as a friend and social worker, *but her previous behavior had been unknown to me.* I now know that whatever had transpired in her life in a negative way with the authorities, *had labeled me from the beginning,* Rachel never had the courage to tell me about it, except that she had been forbidden to enter the building where I lived. She gave me this *information while she was inside with me, violating the order not to be there!* I had been judged guilty by association! How sad that there was not enough trust between Christians and Jews to resolve this terrible grievance.

For Israel's future, I believe that *it is equally important to address the enemy within as well as those without.* Many godly rabbis I have heard speak have equated "*slander" with "murder" because slander is the assassination of one's character!* My genuine credibility and character were verbally murdered with no recourse to justice in a modern democratic state!

Israel will always be a part of my life. It makes me very sad to think about *what could have been* in my relationship with the Land and people in the past. Moreover, I hope that Israel will find a solution to the very hurtful religious extremism that not only harms her own people but her image abroad. I know without a doubt, that her God is my God, and her people are my people, and I will stand with her even unto death.

For Zion's sake I will not keep silent.
For Jerusalem's sake I will not remain quiet.
Till her righteousness shines out like the dawn,
Her salvation like a blazing torch.
The nations will see your righteousness and all kings
Your glory; you will be called by a new name that the
Mouth of the Lord will bestow.
Pray for the peace of Jerusalem:
May those who love you be secure.
May there be peace within your walls
And security within your citadels.
For the sake of my brothers and friends,
I will say, "Peace be within you."
For the sake of the house of
Of the Lord our God,
I will seek your prosperity.

*

This is what the LORD Almighty says:
I am very jealous for Jerusalem and Zion, but I am very
angry with the nations that feel secure......
I will return to Jerusalem with mercy.....
...the Lord will again comfort Zion and choose Jerusalem.
Not by might, nor by power, but by my Spirit,
Says the LORD Almighty.(Zech.1:14-17; 4:6)

If I forget you, O Jerusalem,
May my right hand
Forget its skill
May my tongue cling
To the roof of my mouth
If I do not remember you
Psalm 137: 5,

EPILOGUE

On a visit to Israel for the celebration of the Feast of Tabernacles with the International Christian Embassy Jerusalem in 2006 I had a reunion with David. I had previously mailed him the manuscript of my book for his examination before I published it. I also gave him a copy of my husband's book. This visit had begun a dialogue on the telephone between Israel and America. Of course, it was with my husband's awareness.

David confided that his marriage had not survived, and he was divorced. He expressed that he was now available to marry me if I so desired. I told him that no matter how deeply we had loved each other, I could not leave my current husband. He had done nothing to deserve that.

David then shared with me that when he was in America at my family's home, my father had told him that "he had never met another man as loving as David!" I was very touched by this information. My father had never expressed such things to me, but I also agreed that my own father had seen the beautiful warmth of his heart, which I had so greatly admired. In fact, my father had felt that we were a *"perfect match"*. The tragedy was that our story was born "before it's time." Our love story was really a prototype of Christians and Jews needing each other to express the wholeness of God's family in unity together!

The last time I heard from David was in 2006, when I picked up my telephone receiver and received a voice mail. "Yael, I love you!" Many months later I heard from one of his friends that David had died.

Today, I have just received news from Israel that a new law has been enacted concerning Messianic believers. The Supreme Court has ruled that "*being a Messianic Jew in Israel does not prevent one from receiving citizenship in Israel under the Law of Return or the Law of Citizenship if the father is Jewish. In the past, the father did not qualify according to the Law of Return.* Israel has now established the Law of Citizenship which recognizes Jews with either parent being Jewish as legitimate Jews who may receive citizenship. Until now, many Messianic Jews have been excluded from citizenship and denied their rightful heritage as Israeli citizens. Others have been threatened and harassed by extremists. A door has been opened for them to readily return to the land of their forefathers and serve their people. Those I have known have a deep commitment and loyalty to Israel, and they will bring a wealth of resources to bless their nation.

After Golda Meir, Yitzhak Rabin was Prime Minister when I lived in Israel. Rabin was murdered by the hand of a *Jewish religious extremist on the day he had sung the "Song of Peace" with his nation.* In spite of being a national leader who had fought many battles for his nation's survival, he was willing to make major concessions and even heroic sacrifice of his God-given Land to bring peace to his region. His willingness represents just how much *all Israelis do want peace!* However, contemporary history has proven that *the availability of a genuine partner who honestly desires peace with Israel is nonexistent!* To the contrary, Israel's enemies have never renounced the desire for her total destruction! Moreover, they have shown by their actions that they are not interested in peace, but Israel's destruction. *The true spirit of the Israelis I got to know is one of a genuine desire for peace, but not at any price!* To establish peace, it is necessary to have an honest and legitimate partner. Israel has never had such a partner. America's "Road Map" is not only naïve and unrealistic, it defies biblical promise for Israel's future and is a prescription for the destruction of the Nation. It was very clear that while Yassir Arafat was making proclamations of peace to the international media in English, he was saying the opposite in Arabic. Many who know the language translated his speeches. There is plenty of land for the Palestinians in the area, especially of greater Jordan, which is the original area that was mandated for the Palestinians to occupy. Unfortunately the Palestinian leaders prefer Israel's destruction. Moreover, Jordan has not welcomed the Palestinians because of their radical behavior.

Surveys have indicated that the great majority of the Bible believing Christian community in America today clearly believes that God has given Israel her Land as an everlasting Covenant. The Bible clearly states this reality. Israel should also have a right to access her Temple Mount, which the Moslems have continually denied her people. Jerusalem is not even mentioned in the Koran, which originated in the Seventh Century of the Common Era. Israel is willing to share her Land with others, but not at the expense of enemies murdering her sons and daughters. "Enough of blood and tears!" Yitzhak Rabin had cried out in his speech on the day of his assassination by the hand of an Israeli religious Jewish extremist! Today there are multitudes of Christians all over the world who pledge to love and stand faithfully with Israel in her battle for survival in her God given Land. Israel is not the obstacle to peace in the Middle East. Her enemies are!

As Christians we pray regularly for "the Peace of Jerusalem" and all Israel. We join our heart's cry for Israel with the words of Psalm 102 which reflects Israel's broken heart of desperation in the darkest night of the Holocaust, but ultimately ends with a glorious promise that the Lord "will arise and have compassion on Zion, "

I call upon all Christians and Jews everywhere to:

> Pray for the Peace of Jerusalem. The words of Psalm 122:6-9 are an exhortation to all those who love the nation of Israel.

Psalm 122:6-9

Pray for the Peace of Jerusalem: May those who love you be secure.
May there be peace within your walls and security within your citadels.
For the sake of my brothers and friends, I will say, "Peace be within you."

For the sake of the house of the Lord our God, I will seek your prosperity

Through the International Christian Embassy Jerusalem, which represents all Christians everywhere who desire to stand with Israel and bless her people, the voices and actions of Christians worldwide have a vehicle to express their solidarity with Israel and the Jewish people both, in their individual nations and in Jerusalem as well. At the time of the annual Christian celebration of the Feast of Tabernacles in Jerusalem thousands of Christians come together from many countries, as a spontaneous fulfillment of the prophetic word in Zechariah. Today multitudes of Christians from all over the world are supporting Israeli Tourism, speaking out in their native countries on behalf of Israel's welfare and sending financial and spiritual support on a regular basis to Israel. Truly, we are experiencing a healing friendship and genuine reconciliation between Christians and Jews as never before in history! Moreover, there is an increasing number of Arab Moslems who have discovered that the words of the Man of Galilee, Jesus Christ, *"to love one's enemies," have far more power to heal the world than those who choose to hate, murder and destroy.*

CHRISTIAN ZIONISM

The word Zionism comes from the word, "Zion", which very early in Jewish history became another word for "Jerusalem." Its origin probably dates back to the time of prior to the destruction of the first Temple, and it expresses the longing of the Jews for their homeland while they were in exile. The word itself appeared again in a modern sense in the Nineteenth Century, signifying the movement of the return of the Jews to the Land of Israel. Some Christians, as early as the 1600's in Europe expressed their belief in Israel's return after exile, based on what they read in the Bible. They believed that the Jewish people would be restored to their ancient home of Israel one day according to the promises of Scripture. The belief became more widespread among Christians later and did not become a major modern movement, called "Zionism" until the 19th Century in America and England.

These Christians awaited the time when there would be a great return of Jewish people from all the nations where they had been scattered, back to their God-given Land of Israel, according to the promise of God's Covenant with Abraham. These Christians were not surprised when the resettlement of Israel began to take place and the Jewish nation experienced a rebirth as a political State in 1948. Modern Christian Zionism is the belief and active support of Christians for the restoration of Israel and the resettlement of the Jews into their own Land of Israel. The movement has accelerated considerably since the establishment of the modern statehood of Israel and the restoration of Jerusalem back to Jewish control in 1967 in the Six Day War.

Christians worldwide gathered to support the opening of the International Christian Embassy Jerusalem in 1980, comprising numerous denominational backgrounds Today, there are Christians from over 175 nations who represent solidarity with the Jewish restoration of Israel and the Jewish State. There are also many Christian Zionist organizations throughout the world. They enlist spiritual, material, and physical support and solidarity with the Jewish State.

From the beginning, these Christians who adhere to this belief have intervened with their own governments to help bring this transition about politically, as well as practically. The aid of such Christians helped influence the Balfour Declaration of 1917, through which the British agreed to help in the resettlement of Jews in Palestine. At the same time, Zionism for the restoration of the Jewish State was gaining great momentum among the Eastern European Jews. Theodore Herzl spearheaded the move for political Zionism which ultimately birthed the modern Jewish state in 1948. William Hechler, a Christian minister and Zionist was one of Herzl's closest friends, who encouraged him in his efforts to reestablish the modern Jewish State in Israel.

According to the Encyclopedia Judaica, William Blackstone was the most famous of the Christian Zionists in the United States. He attempted a political realization of his ideas through memoranda to the President of the United States in 1891 and in 1916, demanding American intervention for the return of the Jews to the Land of Israel as a solution to the czarist anti-Jewish persecutions in Russia. Hundreds of eminent Americans signed these petitions, which stimulated various reactions in the general and the Jewish press. Blackstone participated in several Zionist conventions in the United States and remained a supporter of the Zionist movement until his death.

Some of these Christians believe in the biblical prophetic restoration of the nation of Israel before the Messiah can return to earth and establish his Messianic Kingdom. Others limit their belief to the actual current struggle for the Jews to reoccupy and live within the land that was promised them through the biblical covenant of Abraham.

They include many denominations of Christianity. There has been a great increase in the numbers of Christians who subscribe to this belief since 1948, when Israel was reborn to statehood in her ancient land, and 1967 when Jerusalem was returned to the Jews. These Christians see this restoration as a fulfillment of biblical prophecy.

"Before she goes into labor, she gives birth; before the pains come upon her, she delivers a son. Who has ever heard of such a thing? Who has ever seen such things? Can a country be born in a day or a nation be brought forth in a moment? Yet no sooner is Zion in labor than she gives birth to her children. Do I bring to the moment of birth and not give delivery?" says the LORD. On May 14, 1948, overnight, the modern State of Israel was reborn in a portion of her own God given Land.

"Do I close up the womb when I bring delivery?" says your God. "Rejoice with Jerusalem and be glad for her; rejoice greatly with her, all you who mourn over her. For you will nurse and be satisfied at her comforting breasts; you will drink deeply and delight in her overflowing abundance."

In the Six Day War, on June 10, 1967, Israel regained control over the capital city of Jerusalem. Truly these events were fulfillment of prophetic promise of restoration of her Land. Christian Zionists believe that there is more to come, and that Israel is the rightful landlord of her land. Moreover, they feel a mandate to support Israel materially and spiritually.

The Hebrew prophets foretold Israel's restoration after long exile outside of her land. This phenomenon that the world and many Jews called "Zionism" is considered the work of the Spirit of God according to the Jewish prophets. The prophet Ezekiel says: "I will put my Spirit in you and you will live, and I will settle you in your own land. Then you will know that I the LORD have spoken and done it." (Ezek. 37:14)

The fulfillment of Israel's Messianic hope in the future promises ultimate realization through the power of the Spirit of God, according to Ezekiel.

"When I have brought them back from the nations and have gathered them from the countries of their enemies, I will show myself holy through them in the sight of many nations. Then they will know that I am the LORD their God, for though I sent them into exile among the nations, I will gather them to their own land, not leaving any behind. I will no longer hide my face from them, for *I will pour out my Spirit on the house of Israel,* declares the Sovereign LORD." (Ezek. 39:27-29).

The God of Israel alone holds the power of permanent and lasting peace for Israel and the world. Both Jews and Christians have Messianic hope and expectation for the world to become a better place and live in peace. I am of the absolute conviction that through the Spirit of the God of Israel and His Messiah, true and lasting peace will one day come. It must first be preceded by a time of repentance and restoration in our relationship with God. *Peace with God is a precursor to peace among men!* This process will be severely opposed by those who hate the one true God and there will be great upheaval and birth pangs throughout the world prior to the Messianic reign which both Christians and Jews are waiting for. The Jewish prophets Joel and Zechariah describe these events.

Christians believe that Messiah first came as a *suffering servant*, choosing to offer his life as atonement for the sins of every individual who believes in his redemption. He left earth in order to send his Spirit to work on earth in the hearts of men and nations until such time that the world was ready for God's reign on earth. The death of Jesus on the cross was his personal obedience to the will of God. Through his death and resurrection, the way has been opened for *all people who believe in him to receive God's forgiveness and be reconciled to God through faith—not perfect performance. Those who believe in him and his atoning death for their sins are offered a "new heart and a new spirit" through the Spirit of God. For all who receive him are given the gift of God's Spirit to indwell them and live in God's power of love and forgiveness, a* **spiritual rebirth!** Both believing Jews and Christians are awaiting the coming of Messiah to be the reigning King of Israel and the world. It will be the long awaited time of true peace on earth.

Gary and Hellen Kosak
Have established a not for profit organization to bless Israel and the Jewish people, as well as foster Jewish and Christian relations.

FOR ZION'S SAKE MINISTRIES

P.O. BOX 82-4004
PEMBROKE PINES, FL
33082-4004

We are available to speak, teach, and present seminars, Arrange events on behalf of supporting Israel and Jewish and Christian relations

OUR BOOKS

For Zion's Sake I Will Not Be Silent
Gary Kosak

*

If I Forget You, O Jerusalem
Hellen Battle Kosak

*

Every Wall Shall Fall
Hellen Battle Kosak

If I forget you, O Jerusalem,
May my right hand
Forget its skill
May my tongue cling
To the roof of my mouth
If I do not remember you
Psalm 137: 5,

Printed in the United States
125648LV00005B/79-174/P

9 781606 470336